GETTING THE JOKE

GETTING THE JOKE

JOKE

The inner workings of
stand-up comedy

Oliver Double

Methuen

Published by Methuen 2005

1 3 5 7 9 10 8 6 4 2

First published in the UK in 2005 by
Methuen Publishing Ltd
11–12 Buckingham Gate
London SW1E 6LB
www.methuen.co.uk

ISBN 0 413 77476 7

Methuen Publishing Limited Reg. No. 3543167

A CIP catalogue record for this book is available from
the British Library

Printed and bound in Great Britain
by The Cromwell Press, Trowbridge, Wlitshire.

DISCLAIMER

The author and publisher gratefully acknowledge the permissions granted
to reproduce quoted extracts within this work. Every effort has been made
to trace the current copyright holders of the extracts included in this work.
The publishers apologise for any unintended omissions and would be pleased
to receive any information that would enable them to amend
any inaccuracies or omissions in future editions.

Contents

Foreword

'Do you wish people to believe good of you? Don't speak.'
Blaise Pascal 1623–62

Old Blaise was full of insighful comments like that one, none of which have any relevance to what's on its way but quoting him makes me look smarter than I am, and who doesn't want that?

OK. Clichés on the table. I don't consider myself a stand-up any more, and not only does it not bother me, but I'll spend a few paragraphs laboriously explaining why it does not bother me.

For everyone who's never done it and no one who has, stand-up is a romantic, vibrant and intellectual pursuit whereby the commonest of individuals can exchange their complex thought processes with audiences chock-full of adoring, cerebrally superior trend-setters; with the added bonus of a handsome cash settlement and a more than healthy chance of a dynamic post-show sexual encounter. Not so.

Well, actually, sometimes so. But mostly not so.

Of the thousands of gigs I did, what I remember mostly is hitch-hiking to Edinburgh and back for a New Year's Eve gig at a warehouse party where we were arrested for breaking into a police facility (which should have been a clue to the organisational abilities of the promoters) and the act before me was introduced with the phrase 'You've all seen him before and he's absolutely rubbish, don't even give him a fucking chance'. They didn't. I went on at two and valiantly earned my ninety quid.

Or, once being canned off before I'd even said a word

when supporting Dr and the Medics as a tender, and tenderised, eighteen-year-old.

Or, exasperating an audience consisting entirely of Blackpool pensioners so much that one stood up mid act and started singing opera! And, by the way, I don't use exclamation marks lightly.

These were abberrations, obviously, and for the majority of my three to four hundred gigs a year I did leave the stage with whatever ludicrously elevated sense of self-worth that all stand-ups so needily seek. But the reason I don't pursue that particular course these days is that even after the second encore of a well-crafted two-hour show in front of a few thousand people I always saw the entire shenanigan as desperately seeking the approbation of people I would never actually want to meet. So nowadays I sit down.

People who have looked into such matters, with far greater attention to detail than I could ever allot the time to, have declared that, somewhat surprisingly, there is more than one way to skin a cat. What these particular cat-skinning methods may be is a mystery that I have contemplated on rainy evenings and sunny mornings alike, to no avail (sorry, I've been reading a lot of Mark Twain recently, I'll get to the point). The point is there are many ways to get a laugh and if, after twenty years of performing comedy including sell-out national tours and two series of my own stand-up show, I'm still not considered a stand-up, it doesn't bother me.

Were Flann O'Brien, W. C. Fields, Groucho Marx, Bob Hope or Peter Cook considered stand-ups? I think not. Was one of the all-time greatest stand-ups, Woody Allen, considered so? Not really. Honest, it don't bother me.

I was the best though. That's our little secret. Even on my first gigs as a kid with a random collection of stolen and borrowed not very funny material, I would stand in the wings watching Paul Merton and confusillate myself. I was obviously a far superior comic mind and graceful stage presence to him, yet somehow rubbish appeared rubbish and my act fell flat on its face. Whereas his acutely polished routines had people losing ribs. Sincerely, I couldn't work it out. It actually took me years to crack that particular nut. Being the best at such a young age was obviously too much responsibility to burden, but as I got older the fact that I was born great, had more greatness thrust upon me and had achieved a greatness surpassing any quantifiable measure then known, my divine right got a little easier to shoulder. That and the fact that, in this particular valley of the blind, I had as good an eye as any of my fellow attention seekers.

It really is the unspoken collective trait of the stand-up. We all think we're the best. You couldn't do it otherwise. Insert your own boxing analogy here. Oh, I understand I've been accused of arrogance in the past, partly because of the nature of the performance style I've adopted, or which adopted me, and partly because by nature I am quite insufferably arrogant. But, here's the fact: that's what makes a performer. Why else do you think they're up there? (And I don't use question marks lightly.)

From the meekest first-timer doing his whimsical 'I'm so stupid that . . . Don't sheep look like clouds . . . My dog is so lazy . . . I can't get a girlfriend . . . Sorry to take up your time, you've been great' routine, to the loudest, angriest, 'I'll tell you precisely to the letter what's wrong with the world AND give you a detailed remedy plan, not only is everyone else so stupid but you are the single stupidest collective group of individuals it's ever been my misfortune not to be pointing an AK47 at; I'm a genius you're lucky to have me, mouthbreathers, you've been great' and every point in between, they all think they're the best.

And they're probably right. Because, well, first get rid of that boxing analogy, you were never entirely happy with it anyway.

Every stand-up has a code of practice. Maybe they will only ever talk of that which matters. Maybe they will only never talk of that which matters. No puns, no impressions, no blue, no anger, no nice, no swearing because it may offend, tons of swearing cos it may offend, no -isms, only -isms. Concentrate on politics, avoid politics, charm your audience, chastise your audience. Pick any permutation from the list, regard it as your arms of valour and judge those with a different code accordingly. Obviously, feel free to transcend any of those yourself, because you woudn't normally do a pun, or a piece with a talking seagull, or an impression of George Bush, but nevertheless strike down with great vengeance and furious anger any other following a similar path.

Very early on in my career, I decided never to discuss any matters which were the common parlance of my peers, after watching four artists in a row outlining the shortcomings of the Northern Line. However, twelve years later I had such a good bit on Riverdance it would have been considered spitting in the face of the gods had I not shared it. And besides which, lots of other turns were discussing said straight-armed phenomenon but their bits were obvious and puny, whereas mine induced both shock, awe and a dangerous emotional cocktail of shock and awe combined. So that was OK. The only self-imposed boundaries I've never crossed are performing a comedy rap or asking an audience if anyone owns a cat, both of which I now plan on doing.

My major taboo, though, was what comics less than euphemistically referred to as the knob joke. Hate the knob joke. Despise the knob joke. It's beneath a performer's creative low-tide mark and the severest insult to the intelligence of even the audience of knuckle draggers one might encounter at a two in the morning, free bar, Billy Bob Thornton in a *Slingblade* look-a-like contest. The only knob jokes I ever approved of were the many hundreds I anomalously created, including my groundbreaking and never to be surpassed minstrel porn website routine.

A few years ago I did a documentary series on American stand-up. Over the course of six weeks I interviewed two or three every day, beginning with the great Carl Reiner and ending with the great Garry Shandling. Reiner was gracious and humble and learned and all the things you'd dream of in an interviewee; Shandling was effortlessly, breathtakingly funny. Almost every other comic I sat near (interview doesn't work because it was all 'view' and very little 'inter') wanted to impress on me their greatness. One even said, without a hint of awareness of a world existing outside of his own ego, 'You know you're talking to a legend.' When I relate these instances the response is always 'That's Americans', whereas, in fact, it should be 'That's stand-ups'.

You can't pass go until you accept that about them (once I would have said us but, honest, it don't bother me) because it is the most necessary mechanism. It all comes down to this. We were trying to get a laugh. We've all crossed our own professional lines; worse, we've all crossed our own moral lines. Almost every performance. So much so that those moral lines become ever fuzzier offstage. Yes, these selfless individuals have given up their own morality for your entertainment. That could well be a definition of comedy, and a pretty poor one at that.

Explaining why something is funny is like trying to explain smell. Maybe they just don't smell it. The great George Carlin once did a bit called 'Rape Can Be Funny' (unfortunately not a great bit, though it does contain the set-up 'The biggest problem an Eskimo rapist faces . . .') and I would guess that when accused of any insensitivity or, worse, humourlessness, the answer must be 'I wrote it as a joke, they laughed, job done'.

Rape patently can't be funny but rape jokes . . . check out the track 'Adolf Hartler' by Carl Reiner and Mel Brooks and get back to me.

My generation of comics was, in restrospect, a particularly fertile one. Within a year or so of my first gig a typical bill would have included Jo Brand, Lee Evans, Jack Dee, Steve Coogan, Harry Hill, Nick Hancock, Frank Skinner, Eddie Izzard and a handful of others. Not all my cup of tea by any stretch of Philip K. Dick's imagination but all undeniably unique. At the time the comedy circuit, such as it was, was very much run as a left-wing cooperative and I rather naively assumed that my fellow travellers were as eager to change the complacent nature of entertainment as I was. Cut to a few years later and my fellow travellers were jumping all over Royal Variety performances and adverts for biscuits like Vanessa Feltz on a Rasta (it would take too long to explain but the reference is both apt and delightful). Cut to a few more years later and my generation are the entertainment elite with No. 1 records, TV series, Hollywood movies and no, not less importantly, spiteful pop quizzes under their belt. I've spent the last twenty years judging that generation with the contempt only a few can muster. But, thinking this out loud I realise the futility of my former romantic projection. They were, after all, just trying to get a laugh. Sometimes you need eight houses to do that.

I don't judge a comic's motives any more, nor do I judge a joke out of context. Nor do I very often even judge a joke in context. I'm laughing or I ain't and so you can't prove to me in a pie chart that Les Dawson wasn't funny cos he just plain was. He may have skun that cat in a different method to me, as did many of my comic heroes, but, I'll stop myself before I make a Korean delicacy pun.

Bernard Manning once gave me this, particularly un-solicited, advice, which he received from the great American insult comic Don Rickles, 'Never apologise, never explain.' Whether he was aware that this comic mantra originated with the Duke of Wellington he obviously didn't explain.

Manning notwithstanding (which would've been a perfectly serviceable title for this book) here you have 300 pages of explanation by my peers (as if any comic would accept he had peers). (See earlier.)

Some I cherish as profound comic minds; some, undeniably, belong in the economic bracket where they have to cut their own hair. A few I would actually leave a dressing room to glance at; others, I would frankly prefer to be watching pensioners parking.

In closing, here's a final collective trait. Every comic was the first: the first to hold the mike a particular way, the first to finish on an impression, the first with a particular put-down. There's even one well-known incident where one comic was accused of stealing someone's timing. They were all the first with a subject, the first to stand side on, the first to personify animals, the first to talk about mums in supermarket queues. Forgive them. Few comics make a study of the lineage of stand-up history and by whatever honest means they may have come by their singularity, and whether they were even aware of its origination, it really all has been done before.

And done better.

By me.

Mark Lamarr, 2005

Acknowledgements

I'd like to thank everybody who has helped me in the writing of this book, even if you've only been one of those people to whom I've tried to explain some bit I've been working on, to the point where your eyes glaze over.

A particularly enormous thank you to those comedians who were kind enough to give interviews: Adam Bloom, Alex Horne, Alexei Sayle, Andre Vincent, Dave Gorman, Harry Hill, James Campbell, Jeremy Hardy, Jo Brand, Mark Lamarr, Mark Thomas, Milton Jones, Omid Djalili, Phill Jupitus, Rhona Cameron, Rhys Darby, Ross Noble, Shazia Mirza, and Shelley Berman. Doing the interviews was fantastic fun, and an invaluable source of information, much of which was unavailable elsewhere. I was hugely impressed by how willing and open these comedians were to discuss the way they work, and found them genuinely friendly and nice to talk to. Thanks are also due to the agents who helped to set up the interviews, especially Brett Vincent at Bound and Gagged who actively suggested people to me. And more thanks go out to those comedians who said they'd do an interview, but I didn't get time to actually follow it up.

I'm very grateful to the University of Kent for giving me study leave so that I had time to write the book, and especially to the SDFVA Research Committee for funding some of the cost of seeing shows and doing interviews. I'd like to thank Jimmy, Katie, Charlie and Gav for letting me talk about their work on the course – keep in touch, guys. Also, thanks to all of the students I've taught on any of my stand-up courses, for drawing my attention to things and making me think so long and hard about all of this stuff.

Professor Chris Baugh gave me moral support and good advice on the general tone of my research, and I'm very grateful for that.

Tony Allen and Jo Evans did a great job keeping the stand-up course going in my absence, so thanks to both of them; and special thanks to Tony for all the chats we had over the last few weeks which definitely helped to keep me sane.

Thanks are due to Alan Story from the Kent Law School for detailed and helpful advice on copyright law, and I mustn't forget James McGhie, who did some emailing for me in this area.

I'm indebted to Louise Arnold for the comedy videos, and to Mark Lamarr for kindly giving me some of his old comedy albums – not to mention writing the Foreword. Thanks for that, Mark.

Thank you to all the people at Methuen, especially Elizabeth Ingrams who helped to set the project up, and even more especially Mark Dudgeon, my editor.

A shamelessly name-droppy thank you to Richard Pryor who actually bothered to reply to my email despite being a comedy legend: 'always only tell the truth!'

Finally, a great big thank you to my wife Jacqui, who read through various drafts despite having better things to do, pointed out typos, made helpful suggestions, and vehemently encouraged me to make my prose zippy, not stodgy. And a final, final thank you to my sons Joe and Tom, who make me howl with laughter, Joe with his excellent philosophical musings ('Why are we in real life?') and Tom for his hilarious clowning ('I'm going to call you Billy today, Dad').

1. *Born Not Made*

'I've Got a Degree in Beckhamology'

One sunny day in the early summer of 1999, I was driving down the M6 when I felt a sudden vibration in my hip. For a moment I panicked, convinced that my overused and under-maintained car was finally falling apart. Then I realised with a shock that it was my pager on vibrate mode for the first time. I wondered who needed to contact me so urgently. At the next services I checked the message. It was the CEEFAX news desk, wanting to interview me about the stand-up comedy module I was to run in my new job at the University of Kent.

It was the start of what was, in reality, a minor flurry of press interest, but to me it felt like a media feeding frenzy. There were articles in the *Daily Mail*, the *Sunday Times*, the *Guardian*, the *Sun* and *The Stage*, as well interviews for local radio and television. The idea of teaching stand-up comedy at university had all the hallmarks of a silly-season classic, and the press went for the hey-you'll-never-believe-what-these-crazy-academics-are-up-to-now angle. The *Guardian*'s piece started:

> I say. I say. Did you hear that they've hired a clown at Kent University? No, really. He's going to be teaching the students stand-up comedy. No. Seriously, laze 'n' gennermen, he's got a Ph.D. in it. Actually, Dr Oliver

Double is not a clown, but he is a practising stand-up comedian. And he will be teaching third-year drama students who want it – and ooh, we all want it, don't we, missis! – the art of rambling into a pub microphone and making people choke on their pints with mirth.[1]

Some of the coverage was more cynical. The *Sunday Times* said: 'Universities, quick to capitalise on the popularity of such subjects as media studies, see comedy as another way to attract students and the funding they bring.' *The Stage*'s line was similar. They argued that 'stand-up is too rich and juicy a pie for the education industry to keep its fingers out of', and quoted a comedian making the same point more vociferously: 'A course like this is an example of a university desperate to attract students in any way it can to get government funding.'[2]

The *Sun* discovered that a module on football culture at Staffordshire University involved studying the career and public image of David Beckham, and decided to put together an article entitled 'I've Got a Degree in Beckhamology', which presented a series of courses 'ranging from the unusual to the bizarre' which they described as 'odd offerings from the wacky world of education'. Obviously, I was delighted to have my stand-up course listed as one of the odd offerings, and also impressed by the fact that they quoted me as if they'd interviewed me, which they hadn't. All of this was good *Sun*-style fun, but there was a hint of a more serious agenda at work in the introduction to the article: '[S]ome of the subjects [university students] choose to study are worthless and will do nothing to help them get jobs.'[3]

This taps into a powerful and widely held belief: stand-up comedy simply cannot be taught. This argument is particularly popular among comedians themselves. Rhona Cameron, for example, says: 'I don't feel you can study stand-up, and learn stand-up from a situation like that. I've got quite strong views on that. I feel like stand-up has to be . . . a thing you have to kind of drift into. I think it's an organic thing, and I think it comes from a kind of crossroads of life, or a feeling that . . . you've never fitted in or you haven't got along with others.'

While teaching stand-up might be seen as a bad idea, there clearly is a learning process involved, unless you subscribe to the notion that comedians' powers are fully manifested the first time they perform to an audience. There are certain technical skills which need to be acquired, as Alexei Sayle points out: 'It is a craft, you know, and . . . there's an immense amount of technical jargon and also technical understanding that you need. How much you can be taught, I don't know. It's not a craft like carpentry where you can, say, teach it, but there is a very strong element of craft in it, you know.' Similarly, Jeremy Hardy acknowledges that 'the tricks in stand-up are something you can learn'.

This learning process usually takes place in front of a live audience. Most comedians begin by being bad at their job, their early performances marred by nerves. They are clumsy and awkward onstage. They fail to get laughs. The bad experiences are usually leavened by the occasional show where the comic clicks with an audience and goes down well. With experience, the act improves. The comedian learns the job simply by doing it. As Alexei Sayle describes: 'I did as many as seven appearances a night, sometimes – one audience would be cold, the next warm, the next one lukewarm, then another cold, then a really hot one . . . In a technical sense it's fantastic training.'[4]

A short history of teaching stand-up comedy

Advice

Comedians may be sceptical about teaching stand-up in a formal setting, but in many cases they are teachers themselves. There's a long tradition of older comedians giving advice and informal tuition to less experienced acts.

Groucho Marx acted as a father figure to many younger comedians, and was an early admirer of Woody Allen's stand-up act. Milton Berle was well established when he first met Henny Youngman, who was working in a print shop at the time and doing weekend shows in the Catskills; Berle gave him advice about timing and delivery.[5]

In 1949, Bob Monkhouse was appearing low down on the bill of a concert at the London Coliseum in aid of war refugees. Max Miller was topping the bill, and Monkhouse asked him for advice. Though feeling unwell, Miller watched the younger comedian's act and afterwards gave what Monkhouse described as 'a master class in patter comedy by its greatest living exponent'. There was advice on delivery, vocal projection, energy, comic authority, timing and using gesture to create a mental picture. Miller even gave Monkhouse detailed advice on how to improve the structure of particular jokes. Monkhouse described absorbing technique from comedians like Miller, Arthur Askey and Max Wall 'by osmosis'.[6]

Speaking on Radio 4 in 2001, John Sessions said that the thought of comedy courses 'really chills me', but went on to describe how John Cleese saw one of his early performances, and phoned him the next day to discuss it in detail. Cleese advised him to give the jokes more space, and to try not to lump too many ideas together in one gag. Sessions found the advice 'fantastic'.[7]

Omid Djalili had a more sustained relationship with his informal comedy mentor: 'It was really Ivor Dembina who then came to see me and took me under his wing and said, "Look, you've obviously got something, and you're not quite there yet, you need someone to help you write some material" . . . And I think he taught me a hell of a lot actually, he taught me how to write jokes . . . to be honest, he taught me how to do it.'

In other cases, it is not so much a case of older comics giving advice to younger ones, as of comedians sharing knowledge among themselves on a more equal basis. Alexei

Sayle remembers: 'In the early days, I think we used to stay up all night. I can remember me and Tony Allen and Andy de la Tour, for instance, round Tony's flat, staying up all night talking about comedy, and the nature of it . . . we talked about the kind of ethical aspects of it, and . . . I can certainly remember talking about the technical [aspects].'

Younger comics also learn from their older counterparts simply by watching them and observing their technique. Chris Rock talks of the need to 'study comedy', and recalls how listening to albums by acts like Woody Allen and Richard Pryor helped him develop.[8] Adam Bloom describes how watching other comics at the Bearcat Club helped him prepare for his first appearance: 'I used to go every single Monday without fail, and just watch, and learn, and suss it out. I kind of learnt by other people's mistakes, in a way. Just, you know, worked out what open spots were doing wrong. And I could see there was a command that the established acts had that the open spots didn't have.'

There's a long tradition of agents and managers helping to nurture and develop the acts they represent, particularly in America. Woody Allen was helped through the sometimes painful transition from successful comedy writer to stand-up act by his managers Jack Rollins and Charles Joffe. They found him bookings in small venues to allow him to develop his performance skills, talked with him about comedy until 4 a.m., and helped him to edit his material. Allen looks back on Rollins as 'a great coach, a great teacher, a great manager'. Later, Joffe and Rollins helped Robin Williams, for example advising him to end a character piece about an old man looking back at the time before World War III with a moment of pathos.[9]

Comedians sometimes get similar help from people who run the venues in which they perform. At the original Comedy Store in Los Angeles, Mitzi Shore would critique each of the new young acts she put on. When George Black ran the London Palladium, he would sometimes offer advice to the acts he booked. He might, for example, criticise a weak routine, telling the comic, 'It's dull . . . You'd better lose your pants or something.'[10]

When fledgling comics progress to appearances on radio or TV, they may find themselves working with people who can help them adjust their acts to the new medium. Hughie Green would help to shape the acts that appeared on his TV talent show *Opportunity Knocks*. Later, when Bob Monkhouse hosted the same show, he would offer detailed advice to comedians, helping them with delivery, joke construction, and the structure of the overall act.

Working on the regional BBC Radio show *Wotcheor Geordie*, Bobby Thompson received detailed coaching from his producer, Richard Kelly, who remembers: '[O]f course, we spent quite a lot of time instructing him, giving him hints and tips on how to handle an audience, on pauses, on timing . . . particularly on emphasis.'[11] When Thompson used up his existing material, Kelly found a writer called Lisle Willis to provide him with more. Thompson found learning the new material difficult, as he had a poor memory. Kelly would spend long hours rehearsing with him, teaching him different ways of working with punch-lines and ensuring he got the emphasis right in particular sentences. One joke had a payoff line which went, 'And leave me outside the way you've always done,' and Thompson kept insisting on placing the emphasis on the word 'done' instead of where it should have been, on 'always'. It could take a whole afternoon's work to iron out such problems.[12]

Acting schools and clown training

Some comedians have had more formal training than this, albeit not specifically aimed at preparing them for stand-up. Shelley Berman trained as an actor at the Goodman Theater School in Chicago, and felt that this contributed to the development of his unique and extraordinary vocal style: 'The study of speech, for example, I felt contributed to my work . . . as a comedian. The placement of my voice

– I don't know why, but somehow I know I can perform in a theatre without a microphone . . . Yes, certainly the education is a contributing factor there. Whatever is natural is natural, but there was considerable vocal development and speech development in my schooling.'

Andre Vincent had a rather more exotic training, studying clowning for six months at the Fratellini Circus School, and later being taught by Keith Johnstone when he performed theatresports with the Loose Moose Theatre Company. Vincent feels that both clowning and improvisational theatre have fed into his stand-up act: 'I mean, there's lots of . . . little tricks . . . with stand-up that're . . . to do with clowning and sometimes to do with improv, where you have . . . structured levels and some sort of status level . . . You've got this . . . status and pecking order, and if you get angry with somebody or you wanna show anger, what you do is you sort of like turn away, and then you turn around and you come back to them. And it's so good to do that . . . within stand-up. If . . . somebody says something quite horrible, [you] don't just sort of go straight into them, because then you become as horrible as them. You turn around, walk away and then just turn around and go, "Hey, hold on," and you know, you make a thing of it. People'll go, "Whoooo!" and they'll go with you.'

'How to' guides

My stand-up course was by no means the first attempt at offering some kind of formal training specifically geared to stand-up comedy. A number of 'how to' guides have been published, which claim to offer the budding comedian useful advice. In 1945, Lupino Lane wrote a book called *How to Become a Comedian*. Lane came from a line of comic performers stretching back to the seventeenth century, and had worked as a silent-film comedian and in stage musicals, as well as having experience of variety. His book covers topics such as 'How to Use an Old Gag', 'Patter' and 'Timing', which might have been of use to fledgling front-

7

cloth comics in variety theatres, as well as 'Female Impersonation', 'Crazy, Acrobatic, Knockabout and Slapstick Comedy' and 'Ventriloquism', clearly aimed at other types of comedian.

In the last twenty years, the number of 'how to' guides has proliferated, but many of them tend to oversimplify the subtle techniques of stand-up and offer dogmatic advice which is sometimes simply wrong. In *Stand-Up Comedy: The Book*, Judy Carter defines modern stand-up as a form of self-expression: 'People confuse stand-up comedy with telling jokes . . . Joke-telling is the old Catskill school of comedy . . . The new school of comedy is personal comedy. Your act is about you: your gut issues, your body, your marriage, your divorce, your drug habit . . .' However, having argued against simply 'telling jokes', and in favour of a freer, more creative approach, she goes on to stipulate 'specific stand-up formulas': 'All stand-up material must be organized into the setup/punch format. If your material isn't organized like this, you're not doing stand-up.'[13]

It is hard to believe that the free-flowing routines of geniuses such as Lenny Bruce, Richard Pryor, Billy Connolly or Eddie Izzard were produced with this rigid, formulaic set-up/punch approach. Carter specifically warns against personal anecdotes, saying 'stories don't work'. If Pryor or Connolly, say, had followed this advice, they would have had to shed some of their strongest material.

Comedy classes

Then there are stand-up comedy classes. The idea of formally teaching comic skills probably originates in the training which took place within theatrical families over hundreds of years. Lupino Lane writes about the knowledge passed down within his own family, with tuition in such areas as acrobatic tricks, juggling and 'The art of miming or expressing the emotions, in "dumb show"'. His father, whom he describes as 'a most patient tutor', taught him comedy skills and specific routines.[14]

Classes aimed at the general public have existed for the best part of a hundred years. In 1907, the young Marx Brothers spent some time in the newly established Ned Wayburn's College of Vaudeville, and appeared in a show-case performance featuring some of those that had studied in it. Like the 'how to' guides, comedy classes have pro-liferated. In 1972, Pete Crofts set up his Humourversity, which describes itself as 'Australia's foremost training institution in the art of humour, comedy and laughter'. It offers courses and workshops on stand-up as well as related topics like comedy writing and public speaking with humour. In America, workshops are offered by comedians such as Judy Carter, or by venues like the Comic Strip in New York, which offers an eight-week programme and private tutoring. Jamie Masada, who runs the Laugh Factory on Sunset Boulevard, has even established a Comedy Camp for Kids, where students from inner-city schools can learn stand-up skills.[15]

In the UK, the idea of teaching comedy has been floating around since the 1970s, when Trevor Griffiths set his play *Comedians* in a night-school class for stand-ups.[16] It's only more recently that classes like this have become well estab-lished outside the world of theatrical fiction. In the late 1980s, when he was just starting out as a comic, Frank Skinner ran stand-up workshops at the college where he was working. Although he looks back at the experience as 'the near-sighted leading the blind', he received media coverage for the course, and this attracted the attention of Jasper Carrott, who turned up to one of the classes and offered advice and encouragement to the participants. Later, Skinner ran workshops as part of a Red Stripe-sponsored tour for Amnesty International, and the class at the Wythenshawe Forum in Manchester was attended by future comics Caroline Aherne and Dave Gorman, who was just nineteen years old. Gorman remembers: 'It was . . . twenty-odd people sitting around, and Frank sort of talked through what he thought about stand-up and showed a little video, and then that was discussed and analysed, and then anyone who wanted to was able to get up and do . . . five minutes in front of everyone else. A few of us did, and I did.' The experience proved to be crucial for Gorman; on the strength of this five-minute performance, he was booked for a benefit gig by Henry Normal, then a stand-up poet on the Manchester circuit. Skinner was headlining that show, and he went on to offer Gorman a paid booking at the 4X Cabaret in Birmingham which he was compèring at the time. This was the beginning of Gorman's professional career.

At around the same time, the Jacksons Lane Community Centre in Highgate ran comedy workshops taught by comics from the London circuit, covering such subjects as improvisation, writing and compèring, in eleven two-hour sessions. Often, the tutors would be performers who had previously been students, such as Ivor Dembina, Patrick Marber and Jim Tavare.

Jacksons Lane no longer runs comedy workshops, but there are still plenty of places to find them. The Comedy School, founded in 1998, offers classes taught by comics such as Paul Merton, Arnold Brown and Adam Bloom. Tony Allen and Den Levett run what is described as 'a crash course in stand-up comedy' made up of six two-hour sessions, and some of the exercises they use are described in Allen's book *Attitude: Wanna Make Something of it?*'[17]

Stand-up goes to university

The press reaction to my stand-up course tends to suggest I was the first to introduce the subject into university teaching. In fact, Middlesex University has been running a comedy course as part of its drama degree since the mid-1980s; and Salford University started a stand-up course in 1993, with Peter Kay as its most illustrious alumnus.

I had started teaching stand-up at Liverpool John Moores

University even before I moved to Kent. This was not the cynical money-making scheme suggested by the *Sunday Times* and *The Stage*, but the result of the peculiar way my life was turning out. I had started working as a stand-up about ten years before I got the job at John Moores, making a living from the regular paid bookings I was getting as well as the comedy club I compèred and co-managed. I had also written my first book on stand-up.

In 1997, a set of unfortunate circumstances meant I had to get a proper job, so I started applying for drama lectureships. It was only after my first term at John Moores that I was asked to develop a stand-up course. I hadn't expected this, although it would have been surprising if I hadn't been asked to draw on my professional experience in my teaching. Initially, the course was modest: one three-hour workshop per week for one term, leading to a single performance in a local pub at the end of it. When I moved to Kent, I was asked to develop a similar course. This time it involved two sessions per week for a whole year, with three performances at regular intervals.

Learning to teach students how to perform stand-up comedy wasn't easy. I had been taught in the traditional way: by experience. Now I had to find ways of passing on this knowledge to students. My first task was to break down what I knew, to try and untangle and identify the skills so they were no longer merely automatic. I started to do this purely by reacting to what the students were doing in class, and, at first, my only way of passing on what I had learnt was simply by telling it to the students. Gradually, I developed a series of simple exercises which helped the students to make discoveries for themselves.[18]

The spirit in which these exercises are carried out is crucial to their usefulness. One of my most basic principles in teaching stand-up is to absolve the students of the requirement to be funny in workshops. The problem is that funniness is seen as a magical quality, rather than as part of a process of communication. Say 'be funny' to somebody, and the chances are they'll flounder about, defeated by the enormity of what they have been asked to do. Or, they'll try too hard, forcing the energy, faking zaniness, or adopting their stereotyped expectations of what a stand-up comic should be.

Learning by doing

The Kent drama degree is a four-year course, and students specialise in just one practical subject for the whole of their fourth year. In 2001, I developed stand-up comedy as a fourth-year option. It was a chance to teach more intensively, and I had the freedom to shape the course exactly as I wanted. Taking advantage of this, I decided that the best way forward was to make the idea of learning by doing much more central. I would ask the students to do their first show ten days into the course, and then perform every week for the rest of the term. In each of the eleven shows, the students would be expected to come up with new material. That way, by the end of the term, they would have had a fair amount of stage experience, and a repertoire of tried and tested routines to choose from.

I knew this would be throwing them in at the deep end, so I had to find a sympathetic venue, which would feel like home territory. I chose Mungo's, a bar in one of the university's colleges. It wasn't perfect. The walls were slatted not solid, so that the corridor outside would act as a natural echo chamber, and people walking past could disrupt the show by shouting. It was too small for a raised stage, so we would have to perform in one corner of the room. Worst of all, the doors stayed permanently open, and we wouldn't be able to charge people to come in. Normally, this is the kiss of death for a comedy night. On the other hand, it was a regular haunt of other drama students, so it felt like home territory, and by working hard at publicity, we thought we would be able to attract only those people who were interested in seeing the stand-up.

In the second term, the students would put together a

twenty-minute set from the best bits they had done in Mungo's, and take it into away territory, doing a show in a Canterbury pub. They would also carry out a research project, and arrange for themselves a series of open-mike performances in real comedy clubs. Again, the idea was for them to perform as much as possible, and even the research project would involve putting on a show.

On 25 September, it was time for the first workshop, and the four students who had opted for stand-up arrived, looking distinctly nervous. Jimmy was a good-looking middle-class chap, who had spent most of the previous three years underachieving by being cheekily lazy. Katie, the polar opposite of Jimmy, was a self-confessed swot who was convinced that everyone thought she was too boring to be a comedian. Gav was a gentle skinhead anarchist with a penchant for the surreal. Charlie had a kind of post-punk chic, and she liked to take risks. Although they were a mixed bunch, they all had the same expression on their ashen faces. I asked what the matter was, and they told me they had all been in the bar together, drinking to calm their nerves. Even the workshop was a scary prospect.

I told them about the no-need-to-be-funny rule and they quickly relaxed into the exercises, laughing and messing about. The atmosphere of the workshops is important. When I was a drama student, the emphasis tended to be on discipline. We wore standard black clothes, worked barefoot, had to arrive strictly on time, and were sometimes forbidden from talking about life in the outside world. Casual chatting and laughter were frowned on.

This may be a productive atmosphere for learning physical theatre skills or the techniques of Jerzy Grotowski, but not for stand-up. Although it's still important to arrive on time, students wear their own clothes, and talking about the outside world is a positive requirement. As long as it is focused, casual chatting can be very productive. There's a feeling of just playing about, and people gently make fun of each other – and me. Maintaining the balance between this

13

casual atmosphere and the task in hand is a delicate matter.

After five sessions like this, the students had to face a live audience for the first time.

The first night

It's Thursday, 4 October 2001, 8 p.m. Mungo's is teeming with people, but I'm not sure they're here to see the comedy. There's a big party of students who are on a fancy-dress pub-crawl, and I really hope they'll be gone by the time we start. I'm already thinking about other venues we might try if tonight's a disaster. I'm going to compère the show myself, to try and make sure the atmosphere is warm and the audience is focused, and I know I'll have a job on my hands.

It's still chaotic at 8.30 when I walk on to start the show. The drunken fancy-dressers have moved on, but eighty or more people are packed into the bar. There's still a lot of background chatter, and I'm distracted by the echoing acoustics. I work hard to bring the room together, taking the crowd through a silly audience participation thing, and playing them Lipps Inc.'s 1979 disco classic 'Funkytown' on the mandolin. After ten minutes, it feels as if I'm in front of an audience rather than a random collection of people who happen to be in the same room together. I introduce Charlie, who's going on first, and there's a huge burst of cheering and applause, with the kind of excitable edge you'd expect from an audience dominated by drama students.

Charlie does well with the story of a one-night stand, and Katie follows by talking about her family. She plays on her swottiness, apologising after she says 'shit': 'I'm sorry, I didn't mean to say the brown word.' The audience like her. Gav is next, and he suddenly shows a control he has lacked in the workshops, where he's tended to veer off all over the place. He gets a big laugh for his opening gag (Gav: 'Anyone here from Chester?' Punter: 'Yeah!' Gav: 'My dad died there.'), then lights himself a cigarette, taking his time over it. It's a high-status gesture: he's quite happy to keep a room full of people waiting until he's ready.

Jimmy goes on last, and it's clear from the beginning that he's a natural. He has the kind of casualness which shows a deep confidence, and he's prepared to play about onstage. He starts by taking the piss out of me, saying I've only set the course up as a kind of revenge for all the times I died onstage when I was a working comic. Then he tells the tale of when he recently 'shit himself' while backpacking around Thailand. It's well structured and beautifully performed. After a Thai curry and some Chang beers, he's in a sleeping bag under a mosquito net. 'And then it came,' he says. There's a laugh of anticipation. 'Blup!' he says, impersonating the noise of his stomach. 'Blululup!' There's another laugh, and he continues, in a genuinely cheerful voice:

My guts were trying to tell me something! [*laughter*] They were! They were telling me I was about to shit myself! [*laughter and applause*] There's a red Thai curry in there that wants to leave! [*laughter*] It wants to explore the world via my anus! [*laughter*] So, yeah, so I just, I thought, 'No, bollocks,' you know, 'I'm tucked away, I've got all my stuff, I'm in my Action Millets Bearproof fucking Sleeping Bag, I'm not going anywhere, cos it's – it's bound to just be a fart. [*laughter*] I'll stand up, I'll get out of bedroom and I'll just go *thhhppp!* [*laughter*] Then I'll have to go back to bed.' So I took the gamble. [*laughter*] So I did the Jimmy, I took the fucking gamble. I decided that I was going to take it on. So I stayed in bed. [*pause*] Silly Jimmy. [*laughter and some clapping*]

The first night is a big success but not all nights are easy. The crowd fluctuates. Sometimes it's big and noisy, and sometimes the students find themselves playing to thirty-odd quiet punters. One week the PA system starts to emit blue smoke while we're soundchecking, then refuses to work. We have to perform acoustic. By halfway through the term, the students are starting to feel the strain of having to come up with new material every week.

The process of teaching them, of helping them through the stresses and strains, starts to raise certain questions for me. I can draw on my previous research to answer the easier questions, like where stand-up comedy came from, but there are fundamental aspects of the art form that rarely get addressed in books: Who do comedians become when they're onstage? What do they do to establish a relationship with their audience? How much do they improvise? Which different techniques do they use to perfect their delivery? And, perhaps most crucial and most mysterious of all, how do comedians actually go about their job?

2. *A Beginner's Guide to Stand-up Comedy*

Fun with definitions

In late 2000, I happened across a fact that shocked me. According to the *Oxford English Dictionary*, the term 'stand-up comic' was first used in an article in the *Listener*, published on 11 August 1966.[1]

Maybe shock is a bit of a strong reaction, perhaps even a little sad, but at the time I had had a keen, not to say obsessive, interest in stand-up comedy for well over a decade. My second reaction, though, was disbelief. Surely the term must have been in use before 1966? After all, by that point, the style of performance it describes had been in existence for at least sixty years, and some of its most famous practitioners were already dead and gone. Indeed, eight days after the article hit the news-stands Lenny Bruce had been found dead on his toilet.

I went straight to the *Listener* article cited by the *OED* as the earliest recorded usage, to look for clues. It's a piece reporting the ideas of the marvellously named Miss Ethel Strainchamps about the effect of television on spoken English, and it contains two references to 'stand-up comics'.[2] However, it couldn't possibly be the actual first usage of the term, because it's a description of an earlier article by Miss Strainchamps which appeared in an American journal called *Television Quarterly*.

Unable to find the *Television Quarterly* article, I started to look for other earlier usages. I found one in the *OED*'s rival: *Webster's Third New International Dictionary*, published in 1961. It gives a definition of the adjective 'stand-up' as: '[P]erformed in or requiring a standing erect position <*stand-up* lunch> <*stand-up* bar> <*stand-up* comedy act> <*stand-up* boxing stance>'.

Great! So the term 'stand-up comedy' was definitely in use in Lenny Bruce's time. In fact, an even earlier usage crops up in a radio interview with Bruce from 1959, in which the interviewer, Studs Terkel, asks: 'Where does this leave the stand-up comics, quote unquote, who have stables of writers?'[3] It's unlikely that Terkel coined the term there and then, or Bruce would probably have asked him what he meant by it, but the chances are its exact origins are impossible to track down. An article in the *Guardian* claims it was first used on Johnny Carson's *Tonight Show*, but Carson only started on that show in 1962, three years after the Lenny Bruce interview. This claim kicked off an Internet discussion, in which someone suggested that Milton Berle did the coining in 1942, but this seems unlikely given that he disliked the phrase.[4]

What's the definition of stand-up comedy?

If finding where the term 'stand-up comedy' came from is hard, it's nothing compared with the difficulty of actually trying to define it. It's an instantly recognisable form of entertainment, but putting a finger on what makes it so easy to recognise is not so simple. You can start with the obvious fact that it's funny, but that doesn't narrow it down far enough. I've fallen into this trap myself. In my first book, I define stand-up as: '[A] single performer standing in front of an audience, talking to them with the specific intention of making them laugh.'[5]

Now, I find myself having to nitpick this to pieces. I say 'a single performer', but couldn't what Morecambe and

Wise did in their routines in front of the velvet curtains be described as stand-up? And aren't there other performers who fit this description, who are not stand-up comedians? What about comic poets? Circus clowns? Storytellers? Performers of character monologues, such as Joyce Grenfell?

Other definitions fall short for similar reasons. The *OED* defines the stand-up comic as 'a comedian whose act consists of standing before an audience and telling a succession of jokes'. This description more or less fits the work of Lenny Bruce, Richard Pryor, Billy Connolly and Eddie Izzard, but doesn't even touch on the extra things they do that make them so extraordinary.

Having thought long and hard about it, I've come up with a list of the three things which define stand-up comedy, besides the fact of it being funny:

Personality
It puts a person on display in front of an audience, whether that person is an exaggerated comic character or a version of the performer's own self.

Direct communication
It involves direct communication between performer and audience. It's an intense relationship, with energy flowing back and forth between stage and auditorium. It's like a conversation made up of jokes, laughter and sometimes less pleasant responses.

Present tense
It happens in the present tense, in the here and now. It acknowledges the performance situation. The stand-up comedian is duty-bound to incorporate events in the venue into the act. Failure to respond to a heckler, a dropped glass or the ringing of a mobile phone is a sign of weakness which will result in the audience losing faith in the performer's ability.

19

Where did stand-up comedy come from?

If this definition of stand-up comedy is any good, then the form has been around a lot longer than the term which describes it. There's been much speculation about the roots of the form, and it's been suggested that its ancestors might include the shaman, jesters, *commedia dell'arte*, Shakespearean clowns like Tarleton, English pantomime clowns like Joseph Grimaldi, circus clowns, British music-hall comedians, American vaudeville entertainers, the stump speeches of American minstrelsy, nineteenth-century humorous lecturers like Mark Twain, and medicine shows.

It's been said that stand-up comedy itself is an American invention. US comedian Richard Belzer, for example, describes it as, '[O]ne of the few art forms indigenous to this country: jazz, abstract painting, and stand-up comedy.'[6] British comedy critic William Cook agrees, adding: 'British comics have adapted American stand-up to their own ends, but . . . our parochial version is still way off the pace.'[7]

As somebody who's resented American cultural imperialism ever since he first heard The Clash's 'I'm So Bored with the USA', I feel duty-bound to challenge the idea that stand-up originated on the other side of the Atlantic. The easiest way to do this is by looking at the evidence, tracing the history of stand-up first in the USA, then in Britain.

American origins

Vaudeville

In America, the story of stand-up starts in vaudeville, a form of popular theatre which began in the late nineteenth century. Growing out of earlier forms of popular entertainment such as dime museums and Yiddish theatre, the first proper vaudeville venue was probably Tony Pastor's New Fourteenth Street Theatre, which opened in New York in October 1881. Pastor was the first to take this type of popular entertainment out of saloons and present it to a respectable audience. Over a decade later, in March 1894, B. F. Keith opened his first theatre in Boston, the first to use the word 'vaudeville' to describe what it offered its customers.

The entertainment took the form of a mixed bill of acts, which might include singers, dancers, speciality acts and comedy quartets. To give a specific example, the Palace Theater, New York, in the week beginning 2 May 1921, offered the following:

1. Fink's Mules, animal act
2. Miller and Capman, singers and dancers
3. Georgia Campbell and Co., in 'Gone Are the Days'
4. Toney and Norman, songs and talk
5. Dorothy Jardon, prima donna

INTERMISSION

6. Kennedy and Berle, youthful entertainers
7. Ford Sisters, dancers
8. Watson Sisters, singing comediennes
9. Robbie Gordon, posing act[8]

There were different grades of theatre, and the organisation of the entertainment in the major theatres differed from that in the smaller venues. Big-time vaudeville changed the bill weekly and ran the show twice nightly. Small-time vaudeville changed the bill twice a week, ran three to six performances per day, had fewer acts per show and lacked headliners. Small-time vaudeville included the venues run by the Theatre Owners Booking Association (TOBA), which booked black acts and attracted black audiences. The need for its existence is an indication of the segregation which afflicted America, although some black acts, notably Bert Williams, did manage to break into the big-time circuits.

Williams was just one of the many legendary comedians that vaudeville produced. Others include Buster Keaton, Charlie Chaplin, the Marx Brothers, Mae West, W. C. Fields, Eddie Cantor, Fred Allen, Bob Hope, Jack Benny and Milton Berle. Some of these were comic singers or sketch comedians, but others did something which we would recognise as a form of stand-up comedy. First, there were MCs, like Frank Fay, who introduced the other acts. By definition, they had to address the audience directly, and they would also make comic ad libs.[9] Then there were the monologists, like Jack Benny, Bob Hope and Milton Berle. These are now thought of as classic stand-up comics in the traditional style, but in a 1991 interview, Berle rejects this idea: 'We were monologists. Not stand-up comedians. That's a new term. You know why they're called stand-up comics today? Because all they do is stand there and take the microphone off the stand.'[10]

Berle is contemptuous of acts who just stand there and tell gags, because he and his contemporaries did more than that. His first solo act, in 1924, was twelve minutes long. As well as gags, it featured two songs, a card trick, a soft-shoe dance and an impersonation of Eddie Cantor. Similarly, Jack Benny's act contained elements not usually normally found in modern stand-up, like a female stooge, described in a 1927 review as 'a nice-looking girl, who plays the role of a self-conscious "Dumb Dora"'.[11]

The monologists were like modern stand-ups because they addressed the audience directly and told jokes, but they probably only started doing this towards the end of the vaudeville era. A 1921 review of Fred Allen's act notes that as well as singing a song and using what is intriguingly described as 'a wabbly umbrella', he told a series of gags: 'His chatter is unrelated and aimed for laughs, which he secured.' This leads the reviewer to conclude: 'Allen is not a monologist.'[12] Clearly, in the early 1920s this proto stand-up element was new to the art of monologism.

Vaudeville was a very popular form of entertainment. In

its heyday, there were at least 1,000 vaudeville theatres in the USA, playing host to 25,000 performers. As it became popular, it also became big business, with huge theatre chains being formed by entrepreneurs such as B. F. Keith, Edward F. Albee and Martin Beck. By 1927, the huge chains had merged into one enormous one, which combined the Keith & Albee circuit with the Orpheum. This meant that all major vaudeville theatres and many smaller ones came under the control of a single organisation.

At this point, vaudeville was facing competition from silent cinema, and some theatres responded by including movies between the acts. The pressure increased when sound cinema arrived in the late 1920s, particularly as big vaudeville stars like Jack Benny, Fred Allen and Bert Lahr started to appear in 'talkies'. Such stars also appeared on the radio, another new medium competing for audiences.

The fact that so many theatres had been amalgamated into one circuit made vaudeville fatally vunerable to competition. When Joseph P. Kennedy, the father of JFK, took control of the Keith-Albee-Orpheum circuit by buying up 200,000 shares in it, vaudeville's fate was sealed. Kennedy had a background in the movie business, and wasn't interested in live theatre. In 1930, he sold his stock to the Radio Corporation of America, which became RKO (Radio-Keith-Orpheum). With virtually all the theatres in the hands of a film company, live vaudeville was over. By 1935, it had virtually disappeared, living on for a while in the form of live acts performing between the films in cinemas.

Borscht and Chitlins
In 1938, Groucho Marx was worried that the death of vaudeville might make comedians 'a vanishing species'.[13] In fact, stand-up lived on in a variety of venues, such as the hotels and resorts in the Catskill Mountains, known as the 'Borscht Belt'. From the 1930s, the Borscht Belt was a favourite holiday destination for New York Jews. There

23

were more than five hundred hotels, including Brown's, the Concord, Grossinger's, Kutsher's and the Tamarack, and the shows they put on were dubbed 'the new vaudeville'.

Comedians who started out in the Borscht Belt include Red Buttons, Danny Kaye and Joey Bishop. In addition to headline comics, newer acts were booked as 'toomlers'. Like the redcoats of British holiday camps, as well as doing a stage act the toomlers had to mingle with the guests, telling them gags and entertaining them as they did so, performing card tricks or jumping into the swimming pool fully clothed. This must have encouraged the key elements of stand-up: an intensely direct relationship with the audience, improvisation and an emphasis on the here and now.

Another arena where stand-up survived was the 'Chitlin Circuit', a series of cabarets, nightclubs and small theatres catering to black audiences in cities like Chicago, Detroit, Cincinnati, Baltimore, Washington DC and Philadelphia. The pinnacle of the circuit was Harlem's Apollo Theatre, which still thrives today. On the Chitlin Circuit, great black comedians like Pigmeat Markham, Moms Mabley and Redd Foxx appeared alongside jazz bands, bluesmen, tap dancers and doo-wop groups.

Then there were the white stand-up comedians like Minnie Pearl, who emerged from the country music scene. The casinos of Las Vegas provided a stage for the big names of comedy, paying them big money. Beyond all of these, would-be stand-ups could try to find work in cafés, bars or strip clubs.

The sick comics

In 1953, a young comic called Mort Sahl made his debut at a venue called the hungry i in San Francisco. Run by a beret-topped bohemian called Enrico Banducci, it was a small cellar club that played host to folk singers and beatnik poets. Behind the stage was a brick wall, and this was the origin of the classic image of the American stand-up comedian telling gags in front of a bare-brick backdrop.

Sahl's act at the hungry i was revolutionary. He eschewed smart suits in favour of slacks, and a casual sweater worn over an open-necked shirt. His delivery was just as informal, and his subject matter was relevant to a young, hip, beatnik audience. Emerging in the context of McCarthyism, he was unafraid of controversy. He joked that he had bought a McCarthy jacket which is 'like an Eisenhower jacket only it's got an extra flap that fits over the mouth'.

Others followed in Sahl's wake: Lenny Bruce, Shelley Berman, Dick Gregory, Mike Nichols and Elaine May, Jonathan Winters, Phyllis Diller, Bob Newhart, and Woody Allen. They played at the hungry i and other hip venues in other American cities, places like Bon Soir, Le Ruban Bleu, Mocambo, the Purple Onion, the Bitter End, Mr Kelly's and the Blue Angel. Hugh Hefner was an enthusiastic fan of the new comedians, and booked them in to his Playboy clubs. They were labelled the 'sick comics', and *Time* magazine described their style: 'They joked about father and Freud; about mother and masochism; about sister and sadism. They delightedly told of airline pilots throwing out a few passengers to lighten the load, of a graduate school for dope addicts, of parents so loving they always "got upset if anyone else made me cry".'[14]

All of these acts were exciting and inventive, but Lenny Bruce stands out for the sheer daring of his act and the frenzied controversy he managed to whip up. Bruce had started out as a Borscht Belt impressionist, doing Peter Lorre, James Cagney and Maurice Chevalier. In the late 1940s, he had what might have been a big break, performing an item called the Bavarian Mimic on the *Arthur Godfrey Talent Scouts*, but his career failed to take off. At this point, he was still a rather conventional comic, but during the 1950s his style began to change. He began hanging out with a bunch of young comics at a luncheonette called Hanson's in New York. They would try out material on each other, and Bruce was particularly taken with Joe Ancis, who never really worked as a professional comedian. Bruce was impressed by Ancis's ability to improvise outrageous comedy routines across the lunch table, and started to reflect this influence in his act.

When Bruce started working as an MC in strip clubs like Duffy's Gaieties and Strip City, he began to try a riskier approach to stand-up. He would improvise, do very obscene stuff, insult the waitresses and wind up the customers. He would talk about jazz, and loved making the band laugh. Famously, one night he came on after one of the strippers, having taken off all his clothes. The audience was outraged, but Bruce was unrepentant: 'What are you all staring at? You see nudity on this stage every night. What's the big deal if I get naked?' When he broke out into more respectable venues, he took with him his improvisational flair, and his willingness to confront taboos, with routines about sex, race and illegal drugs.

Another standout act was Dick Gregory. Gregory started off on the Chitlin Circuit, and got his big break with a booking at the Playboy Club in Chicago on 13 January 1960. Replacing a white comedian who'd had to cancel, and playing to a white audience including a big party of Southern white businessmen, he stormed the gig, presenting an unashamedly black perspective and satirising racism. Gregory's success opened the door for many more black comedians. Phyllis Diller, who started out in venues like the Purple Onion and the hungry i in the mid-1950s, made a similar breakthrough for women. There had been other female stand-ups before her, notably Moms Mabley and Minnie Pearl, but Diller was the first American comedienne to become a big star.

The sick comics massively expanded the possibilities of stand-up, in terms of both presentation and subject matter. They paved the way for comedians to become less formal, wear casual clothes and adopt a natural, conversational delivery. They made room for comedy to be literate and intellectual, as well as letting it into taboo areas. Just one example of how they drew the blueprint for modern stand-up is the observational style of Shelley Berman who, among other things, was the first to talk about the anxieties of flying, a subject which comedians still harp on about today.

Perhaps understandably, older comics viewed these new-comers with suspicion. As Albert Goldman put it, Mort Sahl 'so revolutionised the role of the comic that pro-fessional comedians viewed him with the same mixture of alarm and envy with which professional singers regarded Elvis Presley'.[15] With the taste of sour grapes in his mouth, older comic Joey Bishop dismissed the new generation: 'Those guys . . . tried their hardest to make it our way; when they couldn't, they switched.'[16]

Comedy clubs

The world's first comedy club opened in 1962, in Sheepshead Bay, New York. A comedian called George Schultz capitalised on the new hipness and popularity which the likes of Sahl, Bruce and Gregory had brought to stand-up, and opened up a new venue called Pip's, devoted exclusively to comedy. Here, stand-ups could perform without having to share the bill with dancers, posing acts, performing mules, beatnik poets or folk singers. Pip's still runs to this day, and you can see shows there for $5 (Wednesdays, Thursdays and Sundays) or $10 (Fridays and Saturdays), plus a two-drink minimum. As well as playing host to comedians, it is also supposed to be haunted by the ghost of George Schultz, who died in 1989.

More famous than Pip's is the Improv (or the Improvisation Café to give it its original full name), which, like the hungry i, boasted a bare-brick backdrop. In previous incarnations, it had been a luncheonette and a Vietnamese restaurant, but in 1963 Budd Friedman reopened it as a late-night café aimed at theatre people. Comedians soon began using it as a place to try out new material, and it went on to become a legendary comedy venue, billing itself today as 'America's Original Comedy Showcase and Restaurant'.

Gradually, more comedy clubs emerged. By the mid-

1970s, New York had two more showcase venues, the Comic Strip and Catch a Rising Star, both of which would thrive and become famous. Then there was the Comedy Store on Sunset Boulevard in Los Angeles, which opened on 10 April 1972. It was set up by an ex-comic called Sammy Shore, who had worked in Vegas and opened for Elvis prior to becoming a comedy promoter. Control passed to his wife Mitzi on their divorce in 1974, and she became infamous for putting the fear of God into the new comedians she nurtured there.

Unlike the venues which had preceded them, from vaudeville to the hungry i, the early comedy clubs didn't actually pay the stand-ups who worked in them. The logic was that the clubs offered comedians valuable exposure and the chance to be spotted by TV producers, so paying them in cab fares and free meals was perfectly acceptable. In 1979, Mitzi Shore's refusal to pay the acts at the Comedy Store led to the extraordinary phenomenon of a strike by stand-up comedians. This was no laughing matter. Once the dispute had been settled and Shore had started paying the acts, a comic who believed he was not being booked because of his involvement in the strike committed suicide by jumping off the roof of a nearby building, holding a note which read, 'My name is Steve Lubetkin. I used to work at the Comedy Store'.

In the 1980s, there was an extraordinary explosion of comedy clubs in America. At the beginning of the decade, there were only ten that actually paid their acts, but by 1992 there were over three hundred, playing host to about 2,000 comedians. As in vaudeville, chains of venues were formed, with branches of the Improv and Catch a Rising Star opening all over the country. Small comedy clubs sprung up in every corner of the USA, for example (to pick three at random): the Looney Bin in Walled Lake, Florida; Uncle Funny's in Miami, Florida; and Filly's Comedy Shoppe in Rapid City, South Dakota. The success of stand-up comedy led to the coining of the cliché that it had become 'the new rock and roll'. Perhaps inevitably, by the early 1990s the expansion in the stand-up scene slowed down, and some venues were forced to close, but in spite of the fallback, there are still comedy clubs all over the USA.

British origins

Music hall

However reluctant I am to accept the idea that America invented stand-up comedy, I have to admit it has a good claim. The MCs and monologists of vaudeville were doing something rather like it as early as the 1920s, and the chances are that even if Studs Terkel didn't coin it, the term 'stand-up comedy' is American.

On the other hand, it may be that an embryonic form of stand-up existed in Britain even before it did in America, and that it evolved in parallel with its American counterpart. The story of British stand-up starts in music hall, a slightly older tradition than vaudeville. The generally recognised date of music hall's birth is 1852, when Charles Morton opened the Canterbury Hall in London. Music hall grew out of tavern-based entertainment which had become increasingly formalised even before Morton opened his Hall, and the entertainment took the form of a series of acts, mainly singers, performing to male-dominated, largely working-class audiences who drank and ate as they watched.

Like vaudeville, music hall became popular very quickly. By 1868, there were two hundred halls in London and three hundred in the provinces. As new venues were built and old ones adapted and expanded to cope with bigger audiences, the halls began to look less like taverns and more like theatres. By the beginning of the twentieth century, when venues like the Hackney Empire were built, music halls were pretty much indistinguishable in shape from the theatres in which straight drama was presented.

Meanwhile, significant changes were taking place in the entertainment they presented. A classic music-hall show lasted three or four hours, and customers would come and go, not necessarily staying for the whole show. There would be a huge number of acts on the bill. A programme from the Canterbury Hall in 1887 shows fifty-three items on the bill, including Little Tich, Raffin's Pigs and Monkeys, and the Sisters du Cane. A bill from the London Pavilion, for 29 May 1899, shows an extraordinary eighty-five acts including Florrie Forde, Dan Leno and Marie Lloyd. By the first decade of the twentieth century, this format was being abandoned in favour of a shorter show, presented twice nightly. A bill from the Holborn Empire for the week commencing 3 March 1913, for example, shows just thirteen acts in a show which started at 6.20 p.m. and 9.10 p.m.[17]

The acts themselves had also begun to change. The classic music-hall style of solo performers singing comic or serious songs in character was gradually replaced by a more varied set of acts. For example, if you were at the Holborn Empire in the week commencing 17 December 1934, you could see nine acts, including:

- The Irresistible Houston Sisters (a double act in which they played children)
- The Melvilles (comic jugglers)
- The Radio Three (a singing act)
- Keith Clark (a magician who did tricks with cigarettes)
- Duncan Gray (a comedian with the delightful bill matter, 'ACCUSED OF BEING FUNNY – FOUND GUILTY')
- Gracie Fields (topping the bill, and described on the poster as 'England's Greatest Comedienne')[18]

To reflect the change in the organisation and nature of entertainment, people began to refer to it as 'variety' instead of 'music hall'.

Why is music hall like stand-up comedy?
The roots of stand-up comedy are unmistakably in the

classic music-hall style. Although the latter was largely made up of songs, these were often comic and were sung directly to the audience. Through time, they became more like stand-up, as a patter section was introduced, with the orchestra stopping and the comedian telling a series of gags, before the music struck up again for the final chorus. Gradually, the patter became more important, and the song which bracketed it became more like an afterthought. Dan Leno, probably the most popular British comedian of the late nineteenth century, was acknowledged as the performer who 'shifted the centre of gravity from song to "patter"'.[19]

It seems likely that music-hall comedians related to the audience in the way modern stand-ups do. It's difficult to prove this, because while there are many studio recordings of acts like Dan Leno, Marie Lloyd and Little Tich, they were never recorded live. However, some acts did survive long enough to perform in an era when live theatre recordings had become possible. Music-hall veterans toured around the variety theatres in shows such Don Ross's *Thanks for the Memory*, which featured Randolph Sutton, Nellie Wallace, Ella Shields, Talbot O'Farrell, Gertie Gitana, Billy Danvers and G. H. Elliott. This was recorded for radio in around 1948, and Nellie Wallace's act is particularly interesting.

Wallace had made her music-hall debut in Birmingham in 1888 while in her teens, and was in her late seventies at the time of this recording. She performs just one song, 'Mother's Pie Crust', but manages to spin it out for over seven minutes. The act starts with the musical introduction, and she proceeds to sing the song, getting regular laughs. It finishes, and the audience applaud. Then she launches into a spoken routine, which sounds exactly like what we would recognise as stand-up comedy:

Oh dear, dear! My poor, dear father! I can seem 'im now! I can see 'im so *plainly*! Just before 'e died, he *called* me to his bedside! He said, 'Are you there – my pretty one?'

[*laughter*] He was unconscious! [*laughter*] Ahh. Ahh, poor darling, how he suffered, how he suffered! And in silence! The doctors wanted us to take 'im – to the seaside. But – we couldn't afford it! We hadn't the money! So what do you think I did? His noble daughter. I sat by 'is bedside, *and fanned him with a kipper!* [*laughter*]'[20]

Her delivery is more stylised and melodramatic than that of most modern comedians, her voice high-pitched and wobbling with age and emotion. She *emphasises* certain words or phrases by elongating the syllables, and adopting a sing-song tone. But in spite of this, the energy and rhythm of her speech are distinctly like stand-up. She is as success-ful as a modern comedian in getting laughs, and building them. The laugh she gets with the third joke lasts for ten seconds, about twice as long as for the first joke. The 'Oh dear, dear' which begins the routine is actually a kind of catchphrase, appearing in a number of her patter routines.

As in stand-up, much of the humour comes from putting a personality on display in front of an audience. The audience laugh when she recalls her father calling her 'my pretty one', because they are familiar with her stage persona: a clownishly unglamorous older spinster with delusions of attractiveness. She wore outlandish costumes, with funny hats and flea-bitten furs, her face made comically gawky with exaggerated make-up, and sometimes thick, round-framed glasses. The gag about fanning her father with a kipper fits in perfectly with her grotesque image.

Then there is the directness of communication. She acknowledges the audience and talks directly to them. She goes on to ask them to join in with the song's chorus (which closes the act), getting another laugh by telling them, 'And when we come to that part, "*The deep blue sea!*" don't mess about with it!' Although she is not heckled in this recording, she would certainly have known how to deal with hostile audiences. T. S. Eliot remembered seeing her being jeered and heckled: 'I have seen her, hardly pausing in her act, make some quick retort that silenced her tormentors for the rest of the evening.'[21]

The intense rapport between Wallace and her audience was essential to her act, and this makes her much more similar to a stand-up than to a revue comedian like Joyce Grenfell. Wallace and Grenfell once appeared on the same bill in a wartime concert in a small country cinema. The difference in their approach becomes clear in Grenfell's recollection of the incident, which manages to be affectionate while also portraying Wallace as eccentric and rather bad-tempered. Grenfell says, 'I felt secure only if I was safely behind the footlights and couldn't see the audience,' whereas Wallace talked to the people who had come to see her. Grenfell had others to converse with: 'I'm pretending there is someone else onstage with me and I talk to him. If I pretend clearly enough I should be able to make you, the audience, accept the invisible character I'm imagining.' Wallace found the idea of a solo comedian ignoring the audience bizarre, to the extent that she stood backstage making loud comments about it even while Grenfell was doing her act: '[A]ll was going fairly well when suddenly I heard Nellie Wallace say in a desperate sort of way, and clearly: "What does she think she's doing out there on her own talking to herself?" Somehow I knew she didn't want an answer!'[22]

Music hall turns into stand-up

It was a short evolutionary leap from the classic music hall of Nellie Wallace to stand-up comedy, and some performers straddled the two styles. Will Fyffe, for example, born in Dundee in 1885, started as a classic music-hall comedian, singing character songs which played on his Scottish ethnicity. His trademark was 'I Belong to Glasgow', sung in the character of a drunken Glaswegian. It uses the standard format of the late music hall. Halfway through, the music cuts out, and he goes into a patter routine, complaining about rich 'cap-u-tilists' in slurred tones, before slipping back into the final chorus.

Later, he did routines which weren't bracketed within songs, like this radio recording in which he talks about being chatted up by a widow:

> But I knew she wanted me, sailors have that instinct. I knew it because one night, we were sitting on the die-van together – [*quiet laughter*] all right, the sofae. [*laughter*] This widow and I, we were sittin' on the sofae. And all of a sudden, she looked right up into my dial. [*laughter*] In the way that widows can. Any o' you lads ever had a widow looking at ye? [*laughter*] Eh? Y'ever noticed that sly, sleekit look, you know? You've, you've seen a ferret looking at a rabbit? [*laughter*]'[23]

This is distinctly recognisable as stand-up. It's a conversation with the audience, with the joke–laugh rhythm which is distinctive to the form. His connection with the punters is made more direct by asking the 'lads' if they've had the same experience of widows as he has.

In the variety era, the song-and-patter format of the music hall disappeared, except in the acts of veterans like Nellie Wallace. Instead, comedians like Max Miller, Tommy Trinder, Ted Ray, Billy Russell, Suzette Tarri, Beryl Reid and Frankie Howerd performed something which was stand-up comedy in all but name. These performers were known as 'front-cloth comics'. The name derives from the staging of British variety theatre, in which acts which used the full stage – such as sketch comedians who normally used the set – alternated with ones which could be performed in front of the curtain – the front-cloth comedians. This allowed the show to run smoothly, with no breaks. While one act was performing front-cloth, the stage behind was being set for the next. Front-cloth comedy existed at least as early as the 1920s. A 1926 review describes Max Miller as 'a comedian of the new school', presumably referring to this emerging style.[24]

Variety outlives vaudeville

Front-cloth comedians had a longer run than their US equivalents, the monologists, because British variety survived decades longer than American vaudeville. This was due to a quirk of fate. Whereas control of most vaudeville theatres had fallen into the hands of somebody who had no interest in live theatre, variety theatres came under the control of two people who were passionately committed to keeping the form alive: George Black and Val Parnell.

In the 1920s, variety was in decline, and many performers were convinced that it was doomed. As in America, there was a trend for shows in which variety acts performed alongside films, and when Walter Gibbons took control of the London Palladium, the pinnacle of the variety circuit, he experimented with putting on cine-variety. He was so unsuccessful that the venue changed hands and was taken over by Gaumont-British, which also took possession of the associated GTC circuit of cinemas and theatres. The company put Black and Parnell in charge. The two men were determined to make the Palladium work as a world-class variety theatre, and although Gaumont-British was a film company, unlike RKO in America it was happy to keep running theatres as well as cinemas.

Black realised that he would have to revive the national variety circuit so that it could keep him supplied with experienced acts. With this in mind, he and Parnell made efforts to improve the quality of entertainment in the theatres they controlled. The Palladium was reopened as a pure variety theatre in September 1928, with a bill which included comedians Dick Henderson, Gracie Fields and Billy Bennett. The posters for the relaunch bore the slogan: 'Variety is coming back . . . to the Palladium.'

Later, in 1932, the larger and more prestigious Moss chain of theatres was rumoured to be about to switch from variety to cinema, but instead it was sold to Gaumont-British. They decided to keep the venues as variety theatres so as to avoid competition with their established cinemas.

This meant that more than thirty theatres fell into Black's hands, to add to the twelve GTC halls he already controlled, and the future of British variety was secure.

By July 1938, the entertainment trade paper *The Era* was topping its front page with the headline 'Biggest Variety Boom for Years'. It reported that many more cinemas were booking variety acts, some were converting back into variety theatres, and there were even fears that bookers would not be able to find enough 'star-material' to put on their bills.

When Batley ruled British showbusiness

By the 1960s, variety was giving out its last gasps, killed by competition from television. Whereas American stand-up found a post-vaudeville home in the Borscht Belt and the Chitlin Circuit, in Britain it survived in the working-men's clubs, which had existed since the mid-nineteenth century. When variety died, entertainment in working-men's clubs boomed, leading entrepreneurs to set up bigger, privately owned clubs built around the same model, but with the budget to put on really spectacular shows.

The Batley Variety Club, for example, was opened by James Corrigan in the small Yorkshire town in 1967. Corrigan had worked out that there were about two million people living within a twenty-mile radius of Batley, who would be happy to travel to be entertained. He raised £65,000 from Newcastle and Scottish Breweries and built a club that could hold 2,000 people. This allowed a small Yorkshire town to play host to glamorous, big-name acts, including Gerry and the Pacemakers, Engelbert Humperdinck, Lulu, Matt Monro, the Beverley Sisters, Roy Orbison, Louis Armstrong, Shirley Bassey and Jayne Mansfield.

Big clubs like Batley put on established comedians such as Tommy Cooper and Dave Allen, but the stand-ups who actually started their careers on the club circuit had a distinctive style. In 1971, a group of them including Bernard Manning, Frank Carson, Ken Goodwin and Charlie Williams appeared in Granada Television's *The*

Comedians. Whereas the front-cloth comics on the variety theatres had used catchphrases, costumes and comic personas, their acts fleshed out with songs and even dances, club comics had a more minimal approach: unoriginal, self-contained gags, told one after another, with little else going on.

Singers turn into stand-ups

Meanwhile, there were more interesting stand-ups emerging from Britain's folk-music clubs. Billy Connolly, Jasper Carrott and Mike Harding started as folk singers, but gradually, the comic introductions to their songs grew and became the most important part of their acts, just as stand-up comedy had originally grown out of the patter section of music-hall songs. In folk clubs, stand-up became more conversational, and comics like Connolly and Carrott put personal anecdotes into their acts alongside observational routines.

Victoria Wood was another singer who turned into a stand-up, although she started her career singing cabaret songs rather than folk. After an appearance on the TV talent show *New Faces* in 1974, she struggled to find the right audience. She appeared in revue and wrote successful plays, and by the early 1980s, her act had evolved into stand-up. Successful television shows like *Victoria Wood – As Seen on TV* helped build her audience to the point where she has become one of the most successful stars of British stand-up, having twice sold out a fifteen-night run in the 5,000-capacity Royal Albert Hall. Like Phyllis Diller in America, Wood was not Britain's first female stand-up, but was the first one to become a really big star.

Alternative comedy and beyond

America reinvented stand-up in the 1950s with the rise of the sick comedians, and it started to spawn comedy clubs as early as the 1960s. In this respect, Britain seriously lagged behind. The Comedy Store, the UK's first dedicated stand-up club, didn't open until May 1979, seventeen years after Pip's had made its first customers laugh. The Store was directly inspired by the American model. An insurance salesman called Peter Rosengard had visited the LA Comedy Store in the summer of 1978 and had been extremely impressed. He copied the idea and the name, setting up his own version in a room above a strip club at 69 Dean Street, Soho.

Acts who found a platform there include Alexei Sayle, Tony Allen, Rik Mayall and French & Saunders, the first British comedians seriously to rival the likes of Mort Sahl and Lenny Bruce, because they directly challenged the crusty conventions of traditional stand-up and expanded the possibilities of the form. Despite the argument that British comedians are 'way off the pace' set by the Americans, the first alternative comedians were genuinely groundbreaking. In a 1987 interview, Mark Breslin, who founded the Canadian comedy club chain Yuk Yuk's, said that American comedians like Jay Leno avoided controversial topics like the then-recent Chernobyl nuclear disaster. He went on to say that the same could not be said of 'that guy out of England' – Alexei Sayle – who would 'do a Chernobyl joke and have no problem with it.'[25]

As in America, once the idea of comedy clubs was established, there was a boom. Initially, alternative comedy was a semi-amateur affair. When the Comedy Store first opened, the only act to be paid was the compère. A group called Alternative Cabaret (founded by Tony Allen) toured pubs, arts centres, students' unions and other small venues, thus sewing the seeds for the pub-based comedy clubs that began to flourish, initially in London and then in most large provincial towns and cities. This is where my own small part of the story comes in. From the late 1980s, I worked in small clubs in London and the provinces, and, in 1992, I helped to set up Sheffield's longest-running comedy club, the Last Laugh, in the Lescar pub, Hunters Bar. I co-managed and compèred it until 1997 when I started my first university job, but it still thrives today in the hands of Toby Foster, who played the drummer in *Phoenix Nights*.

By the end of the twentieth century, the stand-up scene was big business. In 1999, the Comedy Store (now run by Don Ward, who had been part of it from the beginning) was making an annual turnover of about £2.5 million in a purpose-built, 400-seat venue in Oxendon Street. In 2000, the Jongleurs chain of venues was sold to Regent Inns in a deal reported to be worth as much as £8.5 million. In 2001, the turnover of the Avalon agency and production company had grown from £250,000 in 1988 to £30 million.

As the new comedy scene thrived, it became absolutely central to British stand-up. Just about every major British stand-up comedian in the last twenty-five years started his or her career in what would once have been called alternative comedy clubs, including Ben Elton, Jo Brand, Jack Dee, Lee Evans, Eddie Izzard, Harry Hill, Peter Kay, Jimmy Carr and Ross Noble.

Then there are the offshoots, like the black comedy scene, which started with a series of shows in Ladbroke Grove, Deptford and Brixton; and the opening of the 291 Club at the Hackney Empire, which took its inspiration from the Live at the Apollo shows at Harlem's famous theatre. From these roots grew a healthy circuit. One of its most important promoters, John Simmit, runs a large number of shows all over the UK, as well as playing Dipsy in the cult children's TV show *Teletubbies*. There's also the Irish comedy scene, which got going when the Comedy Cellar in Dublin's International Bar opened in 1988. A core of performers played there regularly, learning their trade, and constantly trying new material. Some, like Ardal O'Hanlon and Dylan Moran, moved to the UK and quickly became very successful.

When comparing the history of stand-up in Britain and America, it becomes obvious that rather than British comedians adopting and adapting an American invention, the form has actually undergone a parallel evolution in the two countries. The development has been similar in each case, starting in theatres which presented a variety of acts, finding other types of venues when the theatres shut down, undergoing a major reinvention and finally finding a home in dedicated comedy clubs. While America may have been significantly ahead at certain points, there's no evidence that stand-up actually sprang to life there. In fact, if you accept music hall as a form of embryonic stand-up, then Britain was probably the first to come up with it. There may, of course, be other countries which could claim to have originated the form: Australia, for example, had its own music-hall tradition dating back to the nineteenth century, and an alternative comedy scene which started in the early 1980s.

Live performances

Where does stand-up happen?

Throughout the twists and turns of its history, stand-up comedy has occupied a whole range of venues, from the tiny to the implausibly large. Today, a typical location would be the comedy club, but even these vary enormously. Some are purpose-built, others take place in a bar or a pub function room. The audience usually sit around tables drinking alcohol, but they might be any number from thirty to four hundred. The stage might be a corner of the room with a mike stand, or it could be a raised platform with a backdrop and theatre lights. The show might start as early at 8 p.m. or as late as midnight. Generally, it will be introduced by a compère, and there will be three or four acts; but the format varies.

Stand-up works well in small, intimate clubs, but it started its life in big theatres, and since the 1970s, it has followed rock and roll into huge arenas. Live comedy has shown it can exist on a spectacular scale. In 1977, Steve Martin grossed over $1 million for a tour in which he played to a total audience of 500,000 in enormous venues in fifty cities. In 1993, Rob Newman and David Baddiel played the Wembley Arena, with a maximum seating capacity 11,500. A review in the *Guardian* noted that it wasn't completely sold out: 'It was full-ish – but one end was curtained off, the empty spaces acted like fire breaks in a forest, and although it often crackled, it never quite caught fire.' On the other hand, it was the first British gig on this scale, and it paved the way for the likes of Lee Evans and Eddie Izzard to move into arena gigs. In 1998, four comedians from the black comedy TV showcase *Def Comedy Jam* toured the USA as the Original Kings of Comedy, playing to a total audience of one million people.

From the monstrously huge to the ridiculously small: Mark Thomas once did a stand-up show in somebody's living room. In the last episode of his first TV series, he gambled the entire budget for the show on a horse race, which he had also sponsored, naming it 'The Mark Thomas Chum Special Handicap'. His horse lost, giving him no money to make the episode, so he filmed a stand-up show in 'Andy's living room'. It was lit in green and red, with the show's logo projected on to the walls, but it was clearly a real living room, with coving, a picture rail, plants on a shelf and slatted cupboard doors. At one point, Thomas pauses mid-routine to draw attention to the sound of a train going past, getting a laugh by commenting, 'I just want the folks back home to get a bit of social realism.'

At the fringes, stand-up finds its way into all kinds of quirky venues. James Campbell is building a career by performing stand-up to children, and he started doing this in primary schools, doing up to four shows in a day. Milton Jones is a Christian, and he regularly performs to audiences of fellow believers, sometimes even in church. Understandably, it's not an easy place to do comedy, as he points out: '[O]ften, if it's literally in a church . . . people aren't quite sure how to react. Because they have this thing of, "Do we laugh or do we not? Is it appropriate?"'

Standing behind microphones

The classic image of stand-up is that the format is low-tech. All you need is a microphone and perhaps a spotlight. Even more than the bare-brick backdrop, the hand mike has become a symbol of stand-up. Go to a show at the London Comedy Store, and one minute before the show starts, red backlights come on and the microphone is picked out in white, forming a dramatic theatrical image of stand-up with the iconic mike at its centre.

This may be the classic image, but it's not always accurate. For a start, there isn't always a microphone. The earliest stand-ups, in vaudeville and variety, wouldn't have used them, instead developing powerful vocal projection, something which must have involved great physical effort. They weren't introduced into British theatres until the 1930s and, even then, some of the older performers shunned them, seeing them as the hallmark of an inferior performer. Microphones allowed for more subtle performance, but they also restricted physical movement, so comedians were forced to do their act standing in one particular spot.

Even today, when hand mikes are standard in most comedy clubs, comedians don't always use them. In the big theatres, comics often prefer small, wireless clip mikes, attached to their clothes or worn as a headset. Ross Noble, whose act involves a lot of high-energy physical work, wears a headset mike because although it 'cuts down the amount of sound effects you can do', it also allows him to 'be as physical as I possibly can' and 'demonstrate things with my hands . . . right down to [my] fingertips'.

Then there's the fact that, paradoxically, stand-ups don't always stand up. Shelley Berman was probably the first to work sitting down, performing his routines perched on a barstool. A little later, Dick Gregory also worked sitting down, because it helped with his relaxed style: 'The stool was where you sit and you talk and you had a drink.' In the 1970s, Irish comedian Dave Allen became famous on British TV for performing in a chair. By 1990, he had abandoned this and reverted to performing standing up, but the chair was still there onstage with him as a reminder of his former trademark style. Daniel Kitson, who won the Perrier Award at the Edinburgh Fringe in 2002, has a scruffy armchair onstage during his show, and performs some of his act lolling in it, impressively unaffected by the fact that he is onstage being watched by paying punters.

Technology

Stand-up isn't always a low-tech format, either. Some comedians like playing with technology. When Lenny Bruce played Duffy's Gaities, he would bring a telephone on to the stage with him and call the owner of a rival club, getting laughs by winding him up then slamming down the receiver before he could reply. Many later comics have also used telephones in their act, and today, Jack Dee gets the audience to send him text messages on his mobile. At the end of the show, he reads them out, showing disapproval at a particularly distasteful one before conspicuously pressing the save button. Others use less mundane forms of technology. In an appearance on *Def Comedy Jam* in the early 1990s, Bernie Mac's act is rhythmically punctuated with scratches from the DJ. In 2003, Howard Read received a Perrier nomination for a show in which he does a double act with a computer-animated sidekick called Little Howard.

Increasingly, shows in large venues use sophisticated staging very different from the simple, low-tech set-up in most comedy clubs. The programme for Eddie Izzard's *Sexie* tour credits twenty-one people with the running of the show, covering such areas as 'Scenic & Lighting Design', 'Sound Design', 'Music', 'Personal Trainer' and 'Master Carpenter'. The costume alone required the work of three people.

Projection screens are becoming common in enormous stadium gigs, compensating for how tiny the performer looks to the people in the back rows. At Wembley Arena, Lee Evans is backed by three screens, with a close-up in the centre, and a full body shot on either side. He uses his whole body as much as his face, so both shots are necessary for the distant punters to get the full effect of his act.

In theatres, staging is used to provide a physical context which fits the character of the comedian's act. Al Murray performs as the Pub Landlord, a working-class pontificator whose ridiculous patriotism is matched with a hatred of Europe in general and France in particular. In his 2003–4 tour, the backdrop is the character's coat-of-arms, and Murray shares the stage with a bar. Occasionally, he takes drinks or packets of crisps out from behind it, and gives them to members of the audience.

In the *Monster II* tour, Dylan Moran performs in front of a screen on to which his scratchy, Spike Milliganesque cartoons are projected. Every few minutes, the image changes, and sometimes it connects with what he's talking about. A skull-like picture flashes up during a routine about death, for example. The drawings also crop up in the merchandising. They're printed in the tour programme, on mugs and T-shirts on sale in the foyer, and on the sleeve of the subsequent audio CD of the show.

Even Jim Davidson, whose working-men's clubs origins might suggest a very basic approach to stand-up, is not averse to sophisticated staging. His 2003 *Vote for Jim* tour involves the concept of him running for Prime Minister, the show being his attempt to unveil his policies. He performs in front of a projected 'Vote for Jim' logo, and, rather than his usual casual stage clothes, he wears an expensive pinstripe suit, decorated with a purple rosette.

Ross Noble's *Noodlemeister* show sees him performing in front of a tangled mass of giant, multicoloured foam rubber noodles. He is enthusiastic about inventive staging, saying: 'If you're gonna play big theatres then you might as well do a show that they couldn't see in a comedy club. Because otherwise, you're just playing to more people, doing something that you could be doing in an intimate room where everyone could be right on top on you.'

Creating the right expectation

Obviously, the staging, the size of the venue and all of the other circumstances surrounding the show have an effect on the audience's expectations. Mark Thomas is aware of this, and makes sure the circumstances set the scene for his passionate political satire: '[T]he details of everything . . . as they go in, are important . . . What I want is when people come to gigs there'll be stalls outside, and there'll be people talking about ideas and issues and what have you . . . we did some gigs and we had Banksy[26] art works up as people came in and stuff like that . . . [I]t sets the mood that there is a debate going on, that there is a factual content.'

Dave Gorman uses staging to get audiences to shed their default expectations of a stand-up show. He moved away from straight stand-up in the late 1990s in favour a series of one-man shows in which he recalls the extraordinary challenges he has undertaken. These involve travelling the world to find a given number of people called Dave Gorman, or using the Internet to find ten Googlewhacks in a row.[27] He prefers to think of these shows as 'documentary comedy' rather than stand-up, and this is an important distinction, particularly for audiences: 'Everyone thinks they know what stand-up is. And people will come up and go, "You don't wanna bother with any of that fucking clever-clever nonsense, you want some fucking knob jokes." And they think they're right.' The staging helps him distinguish what he does from straight stand-up: 'When they walk into the show, there's two screens, two projectors, no microphone. And just the fact that they don't recognise it means they don't think they know what it is. And they give me a little bit of leeway . . . The minute there's a microphone in the stand and a spotlight, and it's a format they think they know best about, they have a different . . . set of demands.'

Stand-up comedy in a box

So far, I've concentrated on live stand-up, but the form has also enjoyed a long history as recorded entertainment. Comedians have worked on radio since its earliest days, and the fact that audiences could hear acts like Fred Allen and Jack Benny for free on their wireless sets rather than paying to see them in theatres probably contributed to the decline of vaudeville. In Britain, the variety theatres were so afraid of competition from radio that, in 1927, the three main circuits, Moss, Stoll and GTC, launched a campaign against the BBC.

Later, radio co-existed more happily with variety, as theatres realised that radio stars could draw a big live audience, and comedians realised that radio success could bring them more fame than years of touring. Frankie Howerd, for example, first toured the variety theatres in 1946 as a newcomer at the bottom of the bill in a show called *For the Fun of It*. Later that year, he made his first broadcast on a showcase called *Variety Bandbox*. His radio appearances quickly made him famous, so that when he went back to the theatres he was topping the bill.

When television arrived, stand-ups quickly moved into the new medium, discovering that it could transform their careers just as effectively as radio. In the late 1940s, Milton Berle was already an established act, but by getting his own TV show at a time when ownership of sets was mushrooming, he became a huge star. American TV stand-up was revolutionised in the 1970s by the growth of cable. In 1975, Home Box Office made its first broadcast of a stand-up concert, with a film of Robert Klein at Haverford College. Simple economics made the cable channels very keen on comedy concert films. HBO found that it got similar rates of viewer satisfaction from a stand-up show which cost $75,000 to make and a movie which could cost as much as $1 million. A successful HBO special still has the ability to rocket a comedian to the big time.

Stand-ups have also benefited from putting out commercial recordings of their acts. *Mort Sahl at Sunset*, recorded in 1955 at the Sunset Auditorium in Carmel, California, is often cited as the first stand-up comedy album, but it certainly wasn't the earliest commercial live recording of a stand-up act. As long ago as 1938, HMV issued a three-record set of 78rpm discs, containing a recording of Max Miller's act at the Holborn Empire on 24 October of that year. They went on to release recordings of five more live shows between 1939 and 1942, and in 1957 issued a 33rpm ten-inch LP of a performance at the Metropolitan Theatre of Varieties. There is still a big market for audio recordings on cassette and CD today, although they now have to compete for record-shop shelf space with stand-up on video and DVD.

Like radio and TV, a successful commercial recording can turn a stand-up into a star. Comedy albums were hugely popular in America in the 1950s and 60s, and undoubtedly helped to bring the sick comedians to a wider audience. Shelley Berman was one whose career was transformed: 'It was a friend of mine, another comedian by the name of Mort Sahl, who had recorded for Verve, and he talked me into doing mine on record. And at first I resisted. I said, "But people will know my material, what good is that?" [He said,] "Yes, well, let's see what happens." So I did, and the people didn't care if they knew my material. They just wanted to see me do it, and they were with me. So these records were making a lot of money for me, but more important, they were bringing me to the public, and I was pretty happy about that.' Berman had good reason to be happy: his first album was released in 1959, and by 1963 he had produced three gold records.

Bob Newhart owes the very fact of becoming a stand-up to his first comedy album, *The Button-Down Mind of Bob Newhart*. When he came to the attention of record company executives, he had some clever routines, but had never

47

performed them to a live audience. The record company arranged for him to play three nights at a club in Houston, recorded his performances, and edited the results into the album. His first recording session was also his stage debut. The result was the first of a series of hit records that made him famous and allowed him to embark on a successful career as a live stand-up.

TV reshapes stand-up

Inevitably, recording live entertainment changes its nature, and the act the audience at home hears or sees will be different from what they would experience in a theatre or a comedy club. This is a lesson I learned the hard way, by appearing on the lunchtime TV magazine programme *Pebble Mill*.[28] I had seen other comedians I knew on the circuit on the show, and when I heard they were holding auditions, I thought I'd give it a try. I prepared my audition piece carefully.

Someone told me that a gentle, surreal comic whose act I thought would be perfect for a family audience had been rejected just because he'd used a couple of rude words when he was auditioning. I was amazed that the producers hadn't seen beyond the bad language. I knew that much of my act was unsuitable for TV, particularly this kind of bland daytime fodder. I had heard that the studio audience tended to be made up of pensioners, so I'd also have to take out anything which relied on a knowledge of youth culture.

That left me without enough material to fill the three-and-a-half-minute slot, so I had to start going through old routines and assembled was a lumpy ragbag of bits that didn't really fit together properly. The audition, bizarrely enough, was held at the Frontier Club, formerly the Batley Variety Club, and I performed in a huge concert room sparsely filled with other hopefuls: comedians, a circus performer and a bad rock band. A few damp laughs echoed around, and I got the gig.

On 20 April 1994, two days before my twenty-ninth

birthday, I arrived at the Pebble Mill studios in Birmingham, and after an excruciating camera rehearsal doing the act to the unsmiling producer and cameramen, I had time to enjoy the novel experience of being around TV people and minor celebrities.

The programme was broadcast live at about 11.30 a.m., an unnatural hour to do stand-up comedy. My time came, and I went out to face the audience. It was the weirdest crowd I'd ever seen. There were two seating blocks, each of which contained about fifty people. In the right-hand block, they were all pensioners as I'd anticipated, but to the left, they were all teenagers. It was like playing to two different audiences: each side reacted differently to different gags. If this had been a real stand-up show, I could have had a lot of fun by commenting on the bizarre age segregation in the audience, but with only three and a half minutes to play with, I had to just plough on through the set as quickly as possible.

Watching the footage today makes me writhe with embarrassment. It's one of the only records I have of what I used to do, but it's nothing like the act I actually did in the comedy clubs. The material is different, and the way I approach the audience is dictated by the cameras and the time-slot. Worse still, even though I considered this to be a meaningless appearance on an obscure show, I can still see myself trying too hard. I seem too cheerful, I smile too much, and when the show's host, Ross King, thanks me at the end, I stand there clapping him like an idiot, not knowing what else to do. I look like a puppy in a pet shop window, begging the passers-by to give me a home.

If appearing on *Pebble Mill* can change an act so profoundly, the effect of a truly important show, a potential big break, must be enormous. For many American stand-ups, an appearance on one of the big talk shows has long been the crucial step which leads to fame and success. This makes the hosts and producers of such programmes extremely powerful. From the 1960s to the 1990s, *The*

Tonight Show's host Johnny Carson was probably the most influential of them all, as Bob Zmuda recalls:

> If Carson liked your act, at his whim you were invited to the next level, which was to cross the stage and actually sit and chat with His Excellency. If you finished your act and didn't get the wave-over, that is, if Johnny just applauded and thanked you but made no attempt to speak to you, you probably should have considered the insurance business as a new career before you even left the stage.[29]

A 1992 British TV documentary follows the path of an American comic called Al Lubel as he prepares for his first appearance on Carson. He feels the pressure keenly: 'I've got eight years invested in, like, one six-minute appearance with *The Tonight Show*, and *The Tonight Show* is almost like a final exam. This is where you find out if you can really make it in show business.' Building up to the filming, we see him performing at a comedy club in Vegas. He's wearing comfortable clothes: a T-shirt under his jacket, and trainers. His delivery is just as comfortable: he's relaxed and in control, as if talking to friends. Towards the end of the film, we see his Carson spot. He's transformed. His clothing is neat and formal, his T-shirt replaced by a smart white shirt and a tie. His delivery is taut and keen. Just like me on *Pebble Mill*, he smiles too much, as if he's meeting the parents of his future spouse for the first time. Although Lubel is still a working comic today, this clearly wasn't the big break he'd hoped for.[30]

Given how it can change and distort things, it's not surprising that comedians tend to be suspicious of television. Harry Hill, for instance, comments: '[S]tand-up doesn't really work very well on TV, does it?' Ross Noble wasn't sure he wanted to do television, fearing he would lose control of the process. Eventually, he found a way round the problem: 'I actually filmed it all meself, paid for the thing meself, and just put the cameras in, edited it all, went to them and went, "Look, just put that on," and they went, "All right, then."'

Comedy albums reshape stand-up in a more interesting way

Albums and videos place fewer restrictions on stand-up, and comedians often have a reasonable amount of artistic control over the recorded products they put out. Jo Brand, for example, remembers the process behind her last video: 'I went down . . . and sort of sat in the editing suite for as long as I could stand it . . . and said, "Can we put that bit in, can we take that bit out, blah blah blah." . . . How people are editors, I don't know, it takes so bloody long!' Similarly, Harry Hill says his production company, Avalon, 'give you all the control that you want'.

Unlike radio and TV, albums and videos aren't particularly restricted by censorship, which is part of their appeal. They often contain forbidden fruit, jokes too juicy for the broadcast media. In 1950s America, Redd Foxx's albums gave the buying public the chance to experience the thrill of listening to uncensored black comedy. In the early 1990s, the American music industry was coming under pressure from Tipper Gore's Parents Music Resource Center to place warning stickers on albums with controversial content, and Bill Hicks responded to this by putting a label on his debut CD *Dangerous* which said, 'Are we to have a censor whose imprimatur shall say what books should be sold and what we may buy?' In spite of this act of defiance, Hicks acknowledged that warning stickers on albums probably helped sales.

The comparative lack of restrictions means that albums and videos don't draw stand-up comedy's teeth in the way that radio and TV often do. However, they can still have a powerful influence on the art form, albeit a less negative and more interesting one. When comedy albums were at the height of their popularity in the 1950s and 60s, they affected the way that many American stand-ups shaped their acts. Some albums, such as Lenny Bruce's *The Carnegie Hall Concert*, contain what appears to be one entire performance, even if some edits have been made. Others, like *The Sick Humor of Lenny Bruce*, are made up of various routines, clearly separated by silence. In both cases, the live recordings are usually presented like music albums, with the routines named and listed as if they were songs.

This meant that when audiences went to see a comedian, they would often request bits they had heard on an album. Shelley Berman remembers: 'People would come in and they would request certain routines, and of course I had a little joke for them, I would say, "I'll make up my own damn show if you don't mind."' Lenny Bruce was even less happy to do bits from his LPs, and on the album of his legendary Carnegie Hall concert you can hear him tell the audience: 'People say to me, "How come you don't do all the bits on the records?" . . . As soon as it becomes repetitive to me, I can't cook with it any more, man.'

Thinking of routines as if they were songs meant that stand-up shows became like a series of individual items rather than a flowing, seamless whole. Bob Newhart, who started as a recording artist at exactly the same time as he started doing stand-up, would introduce each routine as if it were a song, explaining the basic premise and finishing by saying that the situation he'd described would go 'something like this'. Shelley Berman used a similar structure. Here's how he introduces one of his routines:

Anyway, after a particularly terrible experience in New York in dealing with a department store, I wrote this particular piece of material. While the bit is rather extended, a little elaborate, I think you'll get the point I'm trying to make of the difficulty you may encounter in phoning a *department store*.'

He emphasises the last two words, as if to indicate that this is the title of the routine, and indeed this is the title as it appears on the album *Inside Shelley Berman*.

More recently, the DVD has also influenced stand-up, albeit in a less significant way. On his most recent DVD, *Sexie*, Eddie Izzard jokes to the audience in the venue about the format in which the recorded show will eventually be sold. In a routine about Greek mythology, he does an impression of the Sirens, the joke being that they sound like different types of siren. He then shows Odysseus going past, commenting, 'Someone's trying to break into that island.' Realising that the way he has acted this out makes it seem as if Odysseus is going past in a speedboat, he goes on to show alternative versions of the same moment, involving different modes of transport: a sailing ship, a bicycle, water skis. In each case, he finishes with the same line. Then he gets a big laugh and a round of applause by explaining, 'This is for the DVD, you see – different endings.'

Spoken Word

One of the things that makes stand-up comedy so difficult to define is the fact that its boundaries are fuzzy. Many of the qualities that seem to be central to it – personality, rapport, immediacy, even funniness – are not unique to stand-up, and can be found in a whole range of other types of performance, including straight acting, political oratory and live music from punk to country and western. There are stand-up comedians who have pushed so hard at the boundaries that what they do seems hardly to fit their own category, and other performance styles have emerged that seem so close to stand-up as to differ in name only.

Take Spoken Word, for example. This performance style is relatively young, growing out of the American punk and underground music scene of the early 1980s. Harvey Kubernik, an LA-based journalist who had been involved in the music business, started encouraging musicians and singers to perform in venues like the Llasa Club in

Hollywood: 'I didn't want to put on poetry readings, so I coined this term Spoken Word, and I wanted it to be diary-rants, improv, fragments of song-lyrics, some traditional poetry, excerpts from in-progress books – I wanted it to be narratives, but I took off the straitjacket.'[31] Henry Rollins, then the lead singer of seminal Californian hardcore punk band Black Flag, was one of the performers that Kubernik recruited for the new genre, and Rollins is now as well known for his Spoken Word performances as for his music with the Rollins Band. Later, Kubernik persuaded the Dead Kennedys' lead singer Jello Biafra to take the same path and, like Rollins, Biafra is now as much a Spoken Word artist as a musician.

Not all of the performers drawn into the genre come from music. In 1998, Rage Against the Machine's Zack de la Rocha set up the Spitfire tour, described on its website as 'Musicians, Actors & Activists Speaking Out on Global Affairs'. Its roster of acts includes musicians like Lydia Lunch, Exene Cervenka and Angelo Moore, rappers like Ice T and Michael Franti, actors like Rosie Perez and Woody Harrelson, and campaigners like Ralph Nader.

The main distinction between Spoken Word and stand-up seems to be the title: performers like Rollins and Biafra do not refer to themselves as stand-ups. A 1998 *Time Out* article brings Rollins together with Eddie Izzard to discuss their performances, and Izzard asks Rollins how stand-up differs from Spoken Word. Rollins gives no clear answer, hesitating to define what he does, simply describing it as 'the talking shows, or whatever it is I do up there'. Izzard, a passionate advocate for the art of stand-up, seems slightly put out by not having Rollins in the stand-up camp: 'In a competitive way, it's annoying that you're good, having come from music.'[32]

It's possible to identify three differences between the stand-up and Spoken Word. First, Spoken Word performers start out with an established reputation and image forged in another discipline; when Biafra did his first talking show, he was already well known as a punk singer, and it is inevitable that his performances will be seen in that light. Second, Spoken Word performances tend to be longer than the average stand-up act. Both Rollins and Biafra have regularly done shows of three hours or more. Finally, stand-up comedy is defined by the fact it is funny, but while Spoken Word performers do get laughs, they do not feel obliged to do so.

In Rollins's early Spoken Word performances, he was often as confrontational as he is in his music, and there's an account of a performance at the Llasa Club where he punched a member of the audience. In his earliest recordings, he plays for laughs only intermittently, and the material is far more extreme than most stand-up. On *Sweatbox*, recorded in 1987–88, he recalls an encounter with a cop which finishes with him fantasising about 'an uptight white pig getting wasted by a Mexican'.

In the 1990s, his performances became lighter, less confrontational, and started to contrast strongly with the darkness of his music, although there was still some serious content. I saw a show at the Octagon, Sheffield, in the early 1990s, where he talked about his abusive upbringing in a way that was by turns funny, touching and insightful.

More recently, the shows have been heavily weighted towards humour, and are distinguishable from stand-up only in that many of the anecdotes relate to his being an alternative rock star. A 1999 routine sees him reading out a letter from a Czech fan, and marvelling at the use of language in it, particularly a sentence which reads: 'On two concert, I'm should collective photo, but small, fat, bald-headed technologist be insane.' Taking care not simply to ridicule the fan, who is after all struggling with a second language, Rollins goes on to imagine a feature-length movie with this kind of dialogue. He has an air stewardess making an emergency announcement: 'For making landing immediate time, incredibly! [*laughter*] Broken, moving, not now, stupid motor on flaming! [*laughter*] I declaration: emergency! [*laughter and applause*]'[33] The piece has a classic stand-up structure, setting up the basic premise, then applying the same logic to an imaginary situation. Rollins's rhythm and delivery are those of a stand-up.

Biafra's Spoken Word is different, bearing more resemblance to performance art and political oratory, with a style of delivery that owes more to the cadences and inflections of his punk singing than stand-up comedy. In a show in Sheffield in 2001, he enters in a large overcoat, his eyes obscured by round, reflective sunglasses, reading out an imaginary declaration of martial law in sinister tones. It's less than a month after the aircraft flew into the Twin Towers, and much of the show deals with this new world situation. While there are plenty of jokes and satirical barbs about this in distinctly stand-up-like passages, there is also much political invective as he weaves complex conspiracy theories. Unlike most comedians, he often reads from notes, regaling the audience with what he sees as 'suppressed information'.

Like Rollins's early work, Biafra's Spoken Word bears the hallmark of his punk origins, sometimes delving into shocking material. On his first album, *No More Cocoons*, he imagines a theme park called 'Vietnam Never Happened', which includes such attractions as a petting zoo 'where you can feed overpriced McDonaldland cookies to our pen full of children deformed by Agent Orange'. Some of this gets laughs from the audience, but as he cranks up the horror, the response becomes more uneasy, and at one point, he asks, 'Is that getting a bit much?'

Pushing at the boundaries

If the phenomenon of Spoken Word makes it difficult to define the boundaries of stand-up, comedians who push against those boundaries make it even harder. Historically, the amount of time stand-ups have spent onstage has varied from a few minutes to three hours or more, but at the 2004 Edinburgh Fringe, Mark Watson gave these time limits a big stretch by performing non-stop for twenty-four hours, finishing the show by proposing to his girlfriend. Then there are occasions when the show spills out of the venue itself. Carl Reiner remembers an incident when Steve Martin took an audience of a thousand people at a college show outside to stand in an empty swimming pool, before diving on to them and 'swimming' across them to the other side.

Some comedians mess about with the form, seeing how far stand-up will stretch. Keith Allen had a very short stand-up career in the early days of alternative comedy, and has left behind little evidence of his act except a few video clips and a collection of legendary word-of-mouth stories. Some of these relate to what he did onstage, like smashing plates over his head; or performing a naked ventriloquism act, in the course of which he kept adjusting his penis, eventually pointing out to the audience that while he did this, nobody noticed his lips were moving. In other anecdotes, he didn't even reach the stage, perhaps announcing from the side that he was too famous actually to make an entrance, or replacing himself with a tape recorder which played the beginning of his act. Sometimes, he broke the most fundamental rule of all, by being deliberately unfunny.

Andy Kaufman was also deliberately unfunny at times, although he enjoyed greater success than Allen. He was a big name in America from the mid-1970s until his death in 1984. One of Kaufman's celebrated stunts was to go on at the Improv and start reading *The Great Gatsby* to the audience. Initially, they would laugh, but as it became clear that he really did intend to read the entire novel, they would start to leave. A more tasteless episode saw him make audience members line up and pay him a dollar per person to touch a cyst on his neck.[34]

Perhaps his most famous boundary-stretching moment came at the end of his Carnegie Hall concert in April 1979, when he invited the entire audience to come with him for milk and cookies. The video of the event shows Kaufman, wrapped in a dressing gown, joining audience members as they file out of the theatre and start getting on to twenty waiting buses. 'Come on, everybody!' shouts Kaufman, and you can hear punters shout, 'We're with ya!' and, 'Let's do it!' It cuts to shots of a canteen, with rows of milk cartons, and Kaufman surrounded by punters. 'Tomorrow the show will be continuing . . . at one o'clock at the Staten Island ferry,' he announces. According to Kaufman's collaborator Bob Zmuda, they turned up at the ferry the next day and were joined by about three hundred audience members from the night before, treating them all to ferry tickets and ice creams.

Trying to understand stand-up comedy is a bit like trying to keep hold of a wet bar of soap. Just when you think you've got to grips with it, it slips out of your hands. You can trace its history, but establishing exactly when and where it first sprang to life is very difficult. The origin of the term 'stand-up' is just as hard to pin down, and coming up with a convincing definition is complicated by the fuzziness of its boundaries. The next few chapters take a closer look at some of the defining features of the form.

3. Personality

You may have noticed that I feature quite heavily in this story. When I have an opinion, I make it quite clear that it's my point of view, and I don't try and hide behind some kind of pseudo-objectivity. The fact is, a stand-up's personality is absolutely crucial to his or her act. It provides a context for the material, it gives the audience something to identify with, and it's what distinguishes one comic from the next. Popular entertainers instinctively understand how crucial personality is, and nothing illustrates this point better than the lengths they will go to protect it. For example, in 1938, the Variety Artistes' Federation tried to bring personality under the protection of copyright law. An international conference on copyright was held in Brussels, and the VAF, the British trade union for light entertainers, put its case to the Board of Trade in a letter which said: '[W]e would comment that our particular anxiety is to endeavour to protect entertainers . . . against unauthorised reproduction of their personalities constituted as self-expression and mannerisms, which entertaining value of personality is the greatest asset an entertainer possesses and is the basis of the goodwill on which he earns his livelihood.'[1]

This might seem a bit paranoid, but there have been real cases of comedians having their personalities stolen. In the 1980s, Woody Allen sued National Video and Men's World Outlet for using lookalikes in adverts. By making it look as if Allen endorsed their products, the advertisers were exploiting his personality for commercial gain.

Why we like comedians

Affection

In 1999, I go to see Lenny Henry at the Philharmonic Hall in Liverpool. For me, the best part of the show is when he walks on to the stage at the beginning. I'm not making a cheap jibe here, it's just that I find his entrance an extraordinary moment. I've followed Henry's career since I was a child. I've seen him in a sitcom called *The Fosters*. I've been a huge fan of the anarchic children's television programme *Tiswas*, which saw him invent a crazy, Rastafarian, condensed-milk-obsessed character called Algernon Razzmatazz and engage in all kinds of custard-pie-related mayhem. I've seen him compère the pilot episode of the alternative comedy showcase *Saturday Live*, and star in various shows of his own.

As he walks on to the stage, a huge wave of affection surges through me, strengthened by the fact that he crosses the stage like a star, aware of the applause that greets him, but making no big show of it. His stride is loose, relaxed and unhurried as he makes his way to the mike. His charisma is almost tangible.

At the Brighton Dome Concert Hall in 2004, Dylan Moran radiates a different kind of charisma. He comes across as melancholy and shambolic, his hair unkempt and his speech slurred as if by alcohol. He is misanthropic, yet philosophical and poetic, capable of producing tender moments. He wanders on and straight away, without any kind of introduction, starts talking about the town he's performing in. After a few minutes of this, gruffly and almost as an afterthought, he says: 'Hello, by the way.' It gets a big laugh. The joke is all about his personality. His terse hello comes across like a glimmer of affection peeping out through the crack in his habitually grumpy façade. It's as if he's too shy or awkward to be more openly friendly. The effect is not only funny, it's also curiously charming. It makes me like him more.

Both these examples illustrate an important truth about comedians: we like them. As well as making us laugh, most stand-ups inspire affection. This is something which comedians have always known. Milton Berle, for example, says: 'The first thing is that an audience, I believe, have to like you, before they laugh at you.' Jack Rollins, who represented Woody Allen when he did stand-up, makes a similar point: 'In a cabaret . . . if an audience can sense the personality underlying the comic – if they can make contact with that personality, they'll enjoy him more.' It's a view shared by Allen himself: '[W]hat audiences want is intimacy with the person. They want to like the person and find the person funny as a funny human being. The biggest trap that comedians fall into is trying to get by on material.'[2]

Sometimes the affection the audience feel for the comedian is very obvious. Victoria Wood has hardcore fans who follow her around dressed up as her characters. A *South Bank Show* documentary shows a bunch of middle-aged women dressed in yellow berets, like the Lancashire girl in Wood's act who is always looking for her friend Kimberly. They meet Wood at the stage door, where she signs autographs and poses for a photo with them. Wood comments: 'They think I'm nice and friendly. My husband says they think I'm their best friend, you know. And that's fine – on the stage, I'm happy to be their best friend.'[3]

In some cases, there's a sexual element to the affection. When Dylan Moran used to play my comedy club, the Last Laugh, female punters often came up to me after the show to tell me how attractive they thought he was, even offering to put him up for the night. In spite of his shabby appearance, he was the comic who seemed to inspire the most female lust.

In a TV documentary, Alan Davies is onstage doing his act, when a woman shouts: 'Get your kit off!' He tries to explain the phenomenon: 'I think that's why it's attractive to audiences. Because they're seeing somebody really expressing themself and being very, very vividly alive in a way that many people haven't found a way to be, you know. So those performers become . . . most amazingly attractive. But it isn't really them, it's what they're doing, they're just flying, they're doing the thing that everyone wishes they could do.'[4]

There's also a sexual edge to Eddie Izzard's appeal. Ken Campbell notes that 'all sexes fall in love with him', and this is borne out by the intensity of feeling to be found in fan forums on the Internet. I spend no more than two minutes looking through these before I happen across the following, posted by 'comic-iris': 'Last night I had a dream with Eddie in it. Strangely enough, I was dating him. It wasn't all hot and bothering type of dream, just a really nice, content feeling dream with the feelings that I usually have with my boyfriend (who I have introduced to Eddie, and he is a fan now).'[5]

While it's unlikely that comic-iris will ever actually become Eddie Izzard's girlfriend, the affection audiences feel for comedians can be reciprocated. Bill Cosby, for example, says that he wants get the same response to his act as when he is talking to people round the dinner table, and Victoria Wood describes playing to the Royal Albert Hall as being, 'like having two and a half thousand friends round and you're the funniest one in the room'. For some comics, the relationship is even more personal. Sean Hughes says the beginning of a stand-up gig is 'much like a first date', and Eddie Izzard reveals that the audience offer him a 'surrogate affection thing', compensating for the death of his mother when he was a child.[6]

All of this makes the audience–performer rapport seem very much like the kinds of relationships that grow between people in everyday life. However irrational it may seem, on one level we think of the comedian as somebody we actually know, whether a casual acquaintance, a friend or a lover.

The pressure to be liked by the audience is one of the things that makes doing stand-up so terrifying. Victoria Wood puts it this way: 'If they don't laugh, I feel they don't like you. That's the dangerous path you tread, I think, as a comic, is that it is you. You know, they're not saying, "Oh well, *she* was very good but the *play* was terrible," they say, "We didn't like *her*." '

Physical appeal

If the 'relationships' we have with comedians are akin to those we have with people we know, then we must like them for the same kind of reasons, and part of the appeal must be physical. We can find ourselves irrationally drawn to a stand-up's voice, face, body, mannerisms or posture. I remember first seeing Eddie Izzard on the London comedy circuit when I was doing open-mike spots at the end of the 1980s. Our paths crossed a number of times, and I was blown away by his ability to generate silly, surreal material, much of it seemingly on the spur of the moment.

On a less rational level, though, I loved the fact that his voice was so posh. This was tied up with my personal history. I'd gone through my teens as a middle-class kid in a comprehensive school where any trace of middle-classness in the voice, a vowel sound here or a slightly ostentatious word there, would provoke the other kids to turn up the end of their nose with a finger and emit a ridiculous aristocratic squawk. I was never terribly well spoken, but fear of the squawk made me careful about how I talked. Izzard had a gloriously and unashamedly posh voice without sounding remotely like an upper-class twit. Hearing him talk was like listening to freedom, unfettered and unselfconscious. I'm not the only one who finds the sound of Izzard's voice appealing. Alan Davies has said that, as with Ken Dodd, Izzard's voice is just funny in itself.

Comedians' voices clearly have a powerful effect, inspiring colourful prose from critics. Ben Thompson, for example, says Jo Brand's voice 'rustles with the beguiling timbre of a freshly opened tobacco pouch', and that Jenny Éclair's 'fag-addled voice rasps like sandpaper on a velvet cushion'.[7]

Faces can be just as potent. Dan Leno, the music-hall comedian whose work paved the way for fully-fledged stand-up comedy, had an extraordinary face, as many of his contemporaries commented. Archibald Haddon, for example, said, 'Look at his picture now. That mouth, those eyes, those eyebrows, the knobbly bit on the top! Do you feel an inward chuckle – an inclination to smile?' Marie Lloyd, another great music-hall comic, said that he had 'the saddest eyes in the whole world', adding, 'if we hadn't laughed we should have cried ourselves sick'. Max Beerbohm made a similar observation in his obituary of Leno: '[T]hat face so tragic, with the tragedy that is writ on the face of a baby-monkey, yet ever liable to relax its mouth into a sudden wide grin and to screw up its eyes to vanishing point over some little triumph wrested from Fate, the tyrant.'[8]

Sometimes, it's the whole physical package that appeals. In the variety era, Max Miller's physicality inspired this almost embarrassingly rapturous description from a critic called A. Crooks Ripley:

Max has physical charm equivalent to that of an attractive woman, or, in vulgar terms, sex-appeal . . . Radio is not able to convey to the listener a picture of the finely shaped hands, idle, still, falling their full length as he stands, rarely seeking to aid the voice; most, most satisfying in gesture . . . or the walking movement, strong and limber, elegant, authoritative, overwhelming the incongruity of attire. Television in a close-up shot would show the scrumptious expression Max wears in particularly big moments, pinching his teeth with his cheeks as if he were sucking a pungent acid-drop, the yolks of the eyes looking towards heaven through his panama . . . but it would miss-out the way the expanse of the whites match the collar and white and black shoes.[9]

Billy Connolly loses his beard

Sometimes, the aspect of a comedian's physical appearance that appeals to the audience becomes very obvious, as when Billy Connolly shaved off his beard at the beginning of the 1990s. Throughout his rise to fame, he sported a long, hippie-style, goatee beard, and when he decided to get rid of it for a while, the event received much media attention. A newspaper critic confided: 'I'm worried about the beard . . . It isn't there any more, and it makes Connolly look younger, saner and unpleasantly professional.' Television interviewer Michael Parkinson, an old friend of Connolly's, agreed, saying, 'I feel it took away that wonderful sort of lunatic aspect of him.' Making use of the attention, Connolly appeared in an advert for non-alcoholic lager, peeling back a false beard to reveal the newly-shaven chin beneath.

He was defiant towards his critics: 'When I whipped the beard off, a lot of people were quite distressed. People would ask, "Aren't you concerned about your image?" I gave it a lot of thought, and came to the conclusion that your image is nothing at all to do with you. It's none of your damn business. People who try to get an image are usually astrologers and other fuckwits on breakfast television with funny pullovers.'[10]

Whether it was any of his audience's damn business or not, it was an issue he had to address in his act. Footage from the time shows him coming on to the stage beardless, in a shirt tie-dyed in multicoloured stripes. While taking the applause, there are visible signs of embarrassment. After saying 'Hello', he touches his face, looks to one side, and grunts with good-humoured self-consciousness. Having created a certain expectation, perhaps even a little tension, he says: 'What do you mean, "Who the fuck are you?" It's me!"' The audience laugh, and he laughs with them, but he's still slightly hesitant. He runs his fingers over his chin where his beard used to be, then buries his face in his hands. 'Whaddya think, isn't it fucking *awful*?'[11] There's a big laugh. Showing masterful control, Connolly has brought any tension that might have been generated by his change of appearance out into the open, defusing it so that he can move on.

He's not the only comedian who is aware of the importance of physicality. Ken Dodd is said to have taken out insurance on his teeth, which protrude as a result of a childhood cycling accident. Phill Jupitus is large both in height and breadth. This contrasts nicely with the delicacy of some of his comedy, and he's aware of how effective this can be: '[I]t's odd to have the juxtaposition of a very large, prepossessing person appearing delicate and subtle, and I suddenly realised that had more visual power to it than me coming on as a big bloke, being a big bloke.' Mark Lamarr gives a different kind of testament to the power of physicality. Laughing at his own misanthropy, he explains his preference for comedy albums over videos by saying, 'I think the things that are annoying about humans are just lessened on tape. You've only got their voice to be annoyed by.'

Why we hate comedians

Lamarr's comment reveals an interesting point: if we can like comedians for the same kind of reasons as we like people we meet in everyday life, then we can also dislike them for similar reasons. The voice, the face, the body, the attitude, the onstage manner might make us hate the person behind the microphone. It's certainly true that some comedians, while inspiring affection and admiration from their fans, provoke loathing in others. A. A. Gill writes scathingly about Bob Monkhouse, in terms so luxuriously vicious as to suggest a genuine, personal hatred:

A deep and fundamental loathing of every syllable and nuance of Monkhouse is one of the cornerstones of my critical edifice. If I ever found I liked Bob Monkhouse, my world would collapse; I'd have to question civilisation as we know it . . . It's not that his material is bad; they are jokes as dumb and pointless as contextless jokes invariably are. It's his delivery that's like being touched up by a Moonie encyclopaedia salesman. Every mannerism drips insincerity and smarm. No, it's like having margarine massaged into your hair. No, it's like wearing marzipan socks.'[12]

Understandably, Monkhouse was unhappy about such attacks. A sympathetic interview written shortly after the Gill diatribe notes that Monkhouse has spent 'a lifetime irritating people in the name of light entertainment', with critics using words like 'despicable', 'slimy' and 'chilling' to describe him. Confronted with this, Monkhouse says, 'What I hate is people like A. A. Gill who attack me personally and who are blisteringly unpleasant. I inhabit that persona he rejects – and it hurts. In the same way that someone refusing to shake your hand is hurtful.'[13]

More recently, Jimmy Carr has attracted a similar kind of personal attack. A review of the candidates on the shortlist for the Perrier Award at the Edinburgh Fringe in 2002 sees Veronica Lee describe him as an 'inhabitant of the Planet Twat', saying: 'Jimmy Carr divides critical and fellow comics' opinion – you either love him or loathe him – and I am firmly in the latter camp. I'm not a violent person and am fully aware of comics assuming a stage persona, but whenever I see Carr I have to be physically restrained from smacking his smug face.'[14]

Trying too hard

Some comedians reject the idea of trying to make audiences like them. In a 2004 *Radio Times* interview, Billy Connolly says: 'When you're a comedian, trying to make yourself likeable cancels out what you're trying to do. There's a fine line between doing your stuff properly and being liked. I want my audience to laugh, sure, but I don't necessarily want to be liked.'

This is a useful point: stand-ups who are overly concerned with being liked can make themselves dislikeable. That's exactly the problem I have watching the footage of myself on *Pebble Mill*: I'm trying too hard. It's also probably what lies behind the hatred Bob Monkhouse inspired in some critics. Words like 'insincerity, 'smarm' and 'slimy' suggest they objected to what they saw as his attempts to ingratiate himself with them.

Adam Bloom, who delivers clever, offbeat gags in a mildly hyperactive style, likens performing to his relationships with women. He says he tries too hard with women he fancies, whereas he is more relaxed and natural with women he doesn't, which tends to make him more attractive to them. Different gigs have a similar effect: 'Now I think a nice gig is when you drop your guard and you're just being completely genuine, and you're not trying to impress them . . . The thing is, when you're actually doing a gig where the crowd isn't sure about you, you try a bit hard to impress them, and then you're putting on a bit of a front, so desperation's going to come across.'

Wanting to be disliked

Being disliked isn't always a sign of comic failure, though, and for Alexei Sayle, being dislikeable was a positive choice, which marked him out from the rest: 'What was unique about me as a comic was that what all comics, possibly apart from me, are seeking is . . . affection and love from an audience. I didn't care about that. I didn't want their affection. I didn't wanna be their mate. But I wanted their approval . . . I had a desperate desire for their approval as evinced in their laughter. But I didn't care if they liked me. In fact, I liked it if they didn't like me – but they had to laugh anyway.'

Mark Lamarr, a big fan of Sayle, is scathing about comics who want to be liked: 'It's very easy to just charm some strangers, and I think a lot of comedy is merely that . . . When I watch comics, and they say, "All I wanna do is connect with the audience," [I think,] "Well what's the fucking point of that? You can connect with people in a cake shop!" Anyone can connect with people, you just agree with what they say.'

Lamarr would sometimes make himself deliberately dislikeable as an exercise to test his own ability: '[O]ccasionally (and it was probably a little foolish), sometimes when I was really bored, in like an Edinburgh run or something, I would go on and just be as hateful as possible for the first ten [or] fifteen [minutes], as unfunny, and just spiteful and egregious, like till they just couldn't fucking stand the sight of me, and then I'd go, "I'll make you laugh now." And I would do it. And I generally could pull it off. And there was a real sense of accomplishment . . . "Yeah, they fucking hated me . . . and it must've killed them to've laughed at me so hard throughout that." And . . . I don't know what that is, and I can't explain it and I can't even justify it cos it sounds really horrible, but it was the case.'

It may be that the gags Sayle and Lamarr told were funny enough to override the audience's antipathy, but there's probably more to it than that. If the performer–audience relationship in stand-up is like any other interpersonal relationship, then it must be capable of being just as varied and complex. Hostages can form an emotional bond with their kidnappers. The crazy kid at school who questions the teacher and doles out devastating insults to classmates, or the rebel who bucks the system at work, can be fun to watch from a distance. The people we admire are not necessarily always people we like.

Self-expression

One of the reasons most comics fear being disliked by an audience is because stand-up is seen as a form of self-expression, so the audience's rejection is personal. This is why Bob Monkhouse found A. A. Gill's attack so hurtful. The more authentic the self-expression, the more comedians reveal their true selves onstage, the more painful the rejection.

Stand-up hasn't always been about self-expression, though. Older comics, like the phenomenally successful Bob Hope, did not reveal themselves in this way. Hope paid his writers to come up with comic 'poses' for him, one of them said that he was 'a manufactured personality, constructed out of jokes'. The common view is that Hope never revealed much of himself either onstage or offstage. In the 1970s, Joan Rivers said, 'Audiences nowadays want to *know* their comedian. Can you please tell me one thing about Bob Hope? If you only listened to his material, would you *know* the man?' This distance may have made it easier for Hope to cope with hostile audiences.[15]

It was the sick comedians who introduced the idea of stand-up as self-expression. Part of what made older comics resent and fear Mort Sahl was that he spoke his mind onstage. Sahl himself said that most comedians were 'no more than a card file', whereas he 'acted like a human being rather than like a nightclub comedian'. Some established comedians, like Alan King, saw the new style, realised its potency and adopted it themselves, rejecting a gag-based style in favour of expressing opinions.

Today, the idea that the comedian's act should reflect his or her real personality is commonplace. Comedian turned playwright Patrick Marber argues that stand-up is based on the premise 'This is my view of the world, this is my little angle on life'. Frank Skinner agrees: 'I've never been so crazy about character-comics. You know, people who just play a part onstage. I know it can be really funny but, personally, I like to know the person who's up there. I want their opinions and attitudes . . . If I want characters, I'll watch a play.'[16]

Similarly, surreal comic Harry Hill dismisses the working-men's club comedians of the past whose style was based on unoriginal gags: 'That's not art, that's kind of craft, isn't it? But then I think once everyone started doing their own material, most people are putting over . . . something about themselves, no matter how hidden it is.'

For Shazia Mirza, the very form of the one-liner or similar short gag is a block to self-expression, regardless of originality. Although she became successful with an act based on well-crafted short jokes, she now rejects that style with a view to making her act more authentically self-expressive: 'In the beginning, I would write jokes. So there'd be set-up/punch, and it'd be very tight and it'd be gags, and you know, set-up/punch is enough to make people laugh and it gets people into that rhythm of laughing, but it never actually . . . said anything about me . . . now I feel as though there's so much in my life that I could talk about, and the way to do it is not by telling gags, but by telling my experiences.'

Who is Omid Djalili?

British Iranian comedian Omid Djalili is on the stage, talking in a thick accent which separates the word 'Israel' into three distinct syllables: *Iz-rye-ell*. His delivery is rich with cheerful enthusiasm, which excites the audience. Their laughter is energetic and they frequently break into spontaneous applause:

> But of course, ahhh – I am circumcised. [*laughter*] But I'm having many psychological problem because I've had one-third of my doo-dah removed, er – [*a few laughs*] And many people say, 'You are an Arab, all Arab have one-third of doo-dah removed as child.' I say, 'Yes, but not the third in the middle, you know?' [*laughter*] 'S a prime example of an Arab knob gag, thank you very much, er – [*laughter*]

The laughter comes not just from the joke itself, but also from the fact of who is telling it, and the fact that he lets the audience know what he is doing by stoking up their

71

laughter with little comments like 'Of course!' But the Arab is not all he seems to be:

> Look, I know I give an impression of being a short, fat, kebab-shop-owning, ahh – [*laughter*] I know what you are thinking. Er – but inside of me,

Now, in the space of a comma, he changes his voice to that of a well-spoken, middle-class Englishman:

> there's an English ponce, erm, screaming – [*laughter*] screaming to get out, because, erm – Yeah, no, I don't talk like that at all, ladies and gentlemen, er – And actually, the reason why *I'm* here is, er – Cos – I'll tell you something – at the office, they said I was really funny. [*laughter*] You know what I mean? [*laughter continues and erupts into full applause, cheering and whistles; the response dies down, and then there's another surge of laughter*]

The audience realise that they've been had. The man talking into the microphone does not have the accent he started the act with, he's an over-enthusiastic middle-class office worker, probably like some of them. They clearly recognise the type: 'Thought I'd give it a go, and ahh – [*laughter*] Actually, erm – I'll be honest, I'm not the funniest bloke at the office, erm – [*laughter*] I'm the second funniest bloke, erm – Cos *Keith* is *nuts*! [*laughter*]¹⁷

This is a practical joke at the audience's expense. We have come to expect stand-up to be a form of self-expression, so we tend to assume that the comedians we see onstage are more or less playing themselves. We see an olive-skinned person with the authentically Middle Eastern name of Omid Djalili onstage, so when he speaks with a thick 'Arab' accent, we assume that it is genuine.

When the accent switches, the joke is revealed. Our stereotypes have been challenged as we realise how ordinary this office nutcase is, without any of the ethnic baggage that's been projected on to him. But this is still not the real Djalili. He was an actor, not an office worker, before he became a comedian. It's another fake persona, which Djalili created to get the maximum comic effect out of the practical joke: 'Comedy's all about putting opposites next to each other, so I thought . . . "Who would be the most surprising person to do this really loud character?" and decided [on] the stupid office bloke, you know . . . I just thought to play off the Arab character, you've got to find the most diametrically opposed character . . . that character then becomes a running gag, because then that's not me . . . you merge yourself into it.'

This is a very clever piece of comedy, because it plays on the ambiguity of identity which is at the centre of stand-up comedy. It's tempting to see stand-ups as falling into two categories: character comedians and those who perform as themselves. In fact, there is not so much a clear dividing line between the two as a continuous spectrum of approaches, each shading subtly into the next.

The personality spectrum

Character comedians

At one end of the spectrum are character comedians. There's a clear division between Steve Coogan and the various guises he adopts in his stand-up act: Paul Calf, the drunken, working-class Manchester lad in false moustache and blond wig styled in a way that would shame even a 1980s footballer; Pauline Calf, Paul's sister, telling tales of promiscuity, in cascading blonde curls that reek of trashy glamour; Duncan Thicket, the impossibly crap new comedian in nasty shell-suit top and woolly hat; and Ernest Moss, the tedious northern safety officer in boiler suit and hard hat. The separation between comedian and characters is clearly signalled by the costumes, the wigs, the make-up and the names he gives them.

The distance between performer and character can be

shocking. Harry Enfield, who performed characters in his stand-up act before using them in TV sketch shows, writes about being approached by a man in the street who says, 'You're Harry Enfield, aren't you? I *love* your characters! Stavros cracks me up and as for Loadsamoney – he's the biz! But I saw you on *Wogan* last night – you're a right prat in real life, aren't you?'[18] Similarly, Bob Monkhouse recalls his shock at being introduced to Rex Jameson, the performer behind the comedy drag act Mrs Shufflewick: '[T]he mere idea that this five-foot twenty-three-year-old with a face like a young Buster Keaton could have been dirty old woman I'd seen on the stage of both the Windmill and the Metropolitan, Edgware Road, seemed incredible.'[19] The performer–character distinction means that comedians like Coogan and Enfield enjoy a lot of licence. We know that when Paul Calf says something offensive or ignorant, this is the character's opinion, not Coogan's.

Exaggerated personas

Further along the spectrum are stand-ups who adopt an exaggerated persona but leave the dividing line between performer and persona unclear. Comics like Joan Rivers and Jenny Éclair might have stage names and wear outlandish clothes, but they use both names and clothes offstage as well as on. For the audience, it's easy to mistake the persona for the person. Rivers acknowledges that her act is partly autobiographical, but sees her persona as 'like a party dress I put on'. Éclair has divided her wardrobe into sections, one end for her offstage self, the other for her stage persona. On her car stereo, she has tapes for herself and tapes for her onstage character.

Milton Jones is a mid-spectrum act who is probably closer to the character-comedian end. His appearance is plausible but startling. The hair is gelled into weird, spiky shapes. The pullovers are exquisitely unfashionable. One is a monstrous thing with a zip and a collar, with knitted grey sleeves and black plastic elbow pads. Down the front of it, knitted red panels do battle with ribbed black plastic panels. Jones's delivery suggests somebody who is endearingly unhinged: the voice slow, rather deep and sonorous, the face sometimes wrinkling as though disorientated, or perhaps breaking into an idiot grin. Jones refers to his onstage self in the third person, calling it 'the character'. It's as strange as his material. Here's a typical excerpt. I've split it into lines to suggest the pauses he uses, and noted how long each big laugh is to indicate the efficiency of his comedy:

I was walking along today – [*a few laughs*]
And on the pavement – I saw a small, dead, baby ghost. [*a few laughs*]
Although thinking about it –
It might've been a handkerchief. [*laughter: 19 seconds*]
Before we start – [*laughter*]
I'd just like to say, er – to the old man –
Who was wearing camouflage gear, and using crutches who *stole my wallet earlier* –
You can hide, but you can't run. [*laughter and clapping: 10 seconds*]
Tell me – if you're an earl, and you get an OBE – do you become an earlobe? [*laughter: 9 seconds*]
You know – when you're in a relationship –
What's that like? [*laughter and a few claps: 8 seconds*]
Sometimes I think I should settle down and have a *mature* relationship, but then I think to myself – it's the middle of the *conker season!* [*laughter: 10 seconds*]

It's comedy that disrupts the usual thought processes: normal objects are seen in an extraordinary new light; old sayings are reversed, and words moulded into new shapes; an introduction to an observational bit about relationships becomes an admission of loneliness; a grown man is more interested in childhood games than girlfriends. Jones invented the character to provide a context for his mind-mashing comedy: 'The character didn't really evolve for four or five years. And as I began to do that, I put hair wax in and put on a silly jumper . . . that's provided more of a signpost for the type of material I was doing. Probably sort of helped me, especially in the harder clubs, you know, Romford on a Monday night or something, where some slightly middle-class bloke coming along and doing slightly wordplay stuff was somehow a bit threatening. Whereas if you stick your hair up and put on a jumper, "Oh, 'e's mad!" It's OK then.'

Naked selves

At the far end of the spectrum are acts where the person we see onstage appears to be an authentic human being, unaffected by the process of performance. Jo Brand says that the person she projects onstage differs from her offstage self 'hardly at all, to be honest', chuckling as she qualifies this, adding, 'I mean hardly at all in public anyway.'

This kind of approach means laying the self bare. American writer David Marc puts it this way:

> Without the protection of the formal mask of a narrative drama, without a song, dance, or any other intermediary composition that creates distance between performer and performance, without even, necessarily, some remarkable physical trait or ability to gratuitously display, the stand-up comedian addresses an audience as a naked self, eschewing the luxury of a clear cut distinction between art and life.[20]

Veteran alternative comedian Tony Allen also uses the analogy of nakedness: 'A raconteur comedian walks onstage relatively naked. He speaks directly to the audience in the first person.' Phill Jupitus extends the analogy, likening stand-up to the commercial exploitation of sex: 'I've always had this belief that you have to have something wrong with you to want to do stand-up, because it is putting yourself (particularly as a performer) in possibly the most vulnerable position you can be in, aside from the people that fuck each other in Amsterdam for money, you know. I think it's really baring and putting yourself out there . . . '

For some stand-ups, the self they reveal onstage is actually more naked than their offstage self. Victoria Wood, for example, has said: 'I used to feel that the real me was on the stage and the rest of me was fumbling to catch up . . . That when I was onstage it was talking honestly and communicating with people, that I had difficulty doing the rest of the time.'[21]

The person in the persona

Even the concept of a continuous spectrum from character to naked self, however, does not really capture the subtle interweaving of truth and fiction in the onstage identities of stand-up comedians, as Milton Jones points out: 'I think that . . . there are two types of comedian in the sense that there are some who are completely the same offstage as they are onstage, and then there are those who are more of an act. And even people who appear to be themselves, it's a heightened version . . . it's like part of them, it's them on showing-off mode or whatever it is. And I think that even my character is a part of me. Feeling slightly outside things sometimes. And so rather than attempt to join in, I'll accentuate the outsider in me.'

He's not the only performer from near the character end of the spectrum to feel that the heightened persona presented onstage is actually derived from an authentic part of the self. Johnny Vegas, a shambling, self-pitying, apparently drunken figure who appears onstage wearing an unlikely ensemble of brown leather jacket and old-fashioned gentleman's trousers turned into flares by having shiny yellow triangles sewn into them, seems to be a creature of pure fiction. This is reinforced by the name. Onstage he is Johnny Vegas; offstage, Mike Pennington.

The tales of woe with which he wins over the audience are

wildly implausible. In a northern voice which sounds as if he has smoked forty a day since birth, he shares his delusions about being a great entertainer and recalls his father sneering at his attempts to become a potter. As he gets into the act, the stories become stranger. He tells of a holiday to Wales, where the locals try to burn him as a witch because his Coco Pops have turned the milk brown, forcing him to escape dressed as a sheep, only to be captured, sexually abused and exhibited as a talking animal oddity.

It seems cut and dried that Vegas is a purely fictional character, but the truth is not so simple. Pennington shares more than just a voice and a body with Vegas. Just as he says in his act, he really did study pottery at Middlesex, and he really did get a third-class degree. Offstage, Pennington sounds like Vegas, his accent originating from a working-class upbringing in St Helens. Like Vegas, Pennington is not averse to heavy drinking, and enjoys the ambiguity surrounding the apparent onstage drunkenness: 'My character, Johnny Vegas, drinks onstage, but I think it's better to maintain some sort of is-he-isn't-he mystique, a bit like Dean Martin.'[22]

Harry Hill presents similar ambiguities. Like Johnny Vegas, he is near the character end of the spectrum. It is difficult to reconcile the well-known fact that offstage he is an ex-doctor called Matthew Hall with the dadaesque figure that scuttles around the stage in a flamboyant costume, dispensing bizarre non-sequiturs and myriad catchphrases, face and voice twitching with exaggerated mannerisms. It stretches credibility that he is like this in everyday life: walking down the road to post a letter with trademark beetle crushers on his feet, row of pens protruding from jacket pocket, head disappearing into a voluminous shirt collar; screwing up his face and saying 'mm-mm' while helping his children with their homework; kicking up his leg and shouting 'Goal!' as he opens his bank statement.

The gap between onstage and offstage selves starts to yawn when he is interviewed. Appearing on a documentary in 2000, we see him in pretty much the full stage costume talking about his comedy calmly and rationally, in the guise of the normal human being that lies behind the persona. There are none of the usual verbal or physical tics. Hill prefers the kind of interview he does on the Des O'Connor show. Here, he can fully adopt his stage self because 'He asks me a question that leads directly to a gag'. Appearing as his offstage self is less comfortable: 'I never wanted to do TV interviews or any of that crap, to be honest . . . I've got forced into it . . . I kind of can't be bothered to carry it on . . . I prefer not to do them really, because I think it spoils it, actually, and I always admired that about Tommy Cooper . . . I don't think you ever saw him being serious in anything, you know. Even on, like, *Parkinson*, he'd just do his act.'

But if the person is clearly distinct from the persona, this doesn't mean that there is no point of contact between the two, and Hill explains that the person he becomes onstage is actually an element of his real personality: 'Normally, I'm quite shy (or I *was* a shy person, funnily enough, since doing comedy it's made me more confident), but I think the stage persona is . . . confident, it's the kind of show-off . . . What I love about it is being able to just show off and, you know, do sort of silly things that you can't get away with in your private life, basically. It's a kind of release. It's like going onstage and shouting.'

The fact that his persona is rooted in part of his personality and isn't just a simple fabricated character gives the lie to the criticism which has been levelled at Hill: that we learn nothing about him from his act, that it is not an outlet for self-expression as stand-up should be. Hill defends himself vigorously from this: 'I think that's missing the point, really. Cos I think people always say that . . . [Y]ou could criticise my act by saying, "It's not about anything. You know, it's just silly." But I think it says a lot, actually. Without getting too up-your-own-arse, just about the kind of human condition, really . . . [W]hat I'm saying,

I think, is, "Everyone's an idiot . . . what is the point? . . .
Everyone's as bad as everybody else. It's ridiculous, it's
stupid." Sort of.'

Exaggeration

Just as there are elements of authenticity in exaggerated
personas, so there are elements of exaggeration in
comedians who apparently go onstage as a naked self.
Andre Vincent, who has an irresistible compulsion for sick
jokes, describes his stage self as 'Maybe 10 per cent more.
There might be a slight switch where I just kind of go,
"Whoop!" and I go up one. Just a little bit bolder. But . . .
the evil and spite is there throughout my whole life. It really
is.' Mark Lamarr also talks about exaggerating negative
traits: 'I don't really think of it as a persona, it's a sort of
louder, slightly more vengeful version of me. But it is
certainly me, and there are very few lines I've ever said that
I wouldn't back up.' Mark Thomas says his stage persona is
defined not just by exaggeration, but also by selection: 'You
edit out the boring bits. You know, and you highlight the
interesting bits, and the significant bits and that's what you
do. That's . . . what it is. It's a bigger version of me . . . a
more succinct version of me, without the moaning and the
rambling.'

For many comedians, going onstage brings out the side of
themselves they would show on a social occasion. Rhys
Darby, for example, says: 'I think the onstage self is like an
extreme version of the offstage self. So, like, when I'm
offstage, I'm normally a bit more reserved, a bit more shy,
especially around people I don't know. But if I'm around
people I do know, my friends and people like that, if I'm
comfortable, then I'll be as zany as possible, you know, and
wacky and what have you, so when I'm onstage, it's that
coming out . . . I mean, when I've been at parties and had a
few drinks, or whatever's going down, I've noticed that I've
become that person.'

Shelley Berman explains that in both stand-up comedy

and in social situations, there's an attempt to impress, but also an underlying authenticity: 'I think we all put our best foot forward, no matter what. You go to a party, you are your best self, whatever you are. You're doing your best self . . . I do hope that I'm always honest. I do hope that whatever self is there is shooting straight and not being affected. But I can't swear to it. I think that an audience can smell dishonesty a mile away. I swear that audiences can see the imperceptible. I know that they can see it when you're sweating inside, they can see it if you have a hole in your sock, they can tell, they know it. There's something about when you're talking about a large group of people, you're talking about people who can *see something*. And, you know, I don't believe it's possible to act your way out of it.'

Onstage behaviour

Adapting to the conventions
In his book about acting, John Harrop points out that there's a key difference between the actor who is 'both present on the stage and yet at the same time absent, replaced by the illusion he or she creates', and musclemen, Miss Universe contestants and stand-up comedians who are 'projecting themselves'. However, he qualifies this point by saying that performers who project themselves 'may be making adaptations to the conventions of the performance'.[23]

This is a crucial point: however authentic the person behind the mike may seem, the very fact of being onstage must affect the way they behave. To pick the most obvious example, stand-ups must, by definition, adapt to the convention of being funny onstage. As Mark Lamarr puts it: 'Jack Dee said to me once that I'm the nearest offstage to what I am on. I mean, obviously I'm a lot less funny offstage, because I'm . . . not needed to be.'

I become very aware of adapting to the conventions of performance in a gig at Alexander's Jazz Theatre Bar,

Chester, in the late 1990s. I've done their Saturday shows before, where the punters are packed in so tightly that the place bulges at the seams, but this is the first time I've done their Wednesday-night show. I sit there waiting for the audience to arrive, but it just doesn't happen. When I go on, there are literally only about six paying punters watching the show.

I get down off the stage, gather the tiny audience together around one table, and sit down with them. I've never consciously created a stage persona, and I'm not aware of undergoing any kind of transformation as I make the long walk over to the mike stand, but I find myself having to consciously tone down my delivery so as to avoid alienating them. My normal performance energy would seem bizarre when I'm sitting across a pub table from the people I'm talking to. I force myself into normal conversation mode so that the prepared material sounds even more spontaneous than it usually does. It works: they laugh in the right places. I get to my final routine, a medley of Clash song parodies played on the mandolin, and realise that it just isn't going to work if I'm sitting on a pub stool. I get back on to the stage and adapt once more to the conventions, cranking myself back up into performance mode.

Jeremy Hardy argues that the way comedians change when they get on to the stage is just like the adaptations we make in certain social situations: '[T]here's a persona in as much as we have different personae that we use in our lives, you know, like talking to your mum, talking to the doctor, we adopt slightly different voices . . . people onstage, usually their accents become more common and they swear more. *We* swear more. Because that's one of the aspects of ourselves that we project. So it's not acting in the sense that it's an observed and learnt and performed character, but it's acting in the sense that it's a performance, and you're having to give the impression that this is what you really want to do at that moment, even though you might have been crying in the dressing room a minute earlier . . . We're all kind of performing all the time in a sense, albeit sub-consciously, and [stand-up is] just one of the performances that we give.'

He goes on to admit that he hardly bothers to adapt to the conventions any more: 'The performance has kind of gradually gone from what I do . . . and it gets less affected as I go on, which may or may not be a good thing. It . . . is pretty much me onstage, talking. And if I'm in a bad mood then that's visible . . . That's probably an abuse of the position, it's not giving people their value for money, but, you know, I think it's quite interesting that you go on with the mood that you're in.'

Different kinds of adaptation

Stand-up gigs come in all shapes and sizes, and so demand different kinds of adaptation. Phill Jupitus describes how different gigs brought out different sides of him: 'I think when I did my early telly, I relished this very boisterous Essex Boy image, which . . . was just born out of nerves more than anything. The . . . fear of the crowd, and fear of something new. I would very often hide behind that persona. That was Jongleurs Phill. Jongleurs Phill wore a leather jacket, DMs and told the audience to fuck off. Whereas Phill that did live stand-up shows, on his own, [where] people just came to see *him*, was a delicate little flower.'

For Rhona Cameron, gender politics come into it. Like Jupitus, she finds that theatre gigs allow her to be pretty much herself, but when she used to perform on the male-dominated London comedy circuit, she had to adapt herself because more was demanded of her as a female act: 'It's different for men, cos men can go onstage and mumble and the audience accepts it a bit more, but as a woman you had to be much better than that. When I was doing it, there was only about two women that would even get booked at the [Comedy] Store . . . you had to just go there, bang-bang-bang, use your punchiest material, which was always hard for me because I didn't have punchy material, I was like a storyteller.'

Michael Barrymore's life spills into his act

The key to understanding the distinction between person and persona in stand-up comedy is the boundary between the stage and the rest of the world. Some performers adopt a distinct identity when they cross the boundary, others make subtler adjustments. At the moment of crossing it, the boundary becomes visible. Most comedians look nervous before going on, their faces taut, their speech coming in short bursts. As they walk on to the stage, they become the assured, natural person they present to the audience. Their faces become expressive, their speech fluent.

However stark the boundary may seem, though, it's not impermeable. The comedian's offstage life can easily seep through it. In an essay about popular entertainers, actor and academic Clive Barker points out how a performer's private life can become incorporated into his or her persona, like Judy Garland's troubled private life giving her performances an added pathos.[24]

A classic example of this is the sad case of Michael Barrymore's attempt at a West End comeback in September 2003. Barrymore, whose act falls somewhere between stand-up comedy and all-purpose light entertainment, had featured in tabloid stories about his homosexuality, drunkenness and drug habits for years, and in 2001 the public was scandalised when a thirty-one-year-old man was found dead in his swimming pool.

Barrymore tried to win his audience back with a show at Wyndham's Theatre, but found he was playing to small and hostile crowds. The critics showed him no mercy. The *Guardian*'s Mark Lawson wrote: 'The problem is partly the shadow of that fatal pool party. Legal investigations cleared Barrymore of the more lurid insinuations, but the revelations of his alarming hospitality make the slapstick and silliness of his act harder to take.' Barrymore cancelled the show after a few days, reportedly sitting backstage in tears saying, 'I can't do this any more. I don't feel like Michael Barrymore out there.'

Barrymore was vainly trying to wish away the audience's knowledge of events, but other comedians willingly bring episodes from their offstage life into their acts, no matter how scandalous or traumatic they may be. In 1980, the great Richard Pryor set fire to himself while freebasing cocaine. After recovering from his injuries he didn't avoid the issue. Instead, he starts a 1981 show by asking for a light, then commenting, 'Gotta be careful with these motherfuckin' matches!' The audience, catching the reference, laugh and applaud. He goes on to do extended routines about both freebasing and his experience of recovering from his injuries in hospital.[25]

Jack Dee's act spills into his life

Just as the offstage life can spill into the act, so the act can spill out into the offstage life. Jack Dee's comedy springs from immaculate sullenness and cynicism. His misanthropic persona is so well established that he can get laughs with the simplest of sentences. In a 1997 show, he comments on a minor TV personality of the time. 'What about the *Gladiators*?' he says, emitting a sneering chuckle which gets a laugh. He does the snarl and mimed clawing action which was the trademark gesture of a Gladiator called Wolf. There's a bigger laugh, and Dee smiles along with the audience's enjoyment of his fun-poking impression. 'I'm Wolf,' he says, momentarily taking on the voice of his victim. Then, in his own voice, he replies, 'Are you?'

It's beautifully performed. His eyebrows raise but his eyelids can't be bothered to follow. His mouth remains sullen and down-turned. His voice suggests someone making a tiny effort to be polite, while fighting monumental boredom. There's a huge laugh, which breaks out into applause, the whole response lasting nine seconds. As it builds, Dee smiles and looks down modestly, as if enjoying the way the audience share his disdain.[26] There's no obvious joke here, but Dee has got three laughs, one of them rich and full-bodied, simply by inhabiting his persona with skill and subtlety.

Dee's well-established persona can have a similar effect in his private life, whether he intends it to do so or not. He complains that people assume he's never serious, seeing his behaviour through the filter of his stand-up act: 'I unintentionally make them laugh because they think I'm being funny when I'm not. No one buys "sincere" from me. They always think I'm taking the piss.'[27]

Living up to the image

Some comedians are happy to live up to the stage image, though. Eric Morecambe, for example, felt a compulsion to adopt his stage persona in any public situation. When he was an up-and-coming comedian, Rowan Atkinson met Morecambe and witnessed him in action: 'The first thing that struck me was how funny he was in the house . . . I remember thinking, "God, how oppressive to be expected to be this funny all the time." My other thought was to wonder what it must be like for the family to live with this man . . . Eric's family had to live with this "act" all the time, which must have been difficult. I then started thinking about how difficult Eric must have found it to live with himself . . . what must it have been like when he didn't feel he wanted to be funny and the pressure remained on him to be so?'[28]

In some cases, living up to the stage image is a conscious form of marketing. This tendency goes back to the music hall. The nineteenth-century comedian George Leybourne took on the persona of a 'swell', a well-to-do merrymaker living the alcoholic high life. His most famous song was 'Champagne Charlie'. In 1868, he entered into an exclusive twelve-month contract with William Holland to play the Canterbury Hall for a fee of £1,500. The contract required him to live out the role he played onstage in his private life, stating: 'George Leybourne shall every day, and at all reasonable times and places when required to do so, appear in a carriage, drawn by four horses, driven by two postillions, and attended by his grooms.' He was expected to wear his ostentatious stage costume when he made these appearances, and give out champagne to members of the public. The alcoholic drinks which made him a star also contributed to his demise. He died at the age of forty-two, from liver damage.[29]

'Finding your voice'

The personas which comedians inhabit in their act don't necessarily spring into life fully formed the first time they walk out on to the stage. There's skill involved in presenting the self to a live audience, and it's a skill which can take time to learn. Comedians tend to call this process 'finding your voice'. Richard Pryor says that it's a process that can take fifteen years. Four years into her career, Shazia Mirza feels she is discovering who she wants to be onstage: 'Four years is a short time, really, to be doing stand-up. I mean, in four years, I'm only just beginning to find my voice now, and I'm only just beginning to realise what it is I wanna talk about really, rather than what people wanna hear.'

Lenny Henry was still in his teens when he made a successful appearance on the TV talent show *New Faces*, which quickly led to live touring and further television. He was disorientated by being thrown into show business quickly, and struggled to find his voice: 'I was famous without having achieved anything. The first ten years were really hard . . . I didn't have a personality.'[30]

Les Dawson found his voice suddenly, in response to adversity. Early in his career, he had a week's engagement as a comic pianist and singer at a grim working-men's club in Hull. After a few days of getting nothing more than contempt from the audience, he got drunk and found himself unable to play the piano. Instead, he gave vent to his feelings: 'The silence was quite eerie, and suddenly all the depression I felt pumped out of my mouth.' He glumly told self-deprecating gags and made fun of the place where he was performing. The audience loved it, giving him 'a magnificent ovation'. The next night, though more sober, he tried the same approach 'to see if [he] had "found" a style that an audience would appreciate', and again got big laughs.[31] He had stumbled across the glum persona which would make him famous.

Tony Allen has a theory about how the process of finding the voice occurs: 'Standing on stage in front of a live audience is a situation that appears to trigger a sort of strategic identity crisis. In order merely to survive, various sides of our personality come to our assistance. However idiosyncratic or inappropriate these minority personalities appear to be, they should all be given an audition.'[32]

There's certainly some evidence to support this idea. It's slightly spooky hearing Alexei Sayle talking about his stage persona in the third person, as if it is a minority personality that he's not fully in control of. 'Well, I mean, I always say that, you know, he's completely different [from me] but I write his material,' he explains. He says that his transformation into this other person was 'instantaneous', adding, 'He was there right from the start.' Sayle has now given up stand-up comedy, and is a successful author. This means performing at readings in bookshops and literary festivals, and he has to be careful to avoid slipping back into the stand-up persona: 'The reason I have a lectern is to have a barrier between me and the audience . . . if I just had a microphone, he would start to reappear, I'm not kidding about that . . . if I just have a microphone, he starts to come out.'

In some cases, the stage persona seems to be connected with some kind of emotional trauma or even mental illness. Eddie Izzard has often discussed the effect of his mother's death on his life and work, talking about 'a childlike thing that I keep locked in after six, which is when my mother died . . . There's a kid there that comes in and plays onstage.'

Vaudeville comedian Bert Lahr suffered from manic depression. The manic side of his personality came out onstage, the depressive side in his personal life. Roseanne Barr, who was a biting feminist stand-up before starring in her own sitcom, has a minority personality she calls Cindy, which developed in response to a difficult childhood. She once tried to use Cindy as a character in a sketch on *Saturday Night Live*, but found that 'the other actors were real scared'.[33]

Dressing up, dressing down

Costumes

Because so much of stand-up comedy is about personality, the clothes comedians wear onstage are extremely important, whether these are items from the performer's offstage wardrobe or a distinctly theatrical costume. The great variety comedian Max Miller based much of his comedy on double entendre and innuendo. Skirting around the prevailing taboos about sex and marital infidelity was daring, and his cheeky, audacious persona was reflected in his outrageous costume. This clearly appealed to his audience. The critic A. Crooks Ripley was just as enraptured by Miller's costume as he was by his physique:

> He arrives at the crease as though he were a man come to read the gas-meter, except that he wears a panama and brown and white shoes with red heels, also, his hulk is completely hidden in a polar-coat of crushing, exotic incongruity . . . this outer envelope removed, he is seen in the plumage of a rampant carp . . . then after you've had your laugh, your smile becomes frozen and you feel a little stupid if you're honest with yourself, because the raiment is extraordinarily exciting and most becoming; it is also one of the several elements Mr Miller's imitators have not, as yet, had the temerity to emulate.'[34]

Miller was at the height of his success when wartime rationing and then post-war austerity restricted the clothing choice available to most people, and men's clothing tended to be particularly drab. In this context, it's easy to see how coming on to the stage dressed in yards of colourful cloth could so excite A. Crooks Ripley.

When Eddie Izzard was building his audience in the 1990s, his colourful costumes gained much attention for a different reason. As he puts it himself in his book *Dress to Kill*: 'Probably I am the only transvestite comedian in the world at this moment.' Izzard argues that his transvestism does not involve imitating a woman so much as exercising the freedom to wear clothing society normally denies to men. This is borne out by his stage wear, which sometimes makes him look more like a glam rocker than a drag act. In his *Definite Article* video, for example, he wears shiny black trousers and high-heeled boots, and a thigh-length, double-breasted jacket made of scarlet crushed velvet. Earrings dangle from his ears, his nails are painted, and his face is prettified with eye make-up, blusher and dark lipstick. Certainly, this is not normal male garb, but neither is it any more feminine than the stage wear of, say, the lead singer of The Sweet. Indeed, Izzard points out that 'there's rock stars who'll put on eyeliner', citing David Bowie as an example. In more recent shows, the costumes have been more overtly transvestite. In *Sexie*, for example, he wears false breasts and a leather miniskirt.

The transvestism affects the act in a number of ways. It becomes the source of material, and he's performed a number of routines on the subject. It makes him glamorous and exotic, slightly separating him from the audience, and providing a context for his tangential and often surreal humour. It's also a good source of publicity. It would be wrong to suggest that Izzard has cynically exploited his transvestism, but it has made a good talking point in interviews since he came out to the *Observer* in 1991, and he looks fantastic on tour posters and video covers.

But there's another important effect, which is not to do with how his audience perceives him but with how being open about his transvestism affects his performance. He has said that he decided to wear skirts onstage because 'I should have that freedom'. It certainly seemed to free him up because, having made the choice, one critic noted that he seemed 'so much more physically relaxed', and that previously, 'Izzard's body seemed to be struggling to escape from a stonewashed denim prison'.[35]

Casual clothes

Some comedians prefer more casual clothes than Miller's or Izzard's, and this reinforces the idea that the performer we see onstage is more or less the same person offstage. The notion of stand-up as authentic self-expression may have become firmly established by the likes of Mort Sahl and Lenny Bruce, but the move towards greater naturalness actually started earlier, when comedians started to wear ordinary clothes onstage.

In the late 1920s, when Ted Ray was becoming established, it was normal for front-cloth comics on the variety circuit to wear either formal dress or exaggerated theatrical costumes. Having initially conformed to this, Ray struck upon a startling innovation. He realised that if he wore ordinary clothes, the kind of thing the men in the audience would have been wearing, he would be more like them and so could form a closer relationship with them: 'From the moment I made my entrance I felt a warmth I had never known before. I was one of them. I told my stories casually and intimately as though they were in on the joke. I wore my best lounge suit and, as far as my appearance went, I might have just climbed up on the stage from the front row of the stalls . . . I got laughs and earned them just by being *myself*.'[36]

Later, Frankie Howerd took a similar approach to stage wear, and for similar reasons: 'I wore an ordinary, far from immaculate, brown lounge suit, since for my act it was vital to attempt to give the impression that I wasn't one of the cast, but had just wandered in from the street – as though into a pub, or just home from work . . . Why a brown suit? Because I thought it was a colour that didn't intrude. It's warm and neutral and man-in-the-street anonymous . . . When playing seaside resorts I'd even wear shorts.'[37] The whole presentation of Howerd's act was informal. This made him extraordinary, but also attracted criticism. A provincial critic attacked him for being unprofessional: 'This man wears no make-up, doesn't dress, doesn't even take a bow at the end.'

In the 1950s, the hungry i's owner, Enrico Banducci, advised Mort Sahl to reject a suit in favour of casual slacks, an open-necked white shirt and a sweater. Sahl explains the reason for this choice: 'Well, the hungry i was a cellar. And it cost a quarter to get in, and I really took the uniform of like a graduate student in Berkeley so I wouldn't look like I took myself seriously.'[38]

On the current British stand-up scene, jeans and a T-shirt are a common choice of stage wear. Mark Thomas is probably one of the most successful comedians doing this: 'It got to the stage where I'd just wear whatever T-shirts were around, and it was just what I'd got in the wash, frankly, what was clean. And I quite liked . . . the simplicity of just a T-shirt and jeans.'

Whereas for earlier comedians, dressing casually was an innovation, for today's stand-ups it is taken for granted. This inevitably means an erosion of the onstage–offstage boundary, as any item of clothing the comedian possesses is a potential piece of costume. Adam Bloom says of his stage wear: 'It's whatever I've got on, but I'd never wear something in the afternoon of a gig that I wouldn't wanna wear onstage. Nearly everything I own is clothes that I would wear onstage . . . And my persona's very honest, and therefore I'd rather wear just a T-shirt. *Ironed* T-shirt, because I wanna pay a little bit of respect for the fact that people have paid money to see me . . . I think if somebody's wearing a T-shirt that's creased onstage, what they're saying is, "I didn't care enough about this gig." '

The politics of clothes

Sometimes, the choice of what to wear onstage is political. African-American comedian Timmie Rogers was one of the first black comedians to play to predominantly white audiences. When he started wearing a tuxedo instead of the more clownish clothes black comics traditionally wore, he was making an important point about the dignity of his race. He met with resistance. The owner of the Los Angeles Clover Club fired him.

Stand-up comedy has historically been male-dominated, and this has led a number of female comedians to adopt an androgynous look. Early in her career, Victoria Wood used to wear trousers, a shirt and tie and a blazer. Originally, Jo Brand's look owed something to punk. A typical early costume might involve a bumper crop of spiked hair, bright red lipstick, black T-shirt, black leggings and Doc Marten boots. For her too, the choice was affected by the sexual politics of comedy clubs, where most of the acts and most of the hecklers are men: 'I must say that I felt all the black stuff, it was easy, it was kind of slightly androgynous, and I suppose I kind of always felt that, particularly sort of being a female that the less you drew attention to what sex you were, if you were a woman, the easier it would be in some ways, you know.'

The 1960s and 70s saw elements of the hippie youth culture creeping into stand-up in both Britain and the USA. In Britain, the comics who were emerging from the folk circuit tended to have long hair and wear brightly coloured clothes influenced by hippie fashions. Billy Connolly had wild hair and an equally wild beard, and would push the fashions of the time to the extreme, wearing boots shaped like big bananas, or a shiny orange jumpsuit, flared in both arms and legs. For him, this was a way of distinguishing himself from more conventional comics, and giving him licence: 'I wanted to have an image that was a bit more than just the mohair suit comedian style, the guy with a bow tie or whatever . . . Wearing ridiculous clothes you could say what you pleased, because you didn't represent anything and so you couldn't be blamed for anything.'[39]

On the other side of the Atlantic, George Carlin was an established comedian with a clean-cut image when he transformed himself into a hippie. He was very nervous when he first performed in his new identity, his long, straight hair, beard, tie-dye T-shirt and jeans making him unrecognisable. His act was similarly transformed, with material about drugs and a looser, more physical style. He had found a new, younger audience and, by embracing the counterculture, he was also taking a political stance, rejecting conformity and aligning himself with the more radical elements in youth culture.

Mark Thomas has used costume in a way that is more tangibly political. He builds the politics of his act into the entire organisation of his shows, with campaigning groups selling T-shirts and other merchandise in the foyers of the venues where he performs. Care is taken to make sure that the clothing sold is ethically produced, avoiding sweatshop labour. Thomas found an easy way to help them shift more products: 'War on Want . . . were touring with us and they said, "Can you wear a T-shirt, because we sell more if you're wearing them?" [I said,] "Oh, all right." And so . . . it became a way of generating money for various . . . causes and campaigns.'

Footwear

Audiences probably don't notice what shoes a comedian is wearing on his or her feet, and in many cases the comic's shoes may be well be obscured by tables or other punters; or, in big theatres, simply be too far away to be seen. But all stand-up comedians have to have something to stand up in, and for some the choice of shoe is an important practical consideration.

Ross Noble, for example, says: 'I always wear skateboard shoes. Because . . . they're flat but they're sort of bouncy at the same time . . . cos trainers are too runaroundy, you want something that you can stand flat in.' This is worth quoting purely for the use of the word 'runaroundy', but it also shows how shoes can affect performance energy. The chunky skateboard shoes allow Noble to achieve the extraordinary liveliness of his physical work, while also grounding him and offering him control. Together with his long, curly hair (which he describes as 'heavy'), and the flared shirtsleeves and trousers he wears, the shoes form part of an overall look which he calls a 'cartoony type thing'.

Rhys Darby says he wears sneakers, 'so that I can jump around, you know, because I do a lot of physical stuff'. Phill Jupitus says that changing from heavy boots to plimsolls improved his performance: 'It did feel different, yeah, it just felt that you could scamper a little bit more . . . Whereas with the boots, you'd stomp.'

Finding the right costume

From the clothes they wear to the shoes on their feet, costume is important to stand-up comedians, helping to form their identity, affecting the way they perform, and sometimes even making a political statement. Yet it seems that costume is rarely something that is consciously decided, often being found through trial and error. There was no conscious strategy behind Ross Noble's choice of stage wear: 'Well, it's one of those things where I *didn't* think it out, I just found what worked, and then somebody pointed it out and I went, "Oh yeah, that's what I've done."' Harry Hill's distinctive costume came about in a similarly haphazard way: 'I just used to wear suits, you know, sixties suits from Oxfam, and then I started wearing a tie in my first gig I did. And that was just too kind of hot. Constricting. So I took that off, and I thought, "Well, I should make a kind of, if you're in show business, you make a kind of thing of it that you're not wearing a tie, you know, you shouldn't be like just a bloke without a tie on" . . . so I used to just pull the collar up, really. And then people would say, "Oh, that big collar of yours!" And I was kind of hunched over, so my head would sort of recede into the collar. And then, when people started saying, "You've got that big collar," I had them made, started getting them made big.'

It was a longer process that led Milton Jones to find his bad-taste pullovers: 'I think it was trial and error really, I tried several things, you know, dressing up smart, dressing up rough, dressing up like a tramp, you know, but you want it to be minimal. And just enough to show the way. And not like anyone else.' He now has a selection of nasty jumpers, getting them from charity shops, always for 'under a tenner'. The women who sell them to him often assume he's buying them for everyday use: '[T]he lady says, "That's just you, that is." And I say, "Yes, it is me."' Her mistake may be funny, but it also speaks volumes about the blurring of onstage and offstage identities in stand-up.

Truth

In Eddie Izzard's show *Dress to Kill*, there's an extraordinary routine about Engelbert Humperdinck. After telling the audience that the popular singer was originally called Gerry Dorsey, Izzard imagines the meeting where the change of name was decided.[40] He acts it out, showing Dorsey's managers trying out different possibilities. He has them reeling out a string of bizarre names: '"Zinglebert Bambledack! [*laughter*] Yengiebert Dangleban! [*laughter*] Zanglebert Bingledack! [*laughter*] Winglebert Humptyback! [*laughter*] Slut Bunwallah!" [*laughter*]' He brings the sequence to a climax by having one of the managers reading back over the list of ridiculous names he's come up with, the penultimate one being 'Engelbert Humperdinck'. Another manager turns round and says, 'No, no, go back one, go back one.' There's a big laugh, and the audience applaud.

Then Izzard changes the mood, becoming serious. He

announces, 'But he's dead now. D'you hear that? Yeah, today, on CNN, I heard, just as I was coming out.' He builds the moment, adding a few details. The audience laugh uncertainly. He assures them he's serious, that he saw it on TV before he came out.

Then he shakes his hands, shakes his head, and laughs, saying, 'It's not true!' There's a big laugh. His eyes rise upwards, as if to show him despairing of the audience's gullibility.

Then he's serious again: 'No, it is true, erm –' Another laugh. He adds a few more details. Then he shakes his head and smiles again, showing he's kidding. Another laugh.

He continues to repeat this sequence of confirmation and denial *six more times*. Amazingly, each time he does it, he gets a laugh. There are subtle variations. Sometimes he adds a few words, sometimes he uses gesture alone. He smiles, narrows his eyes, and shakes his hand and his head to indicate he's only kidding. He nods slowly, adopts a serious face and widens his eyes to indicate that he's serious. The eyeliner he's wearing makes the wide-eyed look particularly funny.[41]

There are many things that make this a great stand-up routine, like the childish joy of playing with language, and the perfectly judged performance. But what makes it truly remarkable is that it plays with a central idea of stand-up comedy: that it is about telling the truth.

When Izzard tells the audience that Humperdinck is dead, he convinces them it's true, even if their nervous laughter suggests they are not completely willing to believe. The laughter he gets when he admits he was only kidding is fuelled by the outrageousness of lying about so serious a matter as somebody's death to such a large number of people.

Truth is a vital concept in most modern stand-up comedy because of the idea that it is 'authentic'. The boundary between offstage and onstage is blurred and, in many cases, the audience believe that the person they see onstage is more or less the same as the person they might meet offstage. This inevitably means that there is an assumption that what the person onstage says about his or her life is more or less true. If comedians say they are gay, or they just went on holiday, or they hate Mexican food, we generally believe them.

Some comedians explicitly champion the idea of truth. In a 2004 newspaper article, Richard Pryor was asked whether he used to write to be truthful or just to make people laugh. 'Truthful, always truthful,' he replied. 'And funny will come.'[42] At the Hammersmith Apollo in 2004, Billy Connolly is telling an anecdote when he breaks off to warn us that there's no punchline because it's a true story. He follows this up with a line that perfectly sums up the point: 'Life doesn't have punchlines.'

For comics who started before Mort Sahl and the rest of his generation introduced the idea that stand-up was about expressing the self, the idea that truth could be funny without being varnished by fictionalised jokework was unthinkable. The producer of *An Audience with Bob Monkhouse* argued with the veteran comedian over this. She wanted him to talk about some of the traumatic events he had written about in his autobiography, believing that 'honesty was important and would be appreciated more than fictional jokes'. Monkhouse disagreed: 'While I could deliver a truthful lecture on these topics, it wouldn't be all that comical.'[43]

Audiences have no problem accepting material that is obviously fictional if it is fantastical and surreal. For example, it's hard to imagine that the audiences who watched Woody Allen's legendary stand-up routines really believed that he had taken an injured moose to a costume party or escaped from a chain gang dressed as 'an immense charm bracelet'. Similarly, Milton Jones's exaggerated performance and absurdist material mean he's unlikely to be taken at face value. Having said this, extraordinary as it may seem, there have been occasions where audiences have confused his unhinged persona with his offstage self: 'I have had people come up to me afterwards and say, "Look, I really think you need help." . . . I mean, it tends to be in the less educated environments, but you know [they say,] "You need help, mate, you need to just go and see someone." '

Just as the person onstage is rarely exactly the same as the person offstage, in most cases, the truth comedians tell segues easily into fiction. Shelley Berman, one of the generation that established the ideal of authenticity in stand-up, had a famous routine in which he recreates a telephone conversation he's had with his father. In the introduction, Berman recalls being about eighteen years old and belonging to a community theatre group. He wants $100 to go to acting school in New York, so he telephones his father, who owns a Chicago delicatessen. We hear only the father's side of the conversation, which is richly characterised in a thick Jewish accent.

Much of the comedy comes from the cultural gap between them. The father is shocked that Berman is too scared to ask him for money face to face ('Did I ever lay a hend on you? In my whole life, did I ever lay one feenger on you? All *right*, but on those times you deserved it'); he cannot understand his son's ambition ('Shakespeare, Schmakespeare, I didn't understand one word'); and he's worried about the company he'll be keeping ('They are sissy boys, Sheldon, all the ectors are sissy boys'). It's a touching portrayal of the father, who eventually agrees to give Berman $100 for acting school, and offers him an extra $150 for other expenses, if he'll work two Saturdays for him in the delicatessen.[44]

It seems a very revealing, truthful routine, yet it's well documented that the actual events which inspired the piece have been fictionalised. In reality, Berman's father was a taxi driver, and didn't have a Jewish accent. Berman explains the changes he made when turning the event into a stand-up comedy routine: 'In order to create a piece of theatre, especially if one is using himself and his own history, there has to be some licence. So some licence is being taken there. But in fact, in absolute fact, it is not only my father who gave me the money to go to school to study the theatre. It had to be both . . . It had to be my mother and my father. But I couldn't play both my mother and my father. That wouldn't have happened. They both were fearful that there must've been something wrong with me, if I wanted to be an actor. I mean, why in God's name would I want to be an actor, unless I had some weird sexual preference. [*he laughs*] My father was terrified! But these things, I have to angle this piece of material, and I have to also increase the cultural gulf so that people will understand where this father was and where this boy is. So, yes, one could say, "No, it is not absolutely the way it actually happened," but – it's the way it happened. May I tell you, it is the way it happened. It's not fudging. Listen, it's a piece of artistry, it's a piece of work. It's a one-act playlet, it can't be without some focus on the story I'm trying to tell.'

In some cases, the truth and fiction become so inter-twined that even the comedian finds it hard to separate the two. Mark Lamarr used to do a routine about a drunken incident in which he behaved so stupidly, it led him to give up alcohol. After a night out, six men in a jeep, who recognise him from TV, start shouting abuse at him. Being drunk, he decides to take them on ('Oh, it's only six blokes in a jeep'). He tries to come back at them with something 'witty and clever'. They call him 'wanker', and he answers:

Look – don't wank me, I'll wank you, all right, don't – [*laughter*] Don't come round here giving it wank, I'll wank all six of you separately, I'll wank you all at once. [*laughter*] Give me twenty minutes, I'll wank your jeep, all right, so don't come round here – [*laughter*]

Violence threatens as they get out of their vehicle, but Lamarr is still showing ridiculous bravado ('And I thought, "Well, that's their first mistake – no jeep"'). Eventually, because he has stood up to them, they start to like him, admiring his guts. One of them still wants to fight, though, and Lamarr says his stupid response to this ('Look, six – or nothing') is the reason he gave up drinking.[45]

Lamarr starts to explain the interplay of truth and fiction in routines like this: 'Yeah, I mean, you sort of invest so much time getting those stories just right, that you do picture 'em in your mind and they do become real. And I actually can't remember, there probably is some truth in there still.' Then suddenly, a realisation strikes him and he says, urgently, '*No, there is!!* Actually, yeah! No, that is very much based on truth!'

He goes on the explain that, in the actual incident, he was with some members of the pop group the Housemartins, which he couldn't mention because 'it ends up as just "This is a fucking bloke namedropping".' In reality, the men who had abused him were black, which he felt he had to change 'because of those connotations'. Also, far from ending up as an example of his own stupidity, he resolved the situation well, but he realised that 'you've gotta lose in this story or it's not funny'. Having remembered the truth of the incident and the reasons for changing it, he explains: 'That is a really good example of something that completely transmogrified, from when I first started telling it, [when] it was just how I would tell a story to mates in a pub. And it was absolutely true, and it was a really cracking story. But by the end of it, it'd become almost the opposite of what happened and lots of the important elements that made it really funny in the pub weren't in there any more.'

With some comedians truth and fiction don't intertwine so much as sit side by side, one replacing the other when it better serves the aim of getting a laugh. On a TV appearance in 2004, Jo Brand tells the audience:

Now I *can* tell that a lot you, you're sitting there and you've got that kind of *feel* about you: 'Oh dear, it's the lesbian off Channel 4,' right? [*quiet laughter*] Let me put your mind at rest, I *am* married. Yes, I know it's difficult to believe. [*laughter*] And the papers, for years, have been *implying* – nay, not even implying, they've been *overt* – and said I was a lesbian. To the extent, right, that I read it so many times about myself, I thought I prob'ly was as well. [*laughter*]

This is pretty much the truth. Brand has been vilified by some sections of the popular press, and there has been a popular misconception that she is a lesbian. It is also true that she is married. The joke about her starting to believe the newspapers' comments about her sexuality is not literally true, but it's an exaggeration rather than out-and-out fiction.

Brand goes on to talk about her husband, referring to him by his actual name, and shortly afterwards, there's a joke about him which is clearly untrue: 'A couple of weeks ago, right, I had to go and sit in casualty with my husband for *seven hours*. Whilst he waited to have seventeen stitches removed from his face.' The audience laugh, uncertainly. 'That'll teach him to buy me a sewing kit for my birthday.'[46]

Now there's a big laugh. The gag works directly because the punchline is obviously fictional. The set-up is plausible, and describes an unpleasant situation, hence the sense of unease in the audience's laughter. The laugh the punchline gets is fuelled by the release of this tension as the audience realise they're not hearing about real violence, but fictional, cartoon violence. Assaulting her husband with a needle and thread is gleefully outrageous image, typical of Brand's work.

Brand's mixture of truthful information and pure fiction is not a deliberate strategy: 'I'm kind of not at all conscious of mixing kind of complete big lies and truth. I mean, I've always felt . . . I had a very sort of slapdash approach to comedy. I would just sit down, and I would just try and think of some funny things, you know, and if those funny things happened to be a couple of things that'd really happened, I would put them in, you know. And the other thing I would do is I would mix a kind of true build-up with a false punchline as well. Just maybe to give it a ring of truth, but not consciously.'

Ethics

Lenny Bruce's widow, Honey, once said, 'He did bits almost about everything that happened in our life. And a lot of times I wouldn't realise it 'til years later because I didn't hear all the bits that he did.'[47] She didn't say whether or not she was happy about her husband putting personal information about her into his act, but, clearly, there is an ethical issue here. It is important for some comedians to tell the truth in their acts, but what right do they have to tell the truth about other people?

This is not just a theoretical question. In spite of the fact that most of his routines were clearly fantastical, Woody Allen was sued by his first wife for 'holding her up to scorn and ridicule' in his act. The person mentioned in the act need not even be somebody close to the comedian to cause potential difficulties. In one routine, Phill Jupitus tells his audience that 'real life is funnier than anything I can make up', and talks about tragic stories he's seen on the news. He portrays himself as a sick voyeur, taking delight in, for example, a story about a man who has broken into the lion's enclosure at London Zoo. Jupitus impersonates Trevor McDonald announcing the story on the ITN news, 'Viewers of a nervous disposition may like to turn awa –' before interrupting in his own, narrator's, voice: 'This is the point I find myself pressing play and record!'

Most of the routine is about the lions' reaction. Jupitus characterises them like tedious middle managers, showing them taking time to comprehend the situation fully. The lion leader stands with his back to the audience, saying: 'There's a *what*? [*laughter*] Oh *do* grow up, Gavin! [*laughter*]'[48]

Little comment is made about the man himself, but using

tragic real-life material to get laughs does have drawbacks, as Jupitus recalls: '[T]he care worker for the guy who went in with the lions came up to me, yeah. And said, "I was the case worker for that guy" (and she gave me his name) "who jumped in with the lions at London zoo." I froze, and she went, "– very funny".'

Rhona Cameron experienced repercussions closer to home. On a TV appearance in the mid-1990s, she performs a delicate, beautiful routine in which she reads out a letter from her mother. This is not stand-up comedy cliché of the string-of-jokes-disguised-as-a-letter-from-home; in this case, the letter is quite real. Cameron stresses this point, repeatedly saying 'This is true'. When she takes it out of her pocket at the beginning of the routine, she draws our attention to the fact that it's a bit shabby 'because I have had many jokes at my mother's expense with it over the last few months'.

The laughter may be at her mother's expense, but she is not portrayed as mean or stupid. She comes across as a good-hearted middle-aged woman. Most of the laughs come from the precision and enthusiasm with which she describes the mundane details of a party she has organised. She gives a long list of the food she prepared, and this is funnily precise. One of the items listed is 'various salads brackets coleslaw not my own close brackets'. She describes trying to get the cream to whip up and set as 'a nightmare'.

Cameron shows considerable skill in breathing comic life into this. The letter probably wouldn't raise many laughs as a printed text. The comedy it contains is subtle, and it's really only drawn out by her performance. In fact, she has taken the common phenomenon of grown-up children making fun of their parents and made it work in a more public context.

We do not laugh only at what her mother has written, but also at Cameron's amused reaction. The letter mentions decorating the garden with coloured fairy lights, which are described as 'really very *effective*'. When Cameron reads this sentence, she lowers the paper for these last three words, stressing '*effective*' with disdainful relish. She pauses for a moment, letting the word sink in, a gleam of a smile shining in her eyes as the audience laugh.[49] Like Berman's routine about his father, this is about a cultural gulf between the generations, and it comes across as a fond, amused portrayal of a parent, not a hostile one.

Nevertheless, Cameron now regrets performing the routine, which she sees as the action of a younger, less emotionally mature person: 'Looking back now I cringe at the thought that I read out my mum's letter onstage, because it was kind of an awful thing to do, but it seemed effective and I think people knew it was genuinely authentic and that's why they extra-liked it, as well as it having, you know, comedic value. But she wrote me letters regularly and I just thought they were so bizarre . . . Also, let's face it, I was looking for some material as well, if I'd had scores of my own material I wouldn't've had to read out my mum's letter . . . My mum said, you know, "I'm going to write to you again, but it's not for stage," you know. And . . . oh, I felt so bad when she said that.'

Such are the hazards of an art form that puts a private self on public display and allows material taken from real life to be turned into laughing matter. But in spite of the difficulties, it is stand-up comedy's ability to deal with the truth that make it so powerful and potent.

4. Working the Audience

Take the audience away from stand-up comedy and it starts to look weird. In 1960, the rotund American comedian Buddy Hackett released an album called *The Original Chinese Waiter*. Unlike other records from the time, from the likes of Mort Sahl and Shelley Berman, it was made in a studio, without an audience. There's something quite eerie about hearing the insistent rhythms of his gags going down to total silence, but the really strange parts are when he addresses his 'audience' directly: 'I don't know about you folks, but I'm very fond of Chinese food.' It sounds rather desperate, an impression reinforced by the first line of the final track: 'Uh, I guess you folks is laughin' pretty good by now.' Hearing this ring out in my silent office forty-four years after the recording was made makes Hackett's guess sound pretty much like wishful thinking.

I'm not trying to put him down, it's just that stand-up comedy without an audience is only half there. Ben Elton has argued that, 'It's a dialogue, it's just very one way.'[1] Without the laughter half of the dialogue, there is nothing. I know this from personal experience. Running through the act without an audience is rather like leaving a message on somebody's answerphone; it's difficult to keep up the energy you need to express yourself, and you often end up collapsing into total inarticulacy. As Mark Thomas points out: 'You can't do the gig in a vacuum, because it is specifically about the performer and the audience, and

106

it's specifically about generating the prerequisite number of responses. And they're very audible responses. And if you're not getting that, really you should stop.'

Exchanging energy

Kiwi comedian Rhys Darby describes what he does: 'You become the energy of the whole thing, you just go out there and switch on.' Some have compared the exchange of energy between performer and audience with electricity.[2] Phill Jupitus paints a beautiful picture of just how wonderful the energy exchange can be: '[There's] this odd dynamic of just a thousand people in a room . . . I'm the one and you're the 999. And you're just like a lightning rod for the feeling in the room, really, as a stand-up . . . And it's two way. Cos you need them as much as they need you. There's nothing like a good stand-up gig. There is *nothing* like a good stand-up gig, for that kind of unique, *what-the-hell-just-happened-there?* kind of night, you know. It's like alchemy.'

Funny lines, gestures and mimes flow from the comedian to the audience, and laughter, applause and heckles flow back. The audience is energised and bonded into a group by the comedy and the performer is energised by the audience's responses. Comics must be able to generate this energy in the audience, or there will be nothing to fuel their performance. Dying onstage is a uniquely enervating experience.

As they gain experience, comedians learn to read the audience, to understand their reactions. As Dave Gorman points out: 'What you do isn't *say those words in that order*; it's play the audience. It's feeling the consciousness of the room, and when they're ready to take the dive into the punchline and when they're not, and when they're tense, and you can't feel that unless they're there creating that atmosphere.'

Sometimes the energy of a show can go wrong. I remember being last on the bill at the Banana Cabaret in

Balham in the early 1990s. The second act is an open-mike spot, filled by a four-person black comedy troupe called They Wouldn't. They generate huge energy between the four of them, and leave the stage after six minutes to the kind of ovation a proper paid act would be proud of. They're followed by accordion-playing Scots oddball Lindsay Moran, who manages to catch the wave of energy they have created, and ride it even higher. The show has climaxed by the end of the first half. After the interval, the audience are tired, and the comedian who follows Moran can't rouse them. I am similarly unsuccessful, getting a few laughs, but unable to waft away the stink of anticlimax. I remember seeing Johnny Vegas doing an open spot in a cellar bar called Mulberries in Manchester a few years later, and being similarly unfollowable.

James Campbell finds that playing to audiences of children means he has to pay particular attention to energy levels: 'With an adult stand-up gig, you try and build it and build it and build it until you've got people literally rolling around in the aisles with tears streaming down their face. You try and do that with a kids' audience, they get hysterical. And the lid just blows off. So you have to keep calming them down every now and again. So you don't get that constant build-up. You can do it to a certain extent, towards the end, but I mean some of them will literally wet themselves . . . There is nothing more horrible than the sound of three hundred children laughing because you've paused. You get that fake laughter, hysterical laughter. They're just laughing because they're supposed to be laughing, and they can't remember why they're supposed to be laughing. It's horrible, it's demonic.'

Shelley Berman learns to talk to the audience

However difficult it is to handle the exchange of energy between performer and audience, it's a defining feature of stand-up comedy. Direct communication allows the comedian to switch on, to generate electricity, to become a lightning rod for the whole room. This is one of the reasons why many actors find the idea of performing stand-up so daunting. Shelley Berman trained as a classical actor, studying Ibsen, Shaw, Shakespeare and Chekhov at acting school. When he started as a stand-up, he brought with him many of the practices of straight acting, and took time to adapt to the demands of the new format: 'I didn't even *address* the audience, because I was used to the Fourth Wall. I was really trained to ignore that, you do not penetrate that Fourth Wall unless you are doing a soliloquy . . . That Fourth Wall was sacred . . . This was incredible, that I would not address the audience. I was afraid to address them, because it was wrong . . . One day, Billy Eckstein, the singer Billy Eckstein, said to me, "When you get onstage tonight" (because I was working with him, I was opening the show for him in Canada) . . . "Will you do me a favour, Shelley, just before you sit down and go to your phone, why don't you just say thank you and good evening to the audience that's welcomed you?" "Well, I can't do that, Billy, I don't do that." "Well, just try it." And he nagged at me, night after night. And one night I tried it, and I got much more laughter. For some reason, the material went over better. And it wasn't just that one night, I tried it again and I saw that there was something. And then I started softening up and relaxing with the audience, telling them about myself . . . and I found that they were enjoying me more than or as much as my material . . . I somehow realised that it's dealing with the audience that the comedian does, and, you know, I'd better stop being such a snob.'

Time and place

The skill of the individual comedian isn't the only thing that can affect the exchange of energy. Another major factor is the particular circumstances in which the stand-up show occurs. The time the show starts has an effect. A seven o'clock start might mean a rather formal, reserved audience, whereas a midnight show can be either lethargic or rowdy. In a Friday-night show, the audience may be bad-tempered or overexcited after a hard week at work; a Saturday show tends to be more relaxed.

Space probably affects energy even more than time. The comedy club I used to run was based in a largish pub function room, which in many ways was ideal for stand-up. There was a small stage at one end, and plenty of tables and chairs to seat the audience. The room had its own bar and direct access to toilets, meaning that paying punters would not have the hassle of having their tickets checked if they wanted to fill their glasses or empty their bladders. In spite of this, the audience tended to take rather a long time to warm up. In the first half of the show, although they seemed to be enjoying themselves, they were not particularly vocal in showing their support. Generally, they were rather quiet until the second half got underway.

A solution to this problem was discovered by Jacqui, the student who sold the tickets and did front of house for the show. She rearranged the tables. The room was longer and thinner than it appeared at first glance, and there was a tendency for a large group of standing punters, up to one-third of the audience, to congregate at the back. Jacqui realised that by putting as many of the tables and chairs as close to the front as possible, the standing punters would be brought forward, and the whole audience would be densely packed around the stage. This made it easier for a really efficient exchange of energy to occur. Needless to say, I went on to marry Jacqui.[3]

I made similar discoveries when I worked with a collective of comedians called Red Grape Cabaret. In the late 1980s and early 90s, we did shows in a motley collection of pubs, students unions and arts centres. College gigs tended to be the worst, often taking place in unsuitable venues, with poor staging and technical facilities. Once we had become confident enough to assert ourselves with the people running the shows, we started to take charge of the situations we found ourselves in. Sometimes this would mean taking obvious steps, like turning off televisions, jukeboxes or one-armed bandits while the show was on. Other times, it would mean rearranging the space, finding the best place for the stage to be set up, adjusting the lighting and rearranging the seating. Usually, this turned an undoable gig into an acceptable one, an acceptable gig into a joy. I don't ever remember discussing the principles behind our decision to move things around, but I do remember developing a strong sense of how a space and the way it was laid out would affect a show.

This acquired knowledge made me sit up and take notice when I came across Iain Mackintosh's book *Architecture, Actor and Audience*. In a history of theatre architecture from Elizabethan times to the present day, Mackintosh argues that its 'chief purpose . . . is to provide a channel for energy'. He suggests a number of rules for theatre design to maximise the flow of energy between actor and audience, including the idea that it's more important for an audience to be densely packed than to be comfortable or have good sightlines, and that the audience should 'enfold the performing area in a welcoming embrace'.[4] This immediately made me think of Jacqui's table layout, and about the general principles of space and energy in stand-up comedy.

One of these principles is that the acoustics of the space are important, and not just to ensure that the audience can easily hear the comedian. Low ceilings are crucial, because they allow the laughter to bounce back and reverberate throughout the room, boosting the energy. High ceilings make things much harder. In 1997, I compèred a series of shows at the Barnsley Civic Theatre, a great barn of a room, both broad and long. I found that even with a big audience, the laughter got swallowed up by the high ceiling, allowing the energy to evaporate.

Demanding venues
Different venues make different demands of a comedian. Variety theatres were laid out in sections, and the comic had

to ensure that he or she was achieving an exchange of energy with stalls, circle and gallery. Frankie Howerd would get his sister Betty to sit in each part of the theatre to ensure he reached them all.

Huge arenas place heavy demands on the performer. In the 1970s, Steve Martin found the experience of playing to stadiums full of screaming fans unpleasant: 'The act got more successful – meaning larger stadiums. Meaning it had a more rock and roll attitude, meaning the audience was wilder. And you can control it up to a point. But there's always annoying people in the audience who won't let the show happen, who think this is about something else. And it eventually ruined it for me . . . You can't treat comedy like rock and roll, it's much more sensitive.'[5]

In 2003, Eddie Izzard embarked on a twenty-one-date UK tour, performing to a total of 200,000 people. He broke his previous record audience (10,500 at an Amnesty International benefit gig at Wembley) by twice selling out the 13,800-capacity Manchester Evening News Arena. A review of his show at the Nottingham Arena mentions the fact that he couldn't hear audience laughter from the stage, thus robbing him of the comedian's most basic method of checking how well the show is going.

Large venues also have a profound effect on the way the audience experience the show. In September 2004, I go to see Billy Connolly at the Carling Hammersmith Apollo. It's a big venue, with a seating capacity of 3,719. I'm in seat 76, row Y, on the second to back row of the circle. It's a long way from the stage. When Connolly comes on at the beginning, he's a tiny figure. He looks like a digital photo taken on the wrong light setting. The white and grey of his hair and beard blend with the complexion of his skin, making it almost impossible to pick out any features on the bleached-out blob of his face. Any raised eyebrows, knowing glances or comic grimaces are lost on the back rows.

However, he's a superb performer, with vast experience

of playing big venues, and his performance works at both short and long distance. People like me in the cheaper seats might miss out on the facial expressions, but Connolly works with his whole body. His long hair flaps about comically when he acts something out, and he habitually strokes it back, running his hands down either side of his head. His legs are very expressive: he demonstrates funny walks and struts about the stage when he gets a big laugh. He has great mime skills, for example illustrating how long it takes a man of his age to urinate, finishing off by pretending to wring out his penis with both hands. He also uses the whole stage, occasionally stepping right up to the front of it and lowering his voice to give the impression he is saying something confidential.

In spite of all this, though, I feel a little distanced from the show because of the way the size of the venue affects the audience. After a punchline, I can hear the wave of laughter rushing through the stalls, but it rarely engulfs me. In my section, there are pockets of laughter or applause from individuals or groups around me, but there are not many moments when we all laugh at once. As individuals, we're more likely to laugh if surrounded by others who are laughing, but here we're on the periphery.

Hostility

Stand-up comedy is shot through with a dark vein of fear and hostility. Comedians tend to fear audiences' ability to judge and reject. Speaking to an audience is a common fear among the general public, and most people are horrified by the idea of performing stand-up. Meanwhile, on the other side of the mirror, audiences also fear comedians. For most events, venues with unreserved seating tend to fill up from the front, whereas in comedy shows they tend to fill up from the back. Punters fear sitting near the front in case they should get picked on or ridiculed. Stand-up jargon has hostility written into it. Comedians who have done well with an audience say they have 'killed'; those who have done badly say they have 'died'. Stand-up has been compared with bullfighting. Comedians say that audiences are 'the enemy', that they can smell the comic's fear.

One of the extraordinary things about watching James Campbell, the stand-up comedian whose act is aimed at children, is seeing how many of the normal expectations of a stand-up show are overturned. The expected rivalry between comedian and audience is simply not there, and there's no question of him having to fight for survival, as his adult status means he is always going to be more powerful than most of his punters. When he asks them questions, rather than shouting out, the children politely raise their hands. There's no way he could seriously ridicule an individual audience member as he might in an adult gig, because the battle of wits would be too uneven.

Campbell avoids all of this by treating the children with skilful delicacy. In a show in Tunbridge Wells, he asks if any of the children are evil, and a little girl puts up her hand. He asks her why she's evil. She says she doesn't know. This leads him into a nice flight of fancy about James Bond villains who have no idea what their plans are. It's a funny bit, which directs the laughter away from the girl whose comment inspired it.

In his influential book *On Aggression*, Konrad Lorenz argues that humour is a veiled form of hostility, but says it is unlikely to regress into 'primal aggressive behaviour'. He drives the point home with a memorable line: 'Barking dogs may occasionally bite, but laughing men hardly ever shoot!' However, there have been incidents in stand-up shows where the fear and hostility that bubbles under the surface has exploded into real violence. Milton Berle once used a couple of standard comic insults on a group of three men sitting at a nightclub table, getting nothing but silence in return. After the show, one of them assaulted him, grabbing him by the tie and sticking a fork into his chin, saying, 'I could kill you right this minute, you little rat bastard.'

Hattie Hayridge, an inoffensive comic with a deadpan act based on offbeat one-liners, was assaulted less seriously while she was onstage at the Tunnel Club in east London. The venue lived up to its reputation for crazy, rowdy hecklers as a punter walked across the back of the stage, stood behind her and lifted up her dress. She responded by repeatedly kicking him, so he came back at her by throwing an egg in her face.

There have also been cases where violence has been started by the comedian. In an uncharacteristically slapstick move, Lenny Bruce once repaid a heckler by inviting him onstage and pushing a custard pie into his face. Milton Berle could give as good as he took. An anti-Semitic heckler started winding him up by shouting 'Kike!', 'Jew bastard' and 'Hitler's right'. Berle leapt off the stage and piled into the man, trying to pass it off as a joke by pretending to dance with him. They were separated by theatre ushers, and Berle was later arrested.

Arguably, the prize for Most Violent Assault on a Paying Punter should go to Bob Monkhouse. In 1977, Monkhouse was performing in Watford when he was persistently heckled by a young man shouting, 'Fuck off!' Eventually, the comedian snapped. 'No more!' he said, before walking tightrope-style along the railing that led from the stage to the punter and kicking him in the head, instantly flooring him. The audience cheered the comic, and his act continued to much greater enthusiasm after the assault. With this in mind, I wonder what would have happened if A. A. Gill had made the comment about marzipan socks to Monkhouse's face?

These incidents may be colourful, but they're also isolated, and it's rare for actual violence to erupt in this way. In fact, for some comedians, seeing the audience as the enemy is a mistake. Dave Gorman argues: 'People always talk about comedy in combative terms . . . it makes it sound like only one of us can be the winner. Whereas, actually, there's only two ways for this to go: we all have a good time, or we all have a bad time. There isn't a middle ground. We're actually all on the same side.'

Shared experiences

Much of what stand-up comedians do is about sharing: shared feelings, shared experiences, creating a sense of community with the audience.

In some cases, the sharing is quite literal. At the Pavilion Theatre, Brighton, in January 2004, Daniel Kitson spends a lot of time talking to a couple of teenage boys in the front row. One of them has been brought along by his father, and Kitson chastises him for bringing his son to such an unsuitable show. He chats to the boys, and goes back to them every so often to ask them more questions. He asks them what music they like, showing his disgust when they tell him they like nu-metal bands like Korn and Slipknot. At the end of the show, he gives them two CDs from his own collection, saying that they can now start listening to 'good music'. It's a surprisingly touching gesture, which shows that, for all the ribbing, he also feels a real connection with the boys.

Observational comedy

A more familiar kind of sharing is observational comedy in which the comedian talks about everyday phenomena that are rarely noticed or discussed. To work properly, the routine must be based on shared experience, as Eddie Izzard observes: 'Your observations need to be something that people can relate to, for the audience to pick up on it.'[6]

Sharing is built into the very language of observational comedy. 'Have you ever noticed . . .?' has become a comedy cliché. Comedians often use the second person in this situation: instead of saying, 'I do this . . .', they say, 'You do this . . .' These linguistic quirks emphasise the importance of sharing, directly asking the audience to compare the comedian's experience with their own.

Observational comedy became popular in America in the 1950s, through the work of comedians such as Shelley Berman. In Britain, it was pioneered by the folk comedians and the Irish comic Dave Allen. In the 1950s, the popular radio comedian Al Read based many of his routines on close observations of northern working-class life, and these often relied on recognition for their effect.

The chances are, though, that observational comedy is older than this, and may even have existed in the music hall. Dan Leno, for example, had a routine called 'The Robin'. It's delivered in Leno's usual, rather theatrical style. In sing-song tones, he tries to be enthusiastic about Christmas, but what he says acknowledges a harsher reality:

> Why, how beautiful it is on a Christmas morning, when a man walks out into the frost and snow, or the mud and the slush as the case might be, and his coat buttoned up, and his nose a beautiful crimson. He meets a friend. Takes him by the hand and he says, 'Merry Christmas!' And the friend takes him by the hand and says, 'Merry Christmas!' And there they stand, hand in hand, looking into each other's face, waitin' to see who's going to stand a drink first.

On one level, the gags are based on the simple premise that Christmas isn't all it's cracked up to be, but there's something about the way he says the last line that suggests that he knows he's striking a chord with the audience. When he describes the experience of meeting a friend in the street and trying to be jolly about Christmas but actually finding yourself in a standoff about who's going to stump up the money for a drink, he seems to be uncovering something the punters will have experienced. It's hard to tell, given that this is, of course, a studio recording made without an audience, but my guess is that working-class Victorian punters would have greeted this observation with the laughter of recognition.

As the routine continues, Leno starts using the second person:

> And then you go home to your Christmas dinner, or other people's Christmas dinners, other people's preferred cos it's not so much expense. And there you sit, with your feet under your friend's table, and your eyes on the bottles and things, and you have that beautiful feelin' in your heart as you're sittin' and eatin' – you know you've got nothing to pay for.[7]

The repeated use of 'you' anticipates a thousand observational routines, and suggests that the audience are being asked to compare Leno's descriptions with their own experiences.

Later, front-cloth comics working the variety theatres would occasionally do something similar. Welsh comedian Gladys Morgan, for example, talks about a seaside landlady who says: 'Now I want you all to enjoy yourselves while you're stayin' with me – get out as much as you can.' The big laugh that follows might be due to the simple gag of the tight-fisted landlady cunningly trying to get her guests to make as little use of her facilities as possible, but Morgan follows it up with a line which suggests she's describing a shared experience: 'Ahhh, they all say that, don't they?'[8]

Embarrassment

In its simplest form, observational comedy works by drawing attention to something. Dominic Holland, described in his publicity as 'The UK's master of observational comedy', does a routine about his toaster. He explains that it is 'very reliable': 'You put the bread in, put it down, and when it's toast, it pops up automatically.' Then, with a hesitant, worried air, his eyebrows arching above the top of his round spectacles, he says: 'But before it pops up automatically, right, there's a compulsion within me – to pop it up beforehand. [*laughter*] To see if it's ready. [*laughter*]'

The audience laughs at the truth of the observation, recognising that they too have behaved in this irrational manner. After pointing out exactly how 'stupid' his behaviour is, Holland then points out how it leads to another irrational action: 'But then I think, "If I put it back down now – [*laughter*] it might reactivate the programme – [*laughter*] and burn the toast." [*laughter*]'⁹ The audience laugh even before he explains his worry about reactivating the programme. They anticipate what he's going to say because they recognise the same neurotic thought process in themselves.

This suggests that in some cases there is a therapeutic element to observational comedy. The situations it describes may involve worry, paranoia or embarrassment, and the act of sharing them allows a release of these tensions. In the late 1950s, Shelley Berman had a routine called 'Embarrassing Moment' which contained such gems as:

Listen, listen – has this ever happened to you, have you ever been talking intimately with somebody and all of a sudden you spit on them, has that ever happened? [*laughter*] Now for the person who's been spat on, it's embarrassing too, you know, because he doesn't know whether to wipe it off or *forget about it*! [*laughter*]¹⁰

There's a slightly hysterical quality to the audience's response. The first laugh lasts for nine seconds, the second for eight. As each starts to quieten down, you can hear individual punters hooting, wailing or shrieking. They seem to find something outrageous about drawing attention to such an embarrassing accident.

Building on an observation
Some observational gags rely less on the observation itself, and more on what is done with it. Adam Bloom offers a good example of this: 'I've actually spent the day in east

London, ha' we got any Cockneys in?' There's a cheer of assent from a few Cockneys in the audience. 'You lot fascinate me, right, what fascinates me about Cockneys is they always laugh at the end of their sentences – right? Even if what they've said isn't funny, that little cackle.'

This observation doesn't get a laugh, even though Bloom asks the audience to identify with it by saying 'right?' But the observation is merely a set-up for what follows:

> And I've worked out what it is. They're trying to com-
> pensate for the aitches they've just dropped. [*quiet
> laughter*] So a Cockney walks in a pub and goes, "Ello,
> 'Arry, 'ow's it goin', 'eard you been on 'oliday, get us 'alf
> a lager, heh-heh-heh-heh-heh-heh!' [*laughter and a few
> claps*][11]

It's a joke that works on more than one level. To start with, there's the energy and rhythm of the final punchline. Bloom's Cockney laugh sounds funny in itself, like a jolly machine gun. Then there's the concept of the gag: Cockneys spewing out dropped aitches at the end of their sentences like a broken machine creates a very funny cartoon image.

Bloom sees the gag as typical of his style, offering a slightly warped view of common experiences. He believes his observations are not so much based on asking the audience, 'Have you ever noticed . . .?', as on telling them, 'You've never noticed . . .' He describes how he relates to an audience: 'I'm one of you, but I'm the odd one of you. I'm the odd one of you. I was nearly one of you, but something twisted and didn't work out.'

Observational parody
Observational comedy is now such an established part of stand-up that some comics parody it. In a twentieth anniversary show at the original Comedy Store in LA, Jim Carrey tells the audience: 'I'd like to do some observational

humour for you now – I hope you can identify with it. Hey – don't you hate – when you're in bed with three women – [*laughter*] And the least attractive one whispers, "Save it for me!" [*laughter and applause*]' It's a glorious subversion of the form, deliberately picking an experience the audience won't be able to 'identify with', while at the same time suggesting that Carrey is a habitual sexual athlete.

A joke by Steve Coogan's character, the dreadful comedian Duncan Thickett, is based on the same idea, but in this case it's not a fantastical boast, but a glimpse of the grimness of the character's life. The bespectacled, woolly-hat-wearing Thickett explains that observational comedy is 'where I observe something, right, and you go, "Yeah – that's true, that"'. Then he goes on:

> Have you ever noticed, when you're walking along the streets at night, you're just walking along the streets, there's always someone, in't there, on the other side of the road, that says, at the top of their voice, 'Hey, you, you four-eyed bastard, where d'you get that hat?' [*laughter*]'

He pushes the gag further by insisting that his observation is a good one, confidently referring to 'one or two laughs of recognition'.[12]

Found comedy

There's another type of stand-up routine which works in a similar way to observational comedy. The comedian finds something from everyday life, recognises its ridiculousness, then takes it onstage and presents it to the audience. Just as the *objet trouvé* is defined by the act of designating it as art, so the comedian creates 'found comedy' by presenting something not designed to be funny as an object of amusement.

When I was working as a comedian, I went through a phase when practically every new routine I came up with worked like this. There seemed to be no end to the things

I'd take onstage with me to get laughs: an English–French phrase book; a misleading headline from the front page of the *Guardian*; the Highway Code booklet; a set of inflatable Spice Girls dolls which came free with a pop magazine; a catalogue full of tacky gift ideas. Best of all was a booklet I picked up in a local government building in Michigan. When I got back from the States, I used it in my compèring at the Last Laugh:

> I picked up this excellent document called 'Crack Down on Drugs Colouring Book', right. [*laughter*] The title, 'Crack Down on Drugs', no pun intended, obviously. [*laughter*] And 'Colouring Book', but nowhere in this is there a warning not to sniff the pens you're colouring the pictures in with, right? [*quiet laughter*] But, aside from that, the thing that caught my eye was this first picture. You probably can't see it, but I've thought of that.

I unroll a large photocopy of the picture, and the audience laugh as they take it in. It shows a respectable-looking man in casual clothes holding out a handful of pills to a kid in a school playground.

> Now as you can see, it's a picture of a drug dealer selling drugs to a kid. Not your, not your stereotypical drug dealer. He looks more like a Jehovah's Witness, or some-thing. [*laughter*] And it says, 'If someone offers you a drug, say no!' And the kid's saying, 'No, I care about myself,' but he's actually, if you look closely, already been taking drugs, cos here is a dog in an overcoat – [*laughter*] and checked trousers, you know. [*laughter and a few claps*]

Sure enough, there is a dog in an overcoat and checked trousers in the background, and a British audience, unfamiliar with the American character McGruff the Crime Dog, share my amusement at the hallucinogenic impli-cations of the picture.

Of course, found comedy isn't my own invention, and a much more celebrated example is Jasper Carrott's 1977 routine, in which he quotes actual statements made on car insurance claim forms:

'The other man altered his mind and I had to run over him.' [*laughter*] 'I bumped into a lamppost which was obscured by human beings,' ha ha ha ha – [*laughter*] Ha – 'Coming home, I drove into the wrong house and collided with a tree I haven't got.' [*laughter*] 'The accident was caused by me waving to a man I hit last week.' [*laughter*]

This is a really efficient bit of comedy, with the audience laughing long and loud at each ridiculous statement. The sentences which Carrott reads out are funny in their own right, but the fact that they're genuine is important. Before he starts, he assures the audience: 'And people say to me, "Surely these are made up," these are not, these are genuinely what people wrote on their claim forms, when they'd had an accident and sent into this insurance office in London, right, and they're all true.'

As with observational comedy, the idea of sharing is important. Carrott shows his own enjoyment of the statements, laughing along with the audience, and occasionally throwing in comments like, 'This is the best one, I think,' or 'Tremendous, I love those, I love those.'[13]

Mark Thomas makes a dull government document funny
In some cases, found comedy is more political. Mark Thomas reads from a book called *The Strategic Export Control Annual Report, 1999*, which lists British arms sales. He acknowledges how unpromising this sounds as a basic comedy premise: 'I know many of you are thinking, "Er – knob gag, please, Mark" [*laughter*]'

He goes on to pick out some choice facts, building on them by imagining tiny cartoonish scenes: 'I found out we

123

sold India anti-gravity suits. [*laughter*] "We shall fight to keep Kashmir!" "How?" "We shall fly above them!" [*laughter*]'

Like Carrott, he points out the absurdity he likes best:

> This is my favourite one: 'General purpose machine guns' [*laughter and clapping*] Cos – I thought they were fairly specific! [*laughter*] 'No, general purpose, you can wear it as evening wear, you can kill people with it' – [*laughter*] Says, 'I'm casual, I'm deadly.' [*laughter*]

The difference is that Thomas is asking the audience not just to share his amusement about what he has found, but also his outrage. He sets up his argument before reading from the book: 'It's 'n incredible link between – it's not incredible, it's fucking obvious – between arms sales that we make as a country and asylum seekers and refugees.'

After getting a laugh with the anti-gravity suits, he comes back to this point, saying that India comes 'in the top fifteen of countries of origin for asylum seekers'.[14] In a context where asylum seekers are being demonised by the popular press and certain politicians, pointing out the UK's own culpability by contributing to unrest in other countries is an important statement to make between the laughter.

Shared history

Another close relative of observational comedy is the type of routine in which comics reminisce about past experiences they share with the audience. Liverpudlian comedian Tom O'Connor provides a classic example. O'Connor built up a loyal following in the working-men's clubs of Merseyside, basing much of his comedy on his understanding of the local culture. Playing the Maghull Country Club in 1975, he talks about the working-class upbringing he shares with his audience: 'D'you remember years ago – when you played in the street and the women used to shout at yer?

"Go on, you! Up yer own end! [*laughter*] Yer like yer mother you are, go on!" [*laughter*] Whaddever that meant. And – [*laughter*]'

The audience laugh, recognising the type of fearsome woman O'Connor describes, and the accuracy with which he has remembered the kind of things she says. As the routine continues, real memories are interspersed with fictional ones, like the game he remembers called 'forwards-backwards-sideways': 'You'd hit a kid on the head with a shovel and – see which way he fell. [*laughter*]'

There's also comic exaggeration, like the memory of the one posh family in every street, with a mother who 'scrubbed the step in her fur coat'. But the biggest reactions are won by the memories themselves, particularly O'Connor's imitations of the way mothers would sing to call their children home: '"Ma-ry/ You're wan-ted!" [*loud, extended laughter and applause*] With – with some of them, you coulda danced! "Joh-nny/ Yer fa-ther's gonna/ Ba-tter yer!" [*extended laughter*]'[15]

In this way, O'Connor forms a strong, warm bond with his audience, identifying himself very much as one of them. His whole act radiates with Merseyside pride. 'Round 'ere we're brilliant,' he tells his audience. Nostalgia is crucial, and his longing to return to the values of his (and the audience's) past is explicit: 'Wasn' it good, when we didn't 'ave any problems like the modern people've got?'

In the 1960s, Bill Cosby used shared history to unite rather than divide his audience. He would look back at his childhood, choosing memories that were not specific to being black. In one routine, for example, he talks about the milk he used to drink in kindergarten, which had been 'sittin' on the radiator for about eighty years': 'Nothin' in the world better for a bunch of five-year-old kids than good old lukewarm curdley milk. [*laughter*] Yes sir, we loved it!'[16]

By avoiding experiences of racism, he allows black and white Americans in his audiences to enjoy shared memories together. This might seem a rather cosy approach, lacking the edge of, say, Dick Gregory, but it's important to realise that for a black comedian like Cosby to ignore issues of race was a radical step in itself in the 1960s; there were black comics before him who had been sacked for not being 'Negro' enough.

Shared references

Another important aspect of sharing is the references which comedians use. Words, places, people, songs and objects might be mentioned in the course of a routine, and these are the references, the basic pieces of knowledge, which audiences need in order to get the joke. When the comedian throws in references and the audience pick them up, it's a process of shared understanding.

Some comedians play it safe by using very broad references, dealing with subjects familiar to audiences across many different cultural boundaries. Some topics have inspired hundreds of stand-up routines, some of them imaginative and funny, others tired and clichéd. Many comics have done observational routines about air travel or pointed out the differences between cats and dogs, for example.

Advertising provides a renewable source of references. Anybody with a television will probably be familiar with a prominent new advert, so it becomes a viable subject for joking, with the added benefit of giving the act currency. The downside is that jokes about TV adverts have a relatively short shelf life. Even though the opening routine from Shelley Berman's 1961 album *A Personal Appearance* is beautifully crafted and skilfully performed, it loses something for audiences unfamiliar with the napkin commercial to which it alludes.

The possibility that the audience won't pick up a reference is always there. This is something that the makers of a documentary called *Lenny Bruce: Swear to Tell the Truth* clearly understand. They use an audio clip of a famous

Bruce routine, in which he imagines facing a white racist with a dilemma:

> You have a choice of spending fifteen years, married to a woman. A black woman – or a white woman. Fifteen years kissing, and hugging, and sleeping real close on hot nights. *Fifteen years with a black woman or fifteen years with a white woman,* and the white woman is Kate Smith – [*laughter*] and the black woman is Lena Horne. [*laughter*] So you are not concerned with black or white any more, are you? [*laughter*]

When Bruce mentions Kate Smith, a photo of a fat, wholesome white woman flashes on to the screen. When he mentions Lena Horne, a slinky, sexy black woman flashes up.

The film was made in the 1990s, and the makers must have realised that a large part of its audience wouldn't necessarily even have heard of the two singers, let alone have a mental image of what each one looked like. Without this shared knowledge, the joke makes no sense. The photos are there to make sure the references are picked up.

Another documentary, made in 2003, shows what happens when live audiences don't share the comedian's references. In *Bernard's Bombay Dream*, Bernard Manning, who is notorious for his relentless racial gibes, is sent to perform for audiences in India. The thinking behind this is clear: wouldn't it be interesting to see how Manning gets on trying to entertain people who are normally the butt of his jokes?

Although he does reasonably well at the first venue, the Jazz by the Bay club in Mumbai, Manning realises he has a problem with his references. In one gag, an Irish working-men's club are having a sweep on a mystery tour, and the driver wins £68. The joke dies, and Manning comments: 'You see, that's fell on flat ears because you don't know what a sweep is, do yer? That's a bet to guess where yer going on this tour, a secret tour, you see.' But the gulf of understanding is deeper than that. The audience doesn't understand the literal meaning of the joke, and its nuances are lost on them as well. The British phenomenon of working-men's clubs and their cultural baggage is entirely alien to the young, hip Indians watching Manning. A later show, at the very refined Gymkhana Club, is an outright disaster. A flat joke about Captain Cook is followed with the comment, 'Now, if you remember, Captain Cook discovered Australia, but you're not fucking bothered, are yer?'

Manning tries to explain terms like 'quid' and 'vicar'. After a few painful minutes, he walks off the stage to the hostile sound of an audience starting to mutter to themselves. Manning has claimed, '[I've] never died on me arse in me life.'[17] Seeing footage of him doing just that at the Gymkhana Club must bring a smile to the lips of anyone who finds his harsh wit distasteful.

Local references

Local references, which rely on knowledge of the particular area in which a show takes place, can help the comedian to develop a rapport with the audience. Frank Skinner's brilliant twenty-month stint as resident compère of Birmingham's 4X cabarets at the beginning of the 1990s saw him making 'profoundly local' jokes about such subjects as 'Bearwood Fruit Market, the mad bloke with the long scarf who hung around the Hagley Road, and the nearby chip shop that sold bright-orange chips'. Skinner was a hero to the audience in those clubs, and the extraordinary affection he enjoyed was undoubtedly helped by his authentic Brummie accent and extensive knowledge of the area.

This kind of thing is not just the privilege of a resident compère. At a show in Sevenoaks in 2004, Jack Dee gets some good laughs by talking about how rough the nearby Bat and Ball is: 'Why do they always keep their kitchen appliances outside the house? [laughter]' A few minutes later, he mentions that he was born in Orpington, a town which is close enough for the audience to know. A woman heckles: 'And you think Bat and Ball's rough?' There's a huge laugh, which Dee rides by smiling sarcastically. Although it might seem like his use of a local reference has backfired, there's still a sense that the woman's jibe binds the comedian and the audience together in shared local knowledge.

There's a really interesting example of a local reference in a 1979 recording of Jasper Carrott.[18] Although performing in central London, Carrott observes that a lot of the audience are from different parts of the country. In a routine about local radio, a mention of Capital Radio receives a cheer, presumably from the Londoners in the audience. It's drowned out by booing, presumably from punters from the rest of the country. A mention of Manchester's Piccadilly Radio inspires cheering and clapping from a single, solitary woman. 'Oh,' says Carrott, getting a laugh by drawing attention to the incongruity of this response. 'There's always one, isn't there?' he adds, getting another laugh.

Later, he gets a big cheer when he mentions Birmingham's BRMB Radio, and gets another just by naming one of the presenters, Tony Butler. The prospect of a Birmingham hero like Carrott playing a big venue in the nation's capital must have attracted a contingent of Brummies and, by mentioning their local station, he allows them to make their presence felt. In this routine, Carrott finds references which are local to different sections of the audience, allowing them to assert themselves by cheering and booing, showing pride and good-humoured rivalry.

References are not just about understanding; they may also provoke an emotional response, getting cheers or boos. Although it must be controlled, this exchange of energy is central to stand-up, and in some ways it is as important as the laughter.

Linguistic references

One of the most basic types of reference is language. Obviously, the audience must be able to understand the words a comedian uses. When the music-hall comedian Harry Lauder started performing in England, he replaced his broad Scots with a gentler accent, giving his audience a taste of his ethnicity while allowing them to understand his jokes. However, he would still use linguistic local references when playing to a Scots audience, such as coming over exaggeratedly posh by pronouncing every syllable of the place name 'Strathaven' instead of using the normal pronunciation 'Straiven'.

Linguistic references can be hazardous for Scots comedians. At a performance in Glasgow's King Tut's, fearless improviser Phil Kay uses the English word 'lake'. A heckler corrects him, shouting 'loch'. Putting his hand over his mouth to draw attention to his blunder, Kay provokes good-natured booing, before getting a big laugh by giving out a heavily accented 'locchhhhh'. He plays the situation well, and it's possible out that his blunder is deliberate. Certainly, he says the word 'lake' twice, stressing it slightly and pausing afterwards as if to encourage somebody to correct him.[19]

As both Lauder and Kay show, language can have particular meanings for particular audiences. It can also help to bond the audience in a feeling of cultural or ethnic kinship. Comedians playing to Jewish holidaymakers in the Borscht Belt hotels in the Catskills would sometimes deliver the set-up of the joke in English, and the punchline in Yiddish. This would allow the audience to feel a sense of belonging, exclusivity and collusion, while making it incomprehensible to outsiders.

Pop songs

Richard Pryor has a routine in which he contrasts the coldness and reserve of white churches with black churches where 'you get a show wit' your money'. This is by way of introducing a typically exuberant impersonation of a black preacher. The first laughs come from the preacher's convoluted language, and the quirky inflection which Pryor gives the character, transforming the phrase 'inferior mind' into a growled 'inferio' *miihhhhhnd*.

Next he reads from the 'Book of Wonder', starting with the line, 'A boy was born in hard time Mississippi.' There's a laugh, some clapping, and a cheer of recognition.[20] The gag is that the preacher has not chosen to read a biblical text, but has instead opted to quote the lyric of Stevie Wonder's 1973 hit single, 'Living for the City'. For the joke to work, the audience must share Pryor's knowledge of popular culture.

Quoting the lyrics of popular songs out of context is a reasonably common joke in stand-up, but nobody has done it as compulsively as Harry Hill. The references in Hill's act are part of what makes it unique, and these come in two obsessive strands. On the one hand, there are references which are cosy, old-fashioned and very English: chops and mash for tea, sleeping bags, lollipop ladies, Savlon, his nan. He explains this as being his own twisted version of the material more conventional stand-ups do about shared history: 'Well, it's a lot of sort of childhood stuff, really, isn't it? It's sort of childhood stuff, without saying, "Do you remember Spangles?" or, you know, "Do you remember chops?"'

On the other hand, he has an almost Tourettic tendency to quote lyrics from pop songs. A five-minute TV spot on *Saturday Live* in 1996 sees him quoting or deliberately misquoting songs by artists as diverse as Mud, Babylon Zoo, the Lighthouse Family, Queen and Ini Kamoze. Hill now works with a keyboard player and a drummer, allowing him actually to sing snatches of songs, albeit in an incongruous, old-mannish style. At a show in September 2004, he performs such unlikely recent hits as Outkast's 'Hey Ya!' and The Streets' 'Dry your Eyes'. Hill started quoting pop songs in 1991, when Bryan Adams' '(Everything I Do) I Do It for You' spent umpteen weeks at the top of the UK charts. Hill decided to speak the opening line of the song in the middle of his act, throwing it in as a non sequitur. It got a big reaction, so he developed it as a technique. He explains why he thinks is works: 'A lot of the time, it's something that everyone knows about, but no one's sort of pointed it out to them. And I'm not even saying anything about it, really – I suppose I am in a way. I'm saying, you know, "We've all seen this, isn't it annoying," I suppose, in a way, but I'm not actually saying that out loud.'

In-jokes

The American comedian Henny Youngman was famous for a minimalist style, based on quickfire one-liners. In a recording of his act, he comes out with the old chestnut, 'Take my wife – please!' A laugh starts but is quickly drowned out by cheering, applause and whistles. This reaction goes on for a full twenty seconds, and doesn't even subside when he acknowledges it by shouting, 'I love this crowd!'[21]

Why such a big reaction? Although this line has been used by many other comedians, Youngman is popularly credited with being its inventor. The recording was made late in Youngman's career, and the audience isn't so much cheering the line, as celebrating his comic longevity and his general contribution to comedy. The joke itself has become the reference.

Once they become well established, comedians are able to use references which are internal to the act. There's an excellent example of this kind of in-joke near the beginning of Eddie Izzard's *Glorious*. He does an impression of God's mum, using a Scottish accent, then comments, rather hesitantly, 'His mum was – Mrs Badcrumble.' As with Henny Youngman's gag, this gets cheers, whistles and applause as well as laughter. In this case, it's an even more explicit reference to previous work, referring back to a routine from Izzard's previous show, *Definite Article*, about an elderly clarinet teacher called Mrs Badcrumble. Presumably, the audience are cheering to show their appreciation of the earlier routine, but they're also showing they belong to a kind of Izzard in-crowd, united by their knowledge of his comedy.

Jasper Carrott relies on a similar sense of insider knowledge with a technique which involves quoting just the punchline of a familiar joke. In a 1983 routine about a trip to Hong Kong, he describes a hair-raising taxi drive from the airport to his hotel, saying that he was a 'darn sight lighter' at the end of the trip than at the beginning. He follows this suggestion of involuntary bowel evacuation with the line, 'Smell it? I was sitting in it!'[22]

This is a reference to a joke which was in common circulation at the time about a man who smelled a funny smell every time he drove his new car. Unable to get to the bottom of the problem, the mechanic asks the man to take him for a drive. The man is a terrifyingly bad driver, and at the end of the trip asks if the mechanic can now smell the smell. 'Smell it? I'm sitting in it!' replies the mechanic.

Unlike the Izzard example, here the audience require knowledge of comedy in general, rather than of Carrott's act in particular. This helps to form an even closer rapport, because by referring to the kind of joke that his audience know from the home, the workplace or the pub, Carrott is showing he's just like them.

The path between popular street culture and Jasper Carrott's stand-up act is not just one-way. In a 1977 routine, he tells the audience about hearing the word 'zit' for the first time, explaining, 'It's American slang for our "spot" or "pimple".'[23] There's no hint that the audience recognise the word, and the definition he offers is received in silence.

In a 1979 TV show, the same routine gets a very different reaction. He segues into it after talking about appearing on *Top of the Pops* and meeting the cult female dance troupe Pan's People who, he says, are 'all covered in zits'. There's a laugh which quickly breaks out into cheering and applause in recognition of the word. Carrott realises that this means the audience must know the routine from his earlier tour, the album of it, or the previous year's TV series, *An Audience with Jasper Carrott*. 'Oh, d'you know about them?' he asks, with mock innocence, then seems slightly flummoxed: 'Oh, hur hur hur! [*laughter*] I think we'd better cut the next ten minutes! [*laughter*]'

In spite of this, he continues with the routine as planned, which goes down every bit as well as if a large section of the audience hadn't heard most of it before. He tells them: 'I'm trying to introduce a word into the English language.' The cheer he gets for his first mention of the word suggests that he's already been pretty successful in achieving this ambition. It seems likely that he is largely responsible for importing 'zit' into British slang. In this way, stand-up draws from street culture but also influences it, with material from comedians' acts spilling out into everyday life.

Alexei Sayle's intellectual references

Lenny Henry was already an established name by the time Alexei Sayle started his career in 1979, but it was the influence of Sayle and others like him at the Comic Strip that led Henry to reject the casual, self-deprecating racism of his early work and develop a more positive style. However, Henry found Sayle puzzling as well as exciting: 'I thought he was funny, but I thought a lot of his reference points were really weird.'[24]

This comment was inspired by the intellectual references which Sayle would liberally sprinkle across his act, namechecking the likes of Karl Marx and Jean-Paul Sartre. A political routine about tower blocks is a classic example. Sayle lays into the architects and town planners who build horrendous concrete estates with the idea of 'designing the working class the perfect fuckin' workers society':

All them fuckin' estates, all them new towns, they're all supposed to be somethin' like William Morris Worker's

Paradise, you know, everybody sittin' in the tower block, weavin' their own fuckin' yoghurt! [*laughter*] Standin' in the windswept concrete piazza discussin' Chekhov! [*laughter*]

[*He adopts a working-class Cockney accent to imagine the discussion*] 'Oh yes, er, I do actually, wiv Chekhov, you know, that erm, 'is alienating use of naturalism, you know, makes one completely reassess one's attitude to the Russian bourgeoisie in the late nineteenth century.' [*laughter*] 'Fuck off, you cunt!' Wallop! [*laughter*][25]

The basic gag of having working-class people discussing intellectual ideas in highfalutin language had already been used by Monty Python, who showed charladies discussing philosophy, but most of the Python team were middle-class intellectuals, emerging from the Oxbridge revue tradition. This is different. There's an interesting tension between the Sayle's foul-mouthed, Scouse persona and the references to William Morris and Chekhov's 'alienating use of naturalism'.

The political point of this is not that working-class people are too stupid to discuss Chekhov, but that middle-class people impose a ridiculous set of idealised expectations on the working class, while providing them with poor housing. Sayle's sympathies are made clear both by what he says (pointing out that you don't catch architects 'living in any of the shit they've been designing for the last twen'y years'), and the way in which he says it (his accent indicating his own working-class origins).

Sayle explains why he was so keen on intellectual references while hoping to attract a popular, working-class audience for his comedy: 'I mean, one of the comedian's tricks is to pretend to be much more erudite than you are. Lenny Bruce used to do that all the time. He used to find the right name to drop. I don't fucking know anything about Kierkegaard, it doesn't matter, I know very little about any philosophy, Sartre, you know, my knowledge is minimal. It doesn't matter. It is a fake, it's a trick, but, you know, it's about finding the telling phrase, the right name.' He rightly argues that comedians should never underestimate an audience's ability to cope with more difficult references, and says that just as he only needed 'minimal knowledge' to drop the names, the punters would only need the same to pick them up. However, he also feels that his quirky references held him back: 'I do also think, though, in a sense, it's harmed my career, because people – like especially journalists and critics – like simplicities.'

Shared misunderstanding

In October 2003, Jim Davidson is doing his *Vote for Jim* show at the Winter Gardens, Margate. At one point, he imagines himself as Prime Minister, being interviewed by Jeremy Clarkson. Neither he nor the majority of his audience realise the mistake; he means Jeremy Paxman (the serious journalist from *Newsnight*, famous for his no-holds-barred interviews with politicians), not Jeremy Clarkson (the car-obsessed presenter of *Top Gear*).

In February 2004, Roy 'Chubby' Brown is playing the same venue. In a routine about the good old days, he fondly remembers a time 'when the royal family were roundheads, not fucking dickheads'. The gag is based on the premise that roundheads were royals, rather than the republicans who temporarily abolished royalty.

In both cases, the references are factually incorrect, but in neither case does it spoil the audience's enjoyment of the joke. This is because although references require shared understanding to be effective, that understanding does not have to bear any resemblance to the truth. A shared misunderstanding can be just as effective.

Sometimes, comedians create comedy which is knowingly based on such shared misunderstandings. Omid Djalili based the accent he opens his act with on that of a distant uncle, a professor of English literature at Oxford, whose voice he had always found funny and endearing. The problem was that the uncle did not have an Iranian accent:

'He was an Iranian who was raised in Lebanon, so he was actually Iranian but had an Arabic accent. And I just kind of said, "Well, people don't really know the difference between Iranian, [and] Arab" . . . what I was doing was actually against my culture. I mean, I was playing an Arab but saying I was Iranian. And most Iranians [would] say, "That's not an Iranian accent." I thought, "Well, look – for now, it doesn't matter, it's just funny." '

Playing with references

A stand-up act might refer to anything from an advert to a Russian playwright, from a slang word to pop song. Factual accuracy is unimportant. All that matters is that the audience share the comedian's understanding of the reference. This basic principle is so well established that some comedians have even made jokes about it.

In a 1977 routine, Steve Martin says that there is a large group in from a plumbers' convention, and that he is going to do a joke just for them. He warns the audience that 'those of you who aren't plumbers probably won't get this', before launching into a gag filled with presumably fictional technical references, like 'a Finley sprinkler head with a Langstrom seven-inch gangly wrench' and 'Volume 14 of the *Kinsley Manual*'. The audience laugh at this deliberate obscurity. The joke ends with a nonsensical punchline: 'It says "sprocket", not "socket"!'

This time, the audience laugh at Martin's own uneasy laughter as he realises that the joke has bombed. After a sticky pause, Martin puts an anxious question to the stage manager: 'Are those plumbers supposed to be here this show, or . . . ?'[26] There's a bigger laugh. The audience is in on the gag from the beginning. It's obvious that the plumbers' convention, the technical references in the gag, and Martin's unease at the end of it are all fake. The real reference in the gag is not plumbing terminology, but the very idea of references, and the need for shared knowledge in stand-up.

Lenny Bruce explicitly refers to this in his act. In a 1961 show, he tells the audience how hard it is for him to reach people over the age of forty, because his language is 'completely larded' with hip, intellectual and Yiddish language, and that for anybody over forty-five, 'all I have to do is hit one word that'll send him off'. He suggests a fantasy solution to the problem: 'I'm gonna have a thing where nobody over forty's allowed to come in to see me. [*laughter*] Have a sign up, man.'[27]

Working an audience means being able to manage the unpredictable exchange of energy between performer and audience. When it goes wrong, laughter can be replaced with hostility and even violence, but when it works the show becomes an occasion for sharing experience, embarrassment, misunderstandings and cultural references. Some of the best comedians don't just use their tricks of sharing and rapport to get laughs and keep the lurking hostility at bay, they also use them to challenge some of the audience's most basic assumptions.

5. *Challenging the Audience*

In the late 1990s, Phill Jupitus created an entire full-length stand-up show about the film *Star Wars*. It started off as 'a Wookiee impression and a joke about Darth Vader', which he threw into a twenty-minute set at the Comedy Store, pretty much on the spur of the moment. This went down well enough for him to develop it further. Every time he watched the film, he thought of more ideas for routines.

It became a stand-alone show at the Edinburgh Festival, entitled *Jedi, Steady, Go*, and went on to tour nationally. The last time he performed it, at the Lyric Theatre, Hammersmith, it lasted one hour and fifty-five minutes, almost as long as the film itself. The show was based on the unusual idea of comedian and audience sharing detailed knowledge of this one particular cultural artefact. Without this, the jokes wouldn't really work, as Jupitus points out: 'I did have a woman at the Edinburgh show once that hadn't seen the film. [To] which I'm gonna say, "This is going to be a very dull hour for you." And it probably was, you know . . .'

Jupitus was pleased to attract obsessive fans of the film to his show: 'The front row always had the *Star Wars* T-shirts. The nerds would come down and, yeah, the geeks loved it.' *Star Wars* fans are notorious for their detailed and pedantic knowledge of the films, and Jupitus would play on this fact,

139

needling them by deliberately mispronouncing things, getting them to tut disapprovingly. By showing a mischievous disregard for the insignificant details of the film so dear to that audience, the comic was, albeit in a tiny way, challenging their values. The fact that he could create a show based on obsessive *Star Wars* knowledge indicates how similar he was to the people who were attracted to go and see it; but the fact that he made fun of their obsession shows that he was also different from them.

Insiders and outsiders

This illustrates a basic choice faced by stand-up comedians. Bob Monkhouse argues that an audience is 'not a community' but a set of 'individuals who have assembled for a single purpose'. The comic 'may impose a temporary bonding upon such a throng' but 'it vanishes as soon as the people disperse'.[1] There's a certain amount of truth in this, but, in some cases, a stand-up audience may be already bound together by some sense of community, even if it's only a shared love of *Star Wars*.

Monkhouse was right, though, to argue that the comedian imposes a temporary bonding on the audience. In many cases, this is achieved by the sharing of common experience. As we saw in Chapter 4, observational comedy, routines about shared history and a well-judged set of references can all help to bond the audience together in temporary feeling of community. With this kind of approach, the comedian is defined as an insider, very much part of the community of the audience. A classic example is Tom O'Connor at the Maghull Country Club in 1975, sharing a common past with the audience, and uniting with them against the debased values of the modern day.

However, comedians can also define themselves as outsiders, distinct from the community of the audience. Sometimes, the comedian becomes an outsider against his or her will. In the variety era, the Glasgow Empire was notorious among English comics for the rough reception they'd get from a drunken Scots audience at second house on a Friday night. In this case, the comedians suffered from a pre-existing hostility based on national rivalry, but in other cases, the comic can become an outsider by making a mistake. In the late 1960s, Bob Hope enthusiastically supported the Vietnam War, and firmly aligned himself with Richard Nixon. Playing to GIs in Vietnam, he misjudged his audience, assuming they would share his hawkish views. At a show at Camp Eagle in 1970, an audience of 18,000 American soldiers responded to his act mostly in silence. He got a similar reception at Long Binh in 1971, where he was faced with heckling, walkouts and banners reading 'Peace Not Hope'.

Being an outsider doesn't always mean dying onstage, and some comedians embrace the role. As a Muslim, Shazia Mirza is easily recognisable as being different from most of her audience: 'Everybody knows I'm not the same as them, because what I'm saying is so different, you know, I say that I don't smoke and I don't drink and I don't take drugs and I don't gamble. And I don't do any of the things that the people sitting in my audience are sitting in front of me doing at that time. So they are all smoking, they are all drinking, and I'm telling them that I don't do those things, and they know that I'm different.'

She's also different from most other comics on the circuit: 'When I saw other comedians talking about themselves growing up, and I thought, "Oh, well, I could talk about something different here, I could talk about my growing up, which would be different to all these white, laddy comedians.' Her difference became a source of material, as well as affecting the way she relates to her audience, but she points out that she is not entirely an outsider: 'For some reason, in some way, they do feel as though we have something in common. We do feel that there is some connection between us.'

The worst audience Bill Hicks ever faaaced

Bill Hicks, on the other hand, was not marked out as an outsider by race or religion, but he willingly accepted the idea of being separate from the community of the audience. His act lambasted the first President Bush, the Gulf War and Christianity, while enthusing about smoking, drugs and pornography, so it was always likely that he would find himself in opposition to audiences in the more conservative parts of America.

Hicks embraced the outsider role, seeing it as a fundamental part of the comedian's job: 'To me, the comic is the guy who says, "Wait a minute" as the consensus forms. He's the antithesis of the mob mentality.'[2] It was not just his material that separated him from his audience, but also his onstage attitude. Hicks's performance exuded high status. He took his time over his delivery, he stroked back his longish hair in the pauses, and he seemed totally assured and absorbed in his own train of thought. He would sometimes approach an audience with an attitude bordering on contempt, for example starting a show at the Funny Bone in Pittsburgh in 1991 by saying: 'Good evening, ladies and gentlemen, I hope you're doing well tonight, I'm glad to be here, I've been on the road doing comedy now for, er, ten years, so bear with me while I plaster on a fake smile and plough through this shit one more time. [*laughter*]' Later in the same show, he announces, 'Y'all are about to win the election as the worst fuckin' audience I've ever faaaced. Ever! Ever! Ever!'[3]

Hicks clearly feels the audience isn't appreciating his act, and many stand-ups must have berated their audiences like this as a desperate response to the horror of dying onstage. The difference here, though, is that Hicks isn't dying. There's laughter throughout the act, albeit patchy at times, so the antagonism which becomes a running theme is something much more interesting than an expression of comic failure. In shows like this, he's the polar opposite of Tom O'Connor.

Hicks enjoyed a following of devoted fans, and sometimes had a less hostile relationship with his audience, though he was never afraid to challenge them. Playing to an excitable crowd in Oxford in 1992, he announces: 'Actually I quit smoking, so er . . .' There's a groan of disappointment from somebody in the audience, and others join in, clearly feeling let down by Hicks's apparent U-turn. On other occasions he has been aggressively enthusiastic about cigarettes. There's also a pantomime quality to this response, as if they're teasing him in the spirit of fun rather than really taking him to task. Nevertheless, he's quick to chide them: 'This ain't Dylan-goes-electric, chill out, OK? [*laughter*]'[4]

Frankie Howerd has nothing against the Establishment

Comedians don't have to be as radical as Bill Hicks to play the outsider role. When Frankie Howerd played at Peter Cook's fashionable satire venue, the Establishment, in 1962, he based his entire act on the idea of being a fish out of water. After huge success in the late 1940s and early 1950s, Howerd's career had gone into a nosedive, largely thanks to being cast in acting roles in a series of theatrical flops. He was on the point of giving up show business when Peter Cook saw him give a speech at the *Evening Standard* Drama Awards, and invited him to appear at the Establishment.

Howerd was an odd choice. Cook's venue was the product of the satire boom which originated in the Oxbridge revue tradition, and was normally the stomping ground of well-to-do satirists. Earlier that year, Cook had imported a genuinely dangerous comedian by booking Lenny Bruce to play a controversial season there. Howerd was far cosier. Although inventive and innovative in his day, he was essentially an old-fashioned front-cloth comic from the variety circuit. Daunted by the prospect of playing such an unlikely venue even in the midst of a major career crisis, he enlisted the help of big-name comedy writers like Johnny

Speight, and Galton & Simpson to provide him with material. From the beginning of the act, he plays on the idea of being out of place and different from his audience.

> Brethren – before we start this little eisteddfod, [*laughter*] I want to make a little, er, apology to you, if I may. Well, I say 'apology', it's really, it's an appeal. Well, it's, no, it's an explanation. Well, no, it's an apology, let's be honest. [*laughter*] I may as well be honest, it's an apology. I'll tell you why. Because erm – you see, ah – I'd like to explain 'ow I happened to get here at this place – [*laughter*] before we start. Because, as you know, if, if, well, if you do know at all, I'm a humble music-hall comedian, a sort of variety artist, you know, I'm not usually associated with these sophisticated *venues*, [*laughter*] and erm –

The word 'venues' is twisted in typical Howerd style. He pronounces it 'vunnyews', finishing the word with a slight, but distinctly camp lisp. Even though he's ostensibly apologising for being the odd one out, the way he says the word gives a hint that he's mocking the pretensions of the place he's playing. He continues:

> And I, *no* – Well, I mean, a lot of people have said to me, you know, 'I'm surprised at you going to a place like *that*.' [*laughter*] And it is a – it is a bit different to a Granada tour with Billy Fury, hoh hoh! [*laughter*] But so I thought if I can explain – I thought if I can explain how I happened to be here, er, it might, er, take the blame off me a bit, you understand, it might disarm criticism a bit, you understand? [*a few laughs*] And you won't expect anything sort of too – sophisticated. Now, erm – [*a few laughs*]

Then, responding to the few punters who have laughed at his apology, he uses one of his classic techniques: he reprimands them for laughing, thus making them laugh more. He goes on to tell a fictionalised version of what happened when Peter Cook approached him at the *Evening Standard* Awards, dispensing a number of bitchy jibes along the way. He clearly separates himself from the fashionable satire which is the Establishment's bread and butter:

I find these days, unless you're sort of, you know, *bitter*, you're not considered artistic, you know. I've always found this, and I mean I'm not that kind of a comedian, I'm more the lovable kind, you know. [*laughter*] Sort of cuddlesome, you know. [*laughter*] *Don't take a vote on it!* [*laughter*]

Having set himself up as not wanting to criticise, he goes on to say some rather uncuddlesome things about the audience:

There's so much bitterness, in any case, I mean I've got nothing *against* this place. I said, the only – Well, I mean, *admittedly* – [*laughter*] admittedly, I think – you get some odd people here. I mean, not that I pry, as I say – I keep to – I keep meself to meself, I think it's best. [*laughter*] Don't you? Keep yerself to yerself, that's what I say, you don't get – I mean you don't get into any mischief, do you? [*laughter*] Unfortunately, [*laughter*] but I mean –[5]

Listening to the recording of the show more than forty years after it was made, it's still exciting to hear Howerd establishing and negotiating his relationship with the audience. Defining himself as an outsider allows him to be cheeky, catty and cutting, sometimes at the audience's expense, sometimes at his own. There's no real antagonism or hostility, and you can feel the affection of a younger generation rediscovering the talent of an older star fallen on hard times. The season at the Establishment was a great success, a turning point in Howerd's career. He was spotted by the Ned Sherrin, the producer of the famous television satire show *That Was the Week that Was* and his satirical spot on TW3 was successful enough to re-establish his reputation.

Inside and outside

While some comedians play the insider and others play the outsider, most play both. In his *Vote for Jim* show, Jim Davidson spends most of his time identifying with the community of the audience, by pushing populist, right-wing buttons, but not all of his imaginary policies go down well. When he asks why he should have to pay 40 per cent tax on most of his earnings, somebody shouts: 'Because you're a rich bastard!' He's unapologetic, explaining he deserves to be rich: 'I'm more talented than you.'

Suddenly, Davidson is separate from the audience, a high-status outsider. Although he isn't cheered for what he says, he doesn't lose the audience. The brazen confidence with which he states his case shows control and asserts his status as somebody to be admired rather than messed with.

For Jo Brand, the choice of defining herself as an insider or an outsider depends on the kind of audience she's playing to. She explains that as she has a family to support and refuses on principle to appear in adverts, she sometimes earns 'shedloads of money' by doing 'these weird corporate gigs with sort of loads of businessmen in them'. In such circumstances, which she describes as 'just fucking weird', her upfront feminism and her penchant for the outrageous clearly define her as being separate from the community of the audience. On other occasions, her audiences are 'very much politically in tune with me and roughly the same age and all that sort of thing'. Sometimes, though, she finds herself shifting between the insider and outsider roles: 'I mean, you might say to an audience, "Oh, isn't so-and-so a pain in the arse," and they'll all agree with you, and then kind of five minutes later you might find you've gone too far, and suddenly you're outside what's acceptable with them, so you then have to relate to them on that basis.'

Surreal comedians have a natural tendency for the

outsider role, portraying themselves as exotic aliens with a skewed outlook on the world. Milton Jones uses hair gel and unpleasant pullovers to achieve this effect. For Harry Hill, though, playing the outsider is what makes him close to his audience, which he describes as 'a room full of outcasts'. He believes his audience collude with him as he unleashes his torrents of silliness on them: 'I think . . . that the audience know that I'm in on it as well.'

Ross Noble, whose act is made up of high-energy cartoon images and surreal trains of thought lubricated by the fluidity of improvisation, sees himself as being both like and unlike his audience. Having started in stand-up at the age of fifteen, he is clearly unlike most of the people who come to see him: 'I'm different from the people in the audience purely because I've never had a job, I've never had a normal existence, and all I've ever done is stand-up . . . I don't live a particularly normal life because I'm always on the road.' On the other hand, the process of touring, with its days spent wandering around city centres, eating in Little Chefs and getting into conversations with people gives him enough experience of normality to identify with his audience. The combination of the surreal and the everyday has its origins in his upbringing in a new town in the north-east: 'I was in this kind of slightly mundane situation, which meant that my head lived in a slightly more sort of fanciful place.'

How far can you go?

Dividing the audience

Dividing up the audience is a basic stand-up skill. A compère may generate energy at the beginning of the show by splitting the audience into sections and getting them to compete for how loud they can shout, cheer or applaud. Comedians playing big theatres may play the stalls off against the balcony, perhaps poking fun at the snobbery of punters who have paid for expensive tickets in the front rows and the tightfistedness of the ones in the cheap seats.

James Campbell's shows have a clearly divided audience: the children his comedy is aimed at, and the parents who have brought them to the show. Campbell doesn't highlight this divide: 'I try and not have separate jokes for separate levels, I try and do stuff that's all funny for everybody. You can't always do that. I've got a few [jokes] that're in the show at the moment which the kids don't get, and there's two of 'em which I've kept in cos I like them. But I feel guilty that the laugh I get is a much deeper laugh than it normally is. Cos you can tell how much of the audience you're getting by the pitch of the laughter, basically. So if you get a deep laugh, you know that was one that the parents got that the kids didn't, and I kind of feel guilty, cos I don't like the idea of kids sitting there sort of looking up going, "What was that? I don't understand that." But I think the occasional one's OK.'

In such jokes, he carefully uses references to make them inaccessible to the children. He says of one gag: 'See, the kids don't get that. Because I've deliberately used the words "public liability insurance". But I don't want them to get that because it's not for them.'

In some cases, the division of the audience is more political. Jo Brand plays differently to the men and women in the audience, sharing experiences with the women, and making out that what she says will be going over the heads of the men. She imagines the husbands of the women in the audience telling their wives: 'This is your one treat this year, I'm coming with you but don't expect me to laugh.'[6]

Similarly, Richard Pryor would relate differently to black and white people in his audience. At the beginning of *Live in Concert*, this starts when he notices punters filing to their seats: 'This is the fun part for me, when the white people come back after the intermission and find out niggers stole their seats. [*laughter, cheering, whistles, and applause*]' He imagines the reaction of a very square, white punter ('Er, weren't we sitting here, er, dear, weren't we?'), and the response of a cool, defiant black one ('Well, you ain't sittin' there now, motherfugger!'). All of this is played out to riotous laughter and applause.

As Pryor gets into the act, it's clear that he identifies with the black punters whose experience he shares, not the white punters who have come along for the ride. He asks, 'You ever noticed how nice white people get when there's a bunch of niggers around?' which leads to an impression of a white man grinning idiotically and introducing himself to a bunch of black people: 'Hi, how ya doin'? [*laughter*] I don't know you, but here's my wife, *hello!!* [*laughter*]'[7]

It's beautifully acted, precisely capturing the ridiculous jollity and underlying anxiety of white people in this situation. Observational comedy may be about shared experience but, in this case, the thing that Pryor is observing is experienced differently by blacks and whites in the audience. For black people, the observation is about the ridiculous behaviour of another group. For white people, it is their own behaviour they are being invited to see as ridiculous. There's clearly a political edge to this, a chance for a black comedian and black punters to enjoy having the upper hand for once, but it's not actually hostile towards the whites in the audience.

Bill Hicks, on the other hand, would single out certain groups and lay into them without mercy. In one routine, he gets laughter and applause by announcing: 'By the way, if anyone here is in advertising or marketing – *kill yourself.*' He repeatedly rams the point home, saying: 'Seriously though – if you are, do. [*laughter*] Ahhhh – [*some clapping*] No, really. There's no rationalisation for what you do, and you are Satan's little helpers, OK? [*laughter*] Kill yourself, seriously.'

Of course, it may be that there are no advertisers or marketing types in the audience, but if there are, he makes sure they can't wriggle off the hook. He imagines them trying to find ways to join in with the laughter, perhaps by thinking he's going for 'that anti-marketing dollar' or 'the righteous indignation dollar'. To laughter, applause and cheering, he calls them 'fucking evil scumbags'.[8]

Overthrowing the government

All of this leads us into the walking-through-a-minefield question of the politics of stand-up comedy, and the effect it might have on the way an audience thinks. There's a long history of comedians who want their act to subvert the status quo. In a show recorded in 1960, Mort Sahl says, almost as an afterthought: 'I'm really not interested in politics as much as overthrowing the government. [*laughter*]'

More than forty years later, Mark Thomas is very clear in the ambitions he has for his work: 'You want to engage people, you want them to walk out having made them change their minds about something or seen something differently, or feel differently about something.'

Those who have theorised about comedy tend to argue that whatever the intention, comedy can never be truly subversive. The anthropologist Mary Douglas, for example, says that although 'All jokes have [a] subversive effect on the dominant structure of ideas', they are ultimately toothless because of the restrictions placed on them:

> Social requirements may judge a joke to be in bad taste, risky, too near the bone, improper or irrelevant. Such controls are exerted either on behalf of hierarchy as such, or on behalf of values which are judged too precious and too precarious to be exposed to challenge . . . [This means that] the joker is not exposed to danger . . . He merely expresses consensus. Safe within the permitted range of attack, he lightens for everyone the oppressiveness of social reality.[9]

It's certainly true that some stand-up comedians do express consensus and work within the boundaries of what is considered acceptable. When Bob Hope talked about politics in his act, he usually kept the gags mild and neutral, aiming them at both parties. He did this because, as he puts it, 'I'm usually selling a product everybody buys and I don't want to alienate any part of my audience'.[10] The problem with Douglas's argument is that, unlike Hope, many stand-ups work by pushing at the edges of consensus. A common technique in contemporary British comedy clubs is to follow an edgy gag which gets a big laugh with the comment: 'I think I've found your level.' Similarly, after an outraged laugh, the comic will often say: 'I think I've gone too far.'

Jo Brand scares men

Comics like Jo Brand base their entire output on a kind of joyful offensiveness. Her 2005 act is a festival of outrage. She delights in creating sexually explicit cartoon images. A vagina is described as 'the old velvet Tardis'. She suggests the *Sun* should produce a page 3 for women, featuring 'a bloke, with his pants on, with a little cheeky testicle poking out the side'. She talks about having a bra fitted by the company which supplies the Queen with underwear, and asking whether the monarch has 'pink nipples or brown ones'.

Brand subverts conventional ideas about femininity. In an anti-matter universe she would be the epitome of lady-like. Her behaviour, as described in the act, is hilariously bizarre and disgusting. She pisses in an estate agent's briefcase, breastfeeds her husband in a café, and eats her children's leftover meals out of the bin. She reverses the classic image of an ideal wife:

> I'd like to say I'm very happily married. Er, my husband's not, unfortunately, but fuck him, you know. [*laughter and applause*] And the thing I find difficult about marriage is that bit where all the nice sort of love and all that's worn off – and you're just left with some twat in your house, [*laughter*] d'yer – d'yer know what I mean?'

Announcing that she's become a parent, she imagines the audience's reaction: 'And I know you're looking at me, going, "I don't think you had sex with your husband for your children. We think, as a group, that you used a turkey baster."' There's a big laugh, mixed with audible groaning, suggesting not disapproval or hostility, but a reaction to the grotesque image. She pushes it further: '"Or perhaps you got a gay friend of yours to get very drunk and turn you against the wall." Well, no!' There's a big laugh, and some people clap. She picks up on this: 'People are clapping that, now that's an interesting reaction, isn't it? "We want you to have done that, and we want to hear more about it, please." [*laughter*]'[11]

She explains that she's always had a penchant for outrage: 'I've always been like that. I mean, again, it's that old cliché of saying, like, "Bum" during assembly when you're at primary school . . . I just always wanted (rather sadly I suppose) to kind of shock people, and I just very much enjoyed . . . the result when I did. Funnily enough, in some ways, I'm not really that sort of person in my personal social life. I am when I'm pissed (you know, well, I suppose we're all a bit like that when we're pissed), but there's always a bit of me that's wanted to be like that, you know. So I suppose it's that bit of me that does the stand-up, really . . . If I actually thought seriously about some of the things I said onstage, I probably wouldn't do it, so I just don't think about it.'

There's a sense in which Brand is licensed to shock. When she picks up on the audience clapping at the joke about being taken from behind by a gay friend, she is bringing into the open the idea that the audience expects her to say outrageous things. It could be argued that this blunts the subversive edge of her full-frontal assault on notions of femininity, that the role of comedian gives her a special licence, but also safely contains her outrageousness, stopping it from spilling out into the wider world.

This argument falls apart in the face of the evidence. Brand may enjoy a special licence but this doesn't defuse the challenge she poses to sexism. Men fear her. She has been persistently and scathingly criticised by Bernard Manning and right-wing tabloid journalist Garry Bushell.

152

She also gets strange reactions from men she meets: 'I'm always surprised when people kind of go, "Oh, you know, I'd better not talk to you cos I'm a bloke, and you know, you might do something." But like what? Punch them? . . . Ridiculous.' At a performance in May 2004, she gets a huge laugh just by saying 'Oh, hello' to a couple filing in late to seats near the front. The audience laugh because they expect her to make fun of them, but, in fact, she leaves them alone and quickly moves on.

She says: 'People will say to me, "Oh, I'm not heckling you," do you know what I mean, as if I can somehow, like, completely destroy them by what I say, which again is, like, utterly ridiculous really.' All of this suggests that what she does in her act makes people see her as having dangerous, almost magical powers. As she puts it: 'The feminist female comedian is a sort of, you know, a witch in some ways.' She believes that this kind of reaction is based on a fundamental misreading of her work, because it is sexism, not men, that she is attacking: 'It's got nothing to do with hating individual men, it's got to do with kind of social roles, you know.'

Sick jokes

At the Carling Hammersmith Apollo, Billy Connolly starts talking about Ken Bigley, the sixty-two-year-old British engineer kidnapped by a terrorist group in Iraq. Just broaching the subject causes a hush to fall over the auditorium. This is a big news story, and a horrible one. The terrorists are threatening to behead Bigley if their demands are not met. Connolly skilfully identifies the unease he's provoked, imagining the audience thinking, 'Oh, God, what's he going to say?'

This punctures the tension for a moment, but he pumps it up again by continuing to talk very seriously about the issue. He mentions that, earlier in the evening, he's seen on the news that the terrorists have released more video footage of Bigley. This makes the story even more current, even more risky. Having built the tension, he walks to the very front of the stage and asks, in a hushed voice, whether we, like him, listen to the news hoping that Bigley has been beheaded. The theatre is filled with the sound of the audience going, 'Ooooo!', in a wave of disapproval that rushes towards the stage, but before it can crash over him, Connolly defiantly shouts, 'Fuck off!', transforming it into a big laugh.

Regardless of the morality of joking about such a thing, it's a beautifully performed piece of taboo-surfing. Connolly manipulates the audience with extraordinary control. Like all sick jokes, his comment derives its power from the fact that it's about a subject deemed inappropriate for joking. It subverts the 'normal' emotional reaction to the Bigley case, replacing horror and sadness with laughter. It's a pure sick joke, in that it has no real motivation other than to play with the tension surrounding a current news story. Connolly is not really telling the joke at Bigley's expense, he's honestly revealing a prurient part of himself that secretly yearns for horror in a news story with which he has no direct connection. It is truly shocking to feel that he might be right in suggesting that many of us share his secret prurience.

Initially, it seems as if Connolly can make this work because, like Brand, he enjoys a licence to say outrageous things in his act. On 3 October, a few days after I see the show, the *Mail on Sunday* publishes a five-star review which says: 'When he provocatively mentions hostage Ken Bigley, he crosses the threshold of respectability, knowing full well he'll get away with it by comedic daring, by force of personality, by reputation.' But a couple of days later, the tide has turned. A number of newspapers report that Connolly has been booed and heckled. A headline in the *Express* screams, 'Audience Jeers Connolly's Sick Joke about Iraq Hostage; That's Just not Funny, Billy'. Bigley's brother, understandably upset, is quoted as saying: 'I don't like his humour anyway.' The Muslim Council of Britain, which has tried to negotiate Bigley's release, says: 'This is the time when everyone needs to be showing solidarity with Ken Bigley's family, to work for his release. The jokes can wait.' A few days after that, the fury provoked by Connolly's joke is swept away by the genuinely disturbing news of Bigley's death.

The idea that humour is controlled by social requirements and consensus is thus shown to be simplistic; social requirements and consensus can shift even in the course of a few days. When comedians push against the boundaries, they use their licence to redefine what is acceptable.

In some cases, sick jokes can go beyond simple outrageousness and say something profound. Bill Hicks provides a classic example of this, in a routine which starts with him talking about how much he enjoyed the special effects in the film *Terminator 2*. He says he thinks they will never be able to better those effects, then uses a single word to qualify his argument: 'Unless . . .'

There's a small laugh, anticipating that something good is coming. He continues: 'They start using terminally ill people –' While the audience laugh, he looks at them quizzically, as if puzzled that they are not taking him seriously. 'Hear me out,' he says, getting another laugh, before finishing his idea: '– as stuntmen in the movies.' There's a few seconds of laughter at this, during which he looks at the audience again, biting his bottom lip, as if eager to see whether they approve of the idea. 'OK, not the most popular idea ever,' he concedes, getting another full laugh. So far, so good. Like Connolly, the way he plays with the audience's reactions to the horrific idea he's suggesting is masterful.

Then he takes the routine to another level. He says the audience probably think it's a cruel idea, then answers back: 'You know what I think cruel is? Leaving your loved ones to die in some sterile hospital room, surrounded by strangers. Fuck that! Put 'em in the movies.' There's a big laugh, and applause. Now he sounds exasperated with them: '*What?* You want your grandmother dying like a little bird in some

155

hospital room, her translucent skin so thin you can see her last heartbeat work its way down her blue vein? Or you want her to meet Chuck Norris?' There's another big laugh and more applause.[12]

Talking about how dying people are treated is far more than a thin justification for a sick routine. The description of the grandmother has a kind of dark poetry which is rare in stand-up. He holds the moment, a pained look on his face. It's a daring performance. He's facing his audience with a true horror, and making an important point about the way our culture treats the elderly. At the heart of a truly grotesque sick routine there's real tenderness and passion.

Andre Vincent tells the audience he's got cancer

There's a long history of comedians who have expanded the possibilities of the stand-up by tackling supposedly unsuitable subjects. Some have broken taboos of obscenity. Frank Skinner, for example, has joked so enthusiastically about heterosexual sodomy that he has been dubbed 'the Billy Graham of anal sex'.[13]

Others have joked about subjects which might seem too esoteric or dull for comedy. In 1990, Tony Allen's act included routines on the financial markets, Heisenberg's Uncertainty Principle and the horticultural habits of rainforest tribes.[14] Dave Gorman had an extensive routine about pure maths, which was inspired by reading *Fermat's Last Theorum*: 'I found myself being fascinated. And I just thought, "I wonder if I can convey this to people." Cos I'm fascinated and I really like this, and I know you're not supposed to, cos it's maths, but if I can convey that, then I think people will find just that funny.'

Then there are the comedians who deal with subjects which might be considered too tragic or uncomfortable for joking, particularly their own physical afflictions. Adam Hills talks about having a metal foot. Paul Merton did a show about his spell in a mental hospital. On his final tour, Richard Pryor joked about the multiple sclerosis that was forcing him to retire. The acclaimed 2002 Edinburgh Fringe show, *Andre Vincent is Unwell*, dealt with the fact that the comedian had been diagnosed with cancer. Vincent decided to tackle the subject precisely because it was unsuitable: '[P]eople were saying, "You can't talk about it," [and] that really became the moment for me where it was like, "I won't be told that. I won't be told that, because it's me. It's me, and I'm a comedian. And I talk about what I know and what I see. And at the moment I've got cancer, so I've gotta talk about it."'

He started talking about it immediately: 'And on the very day that I was told I had cancer, I was doing Southampton Jongleurs, and just before bringing on the second act, somebody heckled me, and I went, "Don't heckle me, I've got cancer!" And it got sort of like a laugh and an "Oo!" And [to] the people that went, "Oo," I went, "What are you oo-ing about?" And one of them said, "You shouldn't say that, that's not nice." I said, "Yeah, but I have." And there was a real lull in the audience. I went, "No, I just found out today, I got cancer of the kidney." And there was no material at that point, there was nowhere for it to go. And bless him, to this day, George Egg, who I brought on next, still never lets me forget about the fact that I brought him on to an audience who were just going, "That poor bloke's got cancer!"'

He went on to find ways of dealing with the subject more successfully. The Edinburgh show includes gags about the absurd things that have happened to him in the course of dealing with the disease, such as the question he was asked about his urine: '"Does it smell or taste different?" I'm like, "*What??* [*laughter*] *Taste??*" [*laughter*]'[15] He also commentates over film footage of his operation.

The show was a big critical success, but, perhaps understandably, it still provoked unease among audiences: 'But even though . . . it was doing so well, it still made people kind of go, "Oo, I'm not sure this is right."' On the Friday, of the first weekend, *The Times* gave me a five-star review, it was the first five-star review that they'd given out. I was on the front page, and there was a full-page interview. It was just brilliant. Couldn't get better coverage. I still only had eighteen people in that night.' This kind of unease only made him more determined to continue talking about cancer in his act: ' "I wanna talk about it now. I *wanna* talk about it. Fuck 'em! I'm not gonna go with the norm. I will talk about it". And I started playing more and more with it. And now I just don't give a fuck about it.'

Keeping comedians under control

Other comedians take a similar attitude to discussing politics. When Mort Sahl told his joke about the McCarthy jacket with the extra flap over the mouth, he divided the audience. According to the hungry i's owner, Enrico Banducci, some people laughed, some stayed silent and some booed. Looking back on those times, Sahl says: 'I had a basically rebellious nature, you know, I always act like, "Well, I'm not gonna fold," but I hit the nerve when I began to talk about the things that really bothered me. You have to conquer your timidity and talk about what people really hate – like, ha ha ha, the government and the police.'[16]

Even while comedians are pushing at the boundaries of acceptability, censors, regulators and private individuals are trying to stop them. The fearless Sahl ran into trouble after the election of John F. Kennedy. He had campaigned for Kennedy but, believing that the role of the satirist was to tell jokes about the government, he continued to do just that, aiming his jokes at the new regime. JFK's father, Joseph, was so incensed by Sahl that he threatened his career, putting pressure on Enrico Banducci not to book the comedian at the hungry i.[17] Ironically, after JFK was assassinated, Sahl moved back to supporting the Kennedy camp, pitching his weight behind the investigation into the supposed conspiracy. He believes he was blackballed for talking so much about the Kennedy assassination in his act.

Comedians working on radio and television face more

organised efforts to restrict them; they are hemmed in by censorship and broadcasting regulations. During the 1980s, before writing musicals with Andrew Lloyd Webber and compèring the Royal Variety Show brought him mainstream respectability, Ben Elton's TV appearances felt edgy. In among observational routines and heavyweight scatology, there were scathing attacks on the Thatcher government and the consumerist culture it promoted so aggressively. Performing such material in a live show had its hazards, as he recalls: 'I used to have to do my act to a lawyer . . . each Saturday, which was a horrible experience because the lawyer never laughed.'

Albums and videos provide fewer problems, and on his classic 1972 album *Class Clown*, George Carlin performs possibly his most famous routine, 'Seven Words You Can Never Say on Television'. Here, he specifically addresses the restrictions posed by television, talking about the importance of words, and then listing the seven unsayable ones in a glorious, obscene, rhythmic stream: 'You know there's seven, don'tcha, that you can't say on television? "Shit", "piss", "fuck", "cunt", "cocksucker", "motherfucker" and "tits", hunh?' There's a laugh and then rapturous applause, lasting for ten seconds. The sense of release is palpable.

There are still some restrictions that apply to albums and videos, though. In the late 1990s, Robert Newman had a significant career change. His comedy superstar phase had culminated in the Wembley Arena gig with his then partner David Baddiel. A few years later, Newman re-emerged playing comparatively low-key shows with a radical political edge. In 2001, he put out a video called *Resistance is Fertile*, in which he does comedy routines about neo-liberalism and globalisation, intercut with real footage of anti-capitalist carnivals, the Seattle protests and the Zapatistas. At one point, he suggests his own 'ethical foreign policy': 'What we do is we ban imports of Nike, Disney, Reebok, Tommy Hilfiger and the Gap until they stop sweated labour.'

Then he starts having fun with the legal restrictions he's working within: 'Cos it's a video, I can't say "children" and "slaves", but they do. I could say "until they stop using children as slaves – although they don't". [*laughter*] 'And then – but then if I went –' Now he wiggles his fingers as if to indicate secretly that he's being forced to lie, getting a laugh. He continues: '– that would be libellous, and I'd have to go into court, and say, "Repeat the gesture." ' He wiggles his fingers again and gets another laugh. Then he makes the judge say: 'No, as you did it before.' This time, he wiggles his fingers, with a sheepish look on his face. Another laugh. He continues with the theme, speaking rather haltingly to show he's taking great care with his words, then says: 'Can you feel it, this is corporate power, you can feel it in the room. [*laughter*]'

Bill Hicks and Lenny Bruce have their careers damaged

Some comedians stretch the boundaries so far that their careers are damaged. In the comedy boom of the 1980s, Bill Hicks's agent Sandy DiPerna found it hard to get him bookings. More clubs meant more competition, and many venues would hand out free tickets for shows early in the week to ensure an audience. A non-paying audience is harder by definition, as people who have got in for free have no investment in listening carefully and joining in. In this context, a comic like Hicks, with an intellectual edge and a compulsion to jab at taboos, must have looked like trouble to club owners.

It was TV, though, that posed real problems. On his third appearance on David Letterman's *Late Night* show in February 1986, Hicks had the end of a joke about a televangelist and a reference to a wheelchair edited from the broadcast, rendering both gags incomprehensible to the viewers at home. Worse was to come. In 1993, Hicks's final Letterman appearance was cut in its entirety from the broadcast. Hicks's set, which included routines about homosexuality, pro-lifers and an imaginary game show in which celebrities are hunted and killed, had gone down well with the studio audience. After the show, its producer, Robert Morton, phoned to tell him that CBS's Standards and Practices department had forced them to cut the act from the show. Hicks was angry and upset, particularly when Morton refused to send him a tape of the act. In a bizarre twist, it turned out that the decision to cut the act had not been made by CBS, but by the show's producers, who had been nervous about how Hicks's jokes would have gone down with the viewing public in middle America.[18]

Lenny Bruce's career was harmed in a more devastating way. Bruce's willingness to cross the boundaries of acceptability was extraordinary, particularly in the late 1950s and early 1960s when he was at the peak of his career. Talking about sex, religion and racism was commonplace for him. He used obscenity very effectively. In one routine, he announces: 'If you've er – ever seen this bit before, I want you to tell me, stop me if you've seen it. I'm going to piss on you.' It takes him ten seconds to say this, but the outraged laugh he gets goes on for twice that long.[19]

He also spoke candidly about illegal drugs. In a 1960 routine, he imagines the dialogue for a radio advert that will never be made. It starts with a grumpy voice: 'I don't know what the hell it is, Bill, I've been smoking the pot all day and I still can't get high on it!' There's a laugh in which you can pick out a female punter shrieking with delight. He then puts on a calm, reasonable voice to reply: 'What kind are you smoking?' Surprised, the grumpy-voiced character replies: 'Well, all marijuana's the same, isn't it?' The calm voice comes in more assertively with the punchline: 'That's the mistake a lot of people make!' There's a big laugh and applause.[20]

Bruce massively expanded the possibilities of stand-up, but his boundary-exploding approach brought him trouble. In 1961, he was arrested for possession of drugs, although he had a prescription for the offending substance. The real reason for the bust was that he had refused to bribe a corrupt official. Five days later, he was arrested after a performance at the Jazz Workshop in San Francisco, after using the word 'cocksucker'. It occurs in a routine about Bruce being asked to play in a club which has changed its policy. He asks the owner, 'Well, what kind of a show is it, man?' After hedging, the owner replies that 'they're a bunch of cocksuckers' and it's 'a damn fag show'. Bruce is apparently nonplussed by this: 'Oh – well, that is a pretty bizarre show, er – [*laughter*] er – I don't know what I could do in that kind of a show. [*laughter*]'[21]

Bruce was tried for obscenity and after an extensive court case, the jury took nearly five and a half hours to decide he was not guilty. He went on to talk about the case in his act, using 'blah blah blah' in place of 'cocksucker'. It's a very funny routine. He says it's bizarre that 'blah blah blah' was interpreted as a homosexual word, because it relates to 'any contemporary chick I know or would know or would love or would marry'. Later, he acts out the court case with the judge, the lawyers and court officials repeatedly saying 'blah blah blah' in shocked tones. He finally makes a realisation: 'Then I dug something. They sorta like saying "blah blah blah". [*laughter*]'[22]

Sadly, there was more trouble to come, and Bruce could not joke his way out of it. On Tuesday, 4 December 1962, he did a show at the Gate of Horn in Chicago.[23] The recording of the performance shows that he wasn't on his best form. Some of the routines are saggy and he sometimes sounds confused. However, there's an amazing bit in the middle of the show where he takes on the character of Adolf Eichmann, describing the workings of a concentration camp with chilling coldness. At the end of this, he has Eichmann say, 'Do you people think yourselves better, because you burn your enemies at long distances with missiles?' Snapping out of the character, he argues that if the Allies had lost the war, President Truman would have been strung up 'by the balls', with mutants left behind after Hiroshima paraded as evidence of his crimes. The audience is deathly silent throughout the routine. Bruce is clearly pushing the boundaries as far as he can, and during the show he draws attention to punters walking out, presumably in disgust.

The end of the performance is extraordinary. The police arrive mid-routine: 'OK! It's the first time they made a bust right in an audience!' As the officers approach the stage to arrest him, he tries to keep joking, pretending he's going to make a daring escape: 'It's Superjew!' The cops make the arrest. They literally stop the show.

The use of the word 'balls' in the devastating Eichmann routine was one of the reasons given for the bust. Bruce was found guilty of obscenity and received the maximum penalty of a $1,000 fine and a year in prison. He never actually had to serve the sentence, but got caught up in a series of legal difficulties from which he could not escape. He was arrested fifteen times in less than two years.

In addition to this, most clubs would not risk booking him. As a result of his arrest, the Gate of Horn had its liquor licence suspended. Clearly, few promoters would want the scandal or economic damage which a Bruce show could bring down on them. His earnings plummeted to a tenth of what they had been. A second engagement at the Establishment in London was cancelled when he was refused entry to the UK on the technicality of failure to obtain a work permit. The Home Office issued a statement saying that 'it would not be in the public interest for him to be allowed in the United Kingdom'. To make matters worse, the few performances Bruce could give were marred by his obsessive ranting about his legal problems. He died of a morphine overdose in 1966, eighteen months before his guilty verdict was overturned. As a final insult, police allowed photographers to take pictures of his corpse.

Clearly, some comedians pay a heavy price for going beyond what Mary Douglas called 'the permitted range of attack', but this does not prove her argument. The fact is that before the authorities clamped down on him, Lenny Bruce had become very successful precisely by ignoring the social requirements which restrict comedy's subversiveness, and going far beyond merely expressing consensus. He also inspired future generations of comedians to do the same.

Uncovering

One of the subversive things stand-up comedy can do is uncovering the unmentionable. Comedians can joke about subjects which are difficult or impossible to discuss in every-day conversation or the broadcast media. Observational comedy is a form of uncovering. As well as being about shared experience, it derives its power from the fact that the comedian has noticed something which the audience pre-viously haven't. Stand-up allows a special kind of frankness. It's not unusual for male comedians to discuss their mastur-bation habits. For some reason, making such confessions to an audience of strangers is acceptable, whereas revealing them to a single stranger would be excruciating.

This kind of comedy can be extremely powerful when it uncovers an important taboo. Chris Rock's 1996 HBO Special *Bring the Pain* includes a routine called 'Niggas vs. Black People', which had an extraordinary impact. In the routine, he tells a black, working-class audience in Washington DC about a 'civil war' between different types of black people, the criminal, anti-social 'niggas' and the honest, hardworking 'black people'. He stalks up and down the stage, smiling broadly, his eyes gleaming with what might be fury or amusement. His voice is loud, abrasive, high-pitched. He punches his consonants percussively.

Rock talks about how niggas ruin things for black people, in a series of razor-sharp barbs which are greeted with laughter, applause and cheering. He says that niggas always 'want some credit for some shit they supposed to do', like taking care of their kids. He imagines a nigga saying, 'I ain't never been to jail,' to which he replies, 'What do you want, a *cookie*?' He talks about the way niggas hate education, coming out with the memorable lines 'Niggas love to keep it real – real *dumb*' and 'Books are like Kryptonite to a nigga'. He also aims some of the jokes at himself, admitting that he failed a black history class at community college: 'That's sad. Cos you know fat people don't fail cooking.' The routine ends with the observation that Martin Luther King, who was against violence, is now remembered as a street name: 'And I don't give a fuck where you live in America, if you on Martin Luther King Boulevard, there's some violence going down.'

Context is crucial here. Performed by a white comedian, this would be grotesquely racist. As it is, Rock delights his audience by acknowledging problems which they recognise but might find difficult to discuss openly. Although the live audience at the show's recording at the Takoma Theatre were predominantly black, when this was shown on TV, it was seen by a wider, racially mixed audience.

The central thesis of *On the Real Side*, Mel Watkins's impressively detailed history of African-American comedy, is that black people have always tended to joke differently behind closed doors than when in the company of whites. Watkins argues that comics like Richard Pryor and Chris Rock are remarkable because they take that private humour and present it publicly. Fellow black comic Dave Chapelle has said of this routine: 'It's the kind of thing that black people say in their living room to one another all the time. All over America. But that's the kind of thing that you never would say in front of a white person.'

Others have been more critical. Russell Simmons, the producer of the early 1990s black stand-up showcase *Def Comedy Jam*, argues that the routine confirms the prejudices of conservative whites. Rock is unafraid of the disapproval his daring comedy attracts: 'If I don't get somebody going "boo", I'm not doing my job.' *Bring the Pain*, and especially 'Niggas vs. Black People', made Rock a comedy superstar, but the routine got so much attention that he has found it difficult to escape its shadow, complaining that it makes him look like 'a one-joke wonder'.

If the impact of a single routine shows how powerful uncovering can be, Shazia Mirza makes the point even more strongly, causing an enormous stir with a single one-liner. Mirza began her career wearing traditional Muslim dress onstage. On 11 September 2001, less than a year after she had started out, the World Trade Center and the Pentagon were attacked. Initially, she was worried her career was over because of the fear and suspicion which Muslims now faced. She cancelled all her gigs for a week, and when she started performing again, she found people afraid to laugh.

Two weeks later, she hit upon a way to uncover the paranoia that was in the air. She went onstage and started her act by announcing: 'My name is Shazia Mirza – at least that's what it says on my pilot's licence.' The audience got to their feet and applauded, but the reaction could not be contained by the walls of a comedy club. It was a joke that rang out around the world. A LexisNexis search using the terms 'Shazia Mirza' and 'pilot's licence' carried out on 28 October 2004 reveals seventy-eight articles which mention the joke, from a list of countries including the UK, Ireland, the USA, Canada, Australia and India, in publications as diverse as the *Yorkshire Post*, the *Times Educational Supplement*, the *Boston Globe*, the *San Francisco Chronicle* and the *St John's Telegram*, Newfoundland. A review in the *Independent* even found it worth mentioning that she had *not* performed the gag in her 2003 Edinburgh Fringe show.

Preaching to the converted

The oldest and most damning accusation that can be levelled at any politically radical artist, comedians as much as anyone else, is that he or she is just preaching to the converted. Accusers say that only people who share the comic's beliefs will be attracted to the shows, so however radical the material might seem, in Mary Douglas's terms, it 'merely expresses consensus'.

At first glance, Jeremy Hardy's act at an Amnesty International benefit at Wembley Arena in 2001 seems like a classic case of preaching to the converted. Hardy, a veteran of the politically radical 1980s alternative comedy scene, specialises in finely crafted satirical barbs, often inspired by events in the news and always underpinned by his strong socialist convictions. He showers the Wembley audience with typically acidic jokes. The police, he says, 'are not normal people. Who d'you know who rides a horse round a shopping centre?' He announces that Prince William is studying History of Art, adding: 'Which is one of those courses they make up for people whose parents were cousins, isn't it? [*laughter and applause*]' The chances are that an audience attracted to an Amnesty benefit are largely drawn from the liberal left, and the laughter and applause that greet these gags suggest that they share some of Hardy's assumptions: that the police are incompetent establishment goons, that the royal family are absurd inbred idiots.

What's interesting about the performance, though, is that while the material might make it look as if Hardy is very much the insider, at one with the community of the audience, he does his best to suggest otherwise. As soon as he comes on, he differentiates himself from the audience and the other comedians. Leaving the microphone in its stand, he says: 'I'm going to stand cos I can't be hopping around like the young ones. I am, I'm middle-aged, I'm having a crisis, I'll admit it, all the old verities are gone.' His manner is cynical and disgruntled. Even though he is not actually significantly older than many of the other comics on the same bill, he makes himself out to be old enough to be puzzled and bemused by the values of the modern world.

So, is Hardy merely expressing the consensus of a liberal audience, or is he, as he suggests, out of step with them? There probably isn't a simple answer to this question. Members of this audience of several thousand might have been attracted to the show for a number of different reasons, including the chance to see a huge comedy event, and perhaps catch a glimpse of Eddie Izzard in the flesh. Although Hardy may be expressing the consensus of the more liberal members of the audience, he might also be challenging the values of other comedy fans who have a certain amount of respect for the police or the royal family.

In any case, the idea that preaching to the converted automatically makes the subversive effect of the comedy null and void is rather simplistic. In his 1972 album *Class Clown*, George Carlin points out 'the sexual side' to the Vietnam War: 'But they're always afraid of pulling out, that's their big problem, you know? [*laughter and some applause*]' A couple of lines later, he uses the same analogy to make an even harder political point: 'Because that is, after all, what we're doing to that country, right?' This time, there's only a smallish laugh, but it quickly turns into a huge surge of applause, cheering and whistling.

As Carlin had recently embraced the counterculture and reinvented himself as a hippie, the chances are that the audience who came to this show would have shared his anti-war sympathies. But I would argue that to allow an audience publicly to express their anger about the war, and to send them home energised and bolstered in their beliefs at a time when America was so bitterly divided over the issue, is distinctly subversive.

Shifting consensus

In some cases, though, comedy can actually change people's minds. When comedians work outside the audience consensus, they can actually help to shift that consensus. In America, black comedians used to be prevented from talking directly to an audience, either by precedent or direct instruction. Dick Gregory points out that when he first moved out of the Chitlin Circuit in the early 1960s, the very act of a black comedian addressing a white audience was extraordinary: 'Black comics was never permitted to work white nightclubs. The racism that existed in America would not permit a black person to stand flat-footed and talk. You could come out as a Sammy Davis and dance, but you could not come out as a human being and talk.'[24]

Even if some of the whites in his audience had enlightened views about race, it stretches belief that all of them did. His first white audience at the Playboy Club in Chicago in 1960 included a large contingent of Southern businessmen and, when this was discovered, the club's management were so worried that they sent a message to Gregory telling him he didn't have to go on. However, Gregory had strategies to win over potentially hostile white punters. He realised that he could make them secure by using jokes about himself to puncture the tension they might feel at being addressed in this way by a black man. He also looked at white humour and seeded his act with what he saw as white jokes. Having won them over, he could then present them with a black perspective.

An early routine describes how Gregory has recently moved into an all-white neighbourhood in Chicago. A new neighbour meets him for the first time when he's shovelling snow on his front path. Mistaking him for a servant, the neighbour asks him, 'Whaddya you get for doin' that?' Gregory replies, 'Oh, I get to sleep with that woman inside.' There's a huge, outraged laugh and some applause. Then Gregory asks the neighbour's husband, 'Hey, baby, you want me to do yours next?' The husband declines with a frightened 'No'. There's another big laugh.[25]

The routine shows a black man outwitting two whites by using their own prejudiced expectations against them, and also hints at interracial sex. For it to get such a positive reaction from a white audience in 1962 shows how skilful Gregory was. It suggests that he was able to shift the consensus of the audience.

Bill Hicks also had methods of winning audiences over so that they would be more likely to accept his perspective. He had lines which he could pull out if he was in danger of losing the audience by going too far. After a particularly obscene gag, he would say, 'My mother wrote that one' or 'I am available for children's parties.' On the other hand, if he felt his audience was getting bored with his political rhetoric, he would say, 'Let me assure you right now – there are dick jokes on the way.'

In some cases, there is actual evidence to suggest that audiences' minds have been changed, that the consensus has shifted. When Omid Djalili plays the *Just for Laughs* festival in Montreal in 2002, he does two shows with a very famous American comedian, at a time when the attacks on the World Trade Center and the Pentagon are still fresh in people's minds. At a show to an audience of about five hundred in a venue called Club Soda, the American makes a series of racist jokes, asking if there are any Arabs in the audience and pretending to take photos of them, saying that the 'towelheads' should have to remove their turbans on aeroplanes. He gets big laughs. When Djalili follows him, he also gets laughs, but the fact that he's Middle Eastern clearly makes the audience uneasy.

The following night, they perform to an audience of 2,500 in the main gala, but this time Djalili goes on first, and it's the American who suffers. Djalili recalls: '[Y]ou could see the panic in his eyes when he came out with this stuff which had been killing for the last two or three months: "Why are they not laughing now?" He didn't even realise there was a Middle Eastern act on . . . in the first half. And I took that as a very big personal triumph, you know . . . Of course, people are gonna do what they wanna do in reaction to events, but there is some kind of comedy which is not really coming from a more humanitarian space, that, you know, will be exposed if you present them with something else. And I showed them a more human face. This is not even a year after 9/11, and still things are a bit raw. It was the first Montreal comedy festival where they were dealing with it. I took that as a huge personal triumph when they clicked into me, and already it meant their minds had changed. Already, the audience had a shift

about Middle Eastern people in general, you know. And
. . . that's why they didn't accept what he said, half an
hour after I'd been onstage. Whereas the night before, half
an hour *before* I'd gone onstage, they were absolutely
loving it.'

6. *The Present Tense*

Show That You're Showing

Jasper Carrott's television set

It's February 1979, and I'm thirteen years old. I'm watching a stand-up show on ITV, by a Brummie comic called Jasper Carrott. It's actually being broadcast live as he performs it. Soon after coming on to the stage at the Theatre Royal, Drury Lane, he capitalises on this, saying: 'People said, "No, it's not *really* live, is it?" and it *is* live, it is live, cos look, look –' He turns on a large television set placed on a stool, which shows the programmes being broadcast on the three channels that exist at the time. When he turns it on, the audience in the theatre take a couple of seconds to take in what the TV is showing, and then there's a really big laugh and some applause. Carrott laughs along, sharing their enjoyment of the gag. Then he changes the channel, announcing: 'That's er, that's BBC1.' There's another big laugh and more applause. This time, the laughter keeps going, coming back in pulses at the audacity of his daring to show what's on the other main channel. Carrott hoots along with them, before commentating on what they're watching: 'It's a, it's a really boring film. [*laughter*] It's got Lauren Bacall in it, and er, actually, she, she isn't a housewife, she's in fact a Russian spy, and she's the murderer. [*laughter*] So if you're thinkin' of switchin' over, forget it, right? [*laughter*]'

Seeing this on TV is a moment that has lived vividly in my memory ever since. What was it that so delighted me? And why have I written about it in the present tense when I actually saw it over twenty-five years ago?

I think that a lot of the appeal was his sense of mischief. In the late 1970s, as the only channels, there was huge rivalry between ITV and the BBC. In this context, the idea of showing what BBC1 was broadcasting while performing on ITV feels naughty. More than this, the fact that it is being broadcast live creates a feeling of freedom that borders on the dangerous. Carrott plays on this in the show: 'The thing is, see, it's live, I can do whatever I wanna do, I can say *anythink*. [*laughter*]'[1]

I find myself having to write about moments like these in the present tense because the present tense is when stand-up comedy happens. The gag with the television works because it knows this simple fact and exploits it. Carrott is playing to two audiences, and by using a TV set to prove he's broadcasting live, he manages to create a sense of immediacy for the audience watching at home as well as the punters in the theatre.

Here and now

As Tony Allen puts it, 'The "Now" agenda defines stand-up comedy.'[2] Straight drama shows events from another place and another time, but with stand-up the events happen right there in the venue. It's normal for stand-up comics to incorporate the here and now into the material of the show. Lenny Bruce starts his Carnegie Hall concert by talking about the prestigious venue in which he's performing. He fantasises about coming on with a violin and playing Stravinsky for an hour, then splitting without saying a word. He imagines that this is a secret gig, that the venue's managers don't know about it, that he's set it up with the help of a corrupt janitor ('All right, but don't make no noise, and clean up after you finish, all right?').

A Ross Noble show in Dartford, Kent, in June 2004

coincides with an important England match in the European Cup. Noble plays on this, saying that all the theatre staff are watching the match on a portable TV backstage. He asks if anyone in the audience is videoing the match, hoping not to find out who's won before they watch the tape. A number of voices shout, 'Yeah.' After the interval, he plays with these punters, announcing a fictitious half-time score, before admitting he's only kidding.

The stand-up comedian has an unwritten contract to address the here and now. If something unexpected happens during the show, whether it's a heckle, a dropped glass, or the ringing of a mobile phone, the comic must react to it. As Milton Jones puts it: 'You learn early on, don't you, that if you don't react to something that happens in the crowd, the audience lose faith in you.'

The present tense is built into the language of stand-up. When a comedian tells the story of something that's happened in the past, it's still related in the present. Even self-contained shows, like Mark Thomas's *Dambusters* or *Dave Gorman's Googlewhack Adventure*, which are entirely based on telling the story of a particular set of events that happened in the past are still told in the present tense. Gorman says: '[E]ven though I'm telling you something which has happened and everyone knows . . . this is six months ago . . . the grammar I use is kind of, "So, I'm on the train, and –" and I try to make it feel present tense. I try not to tell it with hindsight, so that it feels immediate.'

Recorded live

The fact that stand-up comedy has had such a long history of existing in recorded form doesn't alter the fact that it's about immediacy, and has a strong connection to the here and now. It seems absurd to think that you could capture its electric liveness on a shiny disc, put it in a plastic box and sell it at motorway service stations, but, unlike live theatre, stand-up has shown itself highly capable of being recorded and marketed.

When we listen to recordings made decades ago, something about the way the comedian connects with the audience we hear laughing preserves a sense of immediacy. As long ago as the 1930s, an American survey found that 61 per cent of listeners felt that radio comedy was improved by hearing the laughter of a studio audience.[3] People who bought comedy albums in the 1950s and 60s were encouraged to imagine that listening to them was as good as being there for the live show. The sleeve notes to Shelley Berman's first record say: 'This album is a recording of Shelley Berman actually doing one of his nightclub acts. It's a new idea in records . . . Take "Inside Shelley Berman" home, put the record on your gramaphone [sic.], turn the lights down low and there you are – a do-it-yourself night club, with guaranteed laughs.'

Bertolt Brecht, stand-up comedian

The immediacy of stand-up is reinforced by the fact that comics often draw attention to their own performance processes, making the audience aware of exactly what they're doing. As Bertolt Brecht might have said, they show that they are showing.[4] Phyllis Diller, a dispenser of short, self-contained jokes strung together in loose narratives, sets up a joke by complaining that the venue is filthy and advising the audience 'Don't ever eat here': 'I ordered a steak rare, are you ready? [laughter] With a little care, this thing coulda recovered! [laughter]'

The key phrase here is 'are you ready?' By asking the audience if they're ready for the punchline, she's drawing attention to the strict set-up/punchline formula which she uses so heavily. She's making them aware that she's just telling a fictional gag, showing them exactly what she does, like a magician giving away how the trick is done.

At the end of the first half of a show in Brighton, Dylan Moran points out that comedians are supposed to end on a big laugh, but brazenly admits, 'I can't be bothered.' At the end of the second half of the show, he talks about how ritualised encores are, suggesting that the audience should just applaud the show without him having to go to the trouble of going off and coming back on again. They duly oblige. He has pointed out and subverted the conventions of how stand-up shows are framed, in a way which befits his charmingly shambolic persona.

Even mistakes can be pointed out and played with. Daniel Kitson constantly draws attention to the sloppiness of his own technique, making it funny, thus paradoxically showing how razor-sharp his technique is. Someone heckles him halfway through a joke, and after answering them, he says he can't go back and finish it because it's all based on rhythm and the rhythm's been broken. Then he relents and finishes the joke anyway, and his honesty is rewarded. Having been let in on his dilemma the audience appreciate the joke for what it is.

Richard Pryor stumbles over his words at the start of a routine about dating. 'And you know, when you want some pissy –' he says. He has fun with the fact that he's failed to say the word 'pussy' correctly: '"*Pissy*"? H-huh – [*laughter*] "When you want some pissy." [*laughter*] That's a new thing, h-huh. [*laughter*] I hope to get some soon – some pissy. [*laughter and a smattering of applause*]'[5] Again, stumbling over delivery might seem like a sign of weakness in a stand-up, but the ability to get laughs by drawing attention to the mistake is anything but.

Failing to get a laugh can be played with in a similar way. Eddie Izzard has a standard technique for dealing with gags which don't get the response he's hoped for. After a small laugh, one hand becomes a notebook, and the other mimes writing on it, noting his comic failure with a phrase like 'Should be funnier'. He even draws attention to this technique, following it by miming another note: 'Why am I writing on my fingers?'

Like so many aspects of stand-up, the technique of drawing the audience's attention to the performance process can be traced back to music hall. Little Tich is best remembered for his big-boot dance and for being only about four feet tall (the word 'titch' originates from his stage name). His most famous routine involves a series of sight gags using boots with enormous soles, but Little Tich was also a highly skilled verbal comedian, using the standard music-hall format of songs with patter sections, sung in character. J. B. Priestley, who had seen Tich's act, described how he would draw attention to what he was doing: 'He would suddenly take us behind the scenes with him, doing it with a single remark. He would offer us a joke and then confide that it went better the night before. He would drop a hat and be unable to pick it up, because he kicked it out of reach every time, and then mutter, half in despair, "Comic business with *chapeau.*" '[6]

Fake spontaneity

Appearing on *The Comedians* in 1971, Duggie Brown is telling a joke about a plumber talking, unbeknown to him, to a parrot behind the door of the house where he's supposed to be doing a job. The parrot keeps screeching, '*Who is it??*' and the plumber keeps replying, 'It's the plumber, I've come to mend your pipes.' As the sequence is repeated, Brown starts to sound uncertain and hesitant. Then he gets a big laugh by announcing, 'I've forgot the end!' Trying to remind himself, he talks through the set-up to the joke, going through the characters and what they say. The audience laugh along with his confusion, and laugh more when he gives up and goes on to another joke. Eventually, he comes back to finish the parrot gag, saying, 'I 'aven't forgotten,' and explaining where he's gone wrong. When he finally delivers the punchline, he gets a huge laugh and a big round of applause, probably a much better response than the joke deserves.

It seems like an extraordinary moment. On national TV, a comedian is potentially messing up his big break by forgetting the gag, then winning out over adversity by getting laughs from his mistake. But all is not what it seems. The joke, complete with mistake, is a set piece, which is so strong that Brown uses it to conclude his stage act. A book published in 1971 gives an account of the sequence performed at the Batley Variety Club, and it's played out almost word for word as it is on *The Comedians*.[7]

I recall this moment not to criticise Brown for his deception, but rather to praise his ability to pull it off. When he acts as if he's gone wrong, he is so convincing that the audience really believe him. This is a very good example of what happens in almost every stand-up comedy act: the pre-planned is passed off as the spontaneous. As Dave Gorman puts it, 'Although most stand-ups pretend to have an air of casualness about it, you are, on the whole, saying the same words as you said the night before.'

This might seem like a dark secret, but the fact is that what comedians say to their audiences doesn't flow fresh and unfettered from the source of their comic genius, different every show, every word a laugh-getting gem. Inevitably, planning is involved. It might seem naive to think any differently, yet even experienced comedy critics can be fooled by faked spontaneity. William Cook recalls being 'gobsmacked' by seeing Ben Elton repeat an apparently ad libbed response to 'accidentally' spitting on someone in the front row. Cook cites this as an example of what he calls the 'illusion' that 'what is actually pains-takingly prepared is inspired banter'.[8]

Former *Independent on Sunday* comedy critic Ben Thompson, on the other hand, seems to see the illusion of spontaneity as a form of cheating. He squirms at the idea of comics like Paul Merton or Robert Newman repeating material, whether on TV or in a live show, and has a particular dislike of comedians slipping bits of material into TV interviews.[9]

On the other side of the fence, comedians can feel rather sheepish about the fact that apparently spontaneous material is actually planned. Ellen DeGeneres says that 'the whole secret' of stand-up is that the audience 'really think it's something that is brand new', and finds the idea of people seeing her over and over again and hearing the same jokes 'really scary'. In a tour programme, Eddie Izzard is defensive about people saying 'it looks like it's improvised but it isn't', pointing out that he's never claimed his work is entirely improvised. Tony Allen attributes his own inconsistency as a stand-up to the fact that he 'couldn't hack the fundamental deceit' of fake spontaneity.

By contrast, Bill Hicks was daringly candid, and would break the illusion onstage. Raring up for a routine about why women are attracted to serial killers, he mentions an article he read about women at Ted Bundy's trial trying to give him love letters and wedding proposals. 'Docs anyone remember readin' this fuckin' article?' he says. A few people show they do by clapping or shouting, 'Yeah!' Then he lays his process bare:

> That's enough to continue the bit, now – [*laughter*] If no one'd applauded, I'd still be doing it. How? We don't know. [*laughter*] You have to rationalise on your feet. [*laughter*] All I know is I got a script, and I'm headin' towards the ending. [*laughter and applause*][10]

Script vs. making-it-up-as-you-go-along

Given that spontaneity can be so convincingly faked, the big question is, how much do stand-up comedians make it up as they go along, and how much of their acts is scripted? Clearly, the answer will vary from comic to comic. Woody Allen was quite dismissive of improvisation, and it's been claimed that he 'never improvised a syllable onstage'. In most cases, though, while much of the act will be decided in advance, there's still some room for spontaneity. Tony Allen argues that 'an honest stand-up comedian will admit that the moments of pure improvisation account for less than five per cent of their act'. Lenny Bruce, who championed the idea of improvising, once estimated that about eight minutes of his forty-five-minute act would be 'free-form'.

Leaving the security of pre-planned routines seems to be something that comes with experience, and it's difficult to learn. Up-and-coming comic Alex Horne says, 'I think that was the thing I found hardest, was to . . . leave the script, and just react.' Rhys Darby agrees: 'It takes a long time between you being yourself and you doing your orchestrated stuff that you worked out, and finding that bit in between where you can naturally be funny and be relaxed enough onstage to muck around.'

Milton Jones's exaggerated persona made it particularly hard for him to break out from the script: 'I think it took so long because the style is quite honed, and it was very hard then to go into impro that was equally honed. Because it felt like changing character. But I think I've actually got better at that. And just staying in character and having a number of bullets in my gun that are in character should I need them . . . gives me the security to venture out and to talk nonsense.'

Leaving the script behind may be difficult, but it also brings the comedian satisfaction. As Andre Vincent points out, it relieves the potential drudgery of repetition: 'I mean, I suppose the material is a frame that you sort of like hang it off. But to make it interesting for yourself, you're looking for those other things, you know, otherwise it's just there every night.' Adam Bloom argues that the genuinely spontaneous moments are what bring both comic and audience the greatest joy: '[M]y favourite moment of any gig is always an improv moment. Because, firstly, you've surprised yourself with your own, you know, speed of thought or whatever. To make yourself laugh onstage is beautiful, as long as the crowd are laughing too. The biggest laugh of a night will always be an ad lib, I think.'

Planned spontaneity

In Pittsburgh in 1991, Bill Hicks starts working the audience. This is a process in which the comedian starts talking to individual punters, perhaps asking them their names, where they come from, what they do for a living. It's a way of making the conversation of stand-up comedy a little less one-way, allowing the audience to make a bigger contribution. It also allows the comedian to show off how quick-witted he or she is. If a gag arises directly from something somebody in the audience says, surely it must be truly spontaneous? With typical daring, Hicks uncovers the less romantic truth of the situation. 'Whadda you do for a living?' he asks a woman. She's slow to respond. He tells her that answering more quickly would 'really help the timing of the show', then admits that he already has 'pre-planned comedy answers', adding, 'Sorry to pop the spontaneity fuckin' bubble.'[11]

In fact, working the room involves a mixture of the planned and the spontaneous. Bob Monkhouse admits using 'an encyclopaedic collection of laugh lines in [his] memory' as well as 'naturally occurring ad libs'. Performing in Kent in early 2004, Al Murray picks on punters in the first five rows, asking their names and what they do for a living. His Pub Landlord persona gives this an interesting tension, as we know his incongruous conservatism will make him react in particular ways to particular types of people. If somebody says they're a student, he'll be able to make fun of them for lazing around at the taxpayer's expense. If someone says they're a pub landlord, he'll be able to ask them some esoteric question about their trade, accusing them of running a wine bar (a pet hate) if they give an unconvincing answer. The laughs he gets from these people must largely involve responses recycled from other shows.

Some punters, though, give him answers which can't be anticipated. One of the students he picks on tells him she is studying 'contemporary witchcraft'. He bubbles with scorn and incomprehension, and his response is every bit as funny as those he gives to the more predictable answers he gets from punters. To acknowledge that some of Murray's ad libs may not be as spontaneous as this is by no means a criticism. He seamlessly weaves the spontaneous and the semi-spontaneous together with planned routines, frequently reincorporating the punters he has talked to so that they become characters in his show.

In other cases, interaction with the audience can be almost entirely pre-planned. Harry Hill made a 'conscious effort' to talk to individual punters after watching Frank Skinner doing it very effectively, and realising the benefits it can bring: 'I always used to shy away from audience participation. I used to think it was cheap. Which it is. But it's a brilliant thing for kind of breaking the ice.' Hill found ways of interacting with his audience which completely fitted his style: surreal, involving cosy childhood references, and with a delicious hint of menace. Taking out a tub of flying saucers, the old-fashioned rice paper and sherbet sweets which newsagents sell for a few pence each, he picks out a punter in the front row and says, with the slightly patronising manner of an indulgent uncle: 'Hah – Go on then. I know you've been – I know you've been eyeing 'em up! [*laughter*] Ooo, I know you want one!' He walks forward and offers the tub to a woman in the front row. His voice gets softer, encouraging her gently: 'Go on then, flying saucer, go on. [*laughter*] Go on, madam, help yourself, there we are. Go on, flying saucer. There you go. Ha ha!' She takes one of the sweets, and he pauses for a moment. Then his manner changes with a snap, and he's cold and businesslike as he says: 'Two pee, please. [*loud laughter and applause*]'

In another sequence, he asks: 'Why do they put the little tiny holes in the top of the biscuits, though, hm?' He spends some time explaining he means the holes in Bourbon and Rich Tea biscuits ('Yum yum!'), and not the big hole in Jammie Dodgers, then repeats the question: 'Why do they put the little tiny holes – in the top of the biscuits, though?' Rather than going into some surreal explanation of his own, he suddenly points to a punter in the front row and with formidable sternness commands: '*You!! Go and find out!*' There's a big laugh. Nearly ten minutes later, he comes back to the punter and sternly demands: 'What news on biscuits?' There's another big laugh.[12]

Hill admits that the audience interaction he does is 'very prepared', and both of these bits are cleverly designed in that while they allow him to talk to individual punters, the way those punters respond is almost irrelevant to the way the gag plays out. Even if a punter refuses to take a flying saucer from the tub, it's easy enough to find another one who will. The biscuit joke is even more self-contained, not requiring a response from the person picked out.

Speaking your mind

It's shortly after the end of the Second World War and Reg Dixon is onstage in Blackpool. He's feeling unwell, because he's got a painful boil up his nose. In the middle of his act, following a laugh, he decides to tell the audience about it: 'I dunno what you're laughing at. I don't feel very well. I'm poorly. I'm proper poorly. Have you ever had a boil? I bet you've never 'ad a boil where I've 'ad a boil. 'Ave you ever 'ad a boil up yer left nostril?'

It's a moment of pure spontaneity. The comic is literally speaking his mind. He is in pain, and on the spur of the moment, he decides to tell the audience about it. He gets some big laughs. The idea of him suffering from some minor ailment fits with his gentle loser persona, which means he's struck comedy gold with his off-the-cuff comment. 'Proper poorly' becomes his catchphrase or, as he put it, his 'big gimmick'. This is either one of those magical moments where the comedian gives free rein to his or her imagination, creating something unique and special, or it's a good story Dixon invented for publicity purposes. A less successful comic called Roy Barbour also used the 'proper poorly' catchphrase, and also claimed to have invented it.[13]

It's clear, then, that improvisation can be mythologised; but genuinely spontaneous moments do happen. Bill Bailey is onstage at Wyndham's Theatre in the West End in October 2003, and he asks the audience if anybody has had a bad experience with marijuana. A man on the balcony shouts out that he has. Interested, Bailey asks him what happened. The man replies in a deep, clear voice, apparently unaffected by the pressure of having to talk with a theatre full of people listening in. 'I was on a houseboat on a frozen lake in Kurdistan,' he begins, and, as the story unfolds, the audience laugh both at what the man says, and at how Bailey responds. The comedian avoids the usual knee-jerk reaction of trying to make fun of the man, being generous enough to let him have his say and share the audience's attention for a few minutes. For a while, the stand-up act has changed from a fake conversation to a real one.

Once again, such moments can be traced back to music hall. R. G. Knowles, a Canadian comedian who regularly played the British halls from the 1890s to his death in 1919, was known for his quick wit. On a show at the Star in Bermondsey, he is said to have been interrupted in mid-flow by a latecomer noisily taking his place in the audience. Knowles turned to him and said, 'Brother, you're very late; but never mind, you're just in time for the collection.' At another show at the same hall, he did two encores, but even after five songs, the audience still wanted more. 'I only get paid for three, you know,' he said. 'If I do another, they won't give me any more money.' 'Why don't you send the hat round?' shouted a heckler. 'Good idea,' Knowles responded, 'but if I did I wouldn't get it back.' On yet another occasion, he was interrupted by the theatre cat wandering across the stage, leading him to comment, 'This is a monologue not a catalogue!'[14]

Mark Lamarr meets a beetle

Mark Lamarr's stand-up is characterised by an apparently effortless ability to step out of material and create spontaneous comedy from the particular circumstances of the gig. Even in a show that's being filmed for a live video, he's confident to play the situation. Like Knowles, he has an animal encounter, but this time it's not a cat but a beetle that wanders across the stage. Lamarr notices it as it crawls across a white line marked on the stage. He crouches down to look at it, and some of the audience laugh, seeing what he's doing. Then he starts having fun with it:

No, it's all right, I was just trying to talk and this beetle started walking across the stage, [*laughter*] and he's got, ah – he's got all fluff on his back and he's having a hard time. [*laughter*] And, but the thing is, I feel like he's really bored with the show and he's trying to fuck off, so that's – [*laughter*]

[*He gets back on his feet to imitate the beetle, scuttling about the stage.*] He just keeps wandering around and going, 'I'm not into this menstrual stuff, I'm not really,' [*laughter*] and he just – he's got fluff on him, he's just wandering around in circles, and I know exactly how he feels at the moment. [*laughter*]'

[*Now he goes back to the beetle, crouching down again.*] 'He's not like a sacred, er, beetle from this part of the country, is he, like, not one of you brought in the Sacred Bracknell Beetle? [*quiet laughter*] And if I get, you know, if I say anything out of turn, he just – goes into a really big beetle and hits me, or something like that? That's – [*laughter*] I know it's fairly unlikely, isn't it, I'm just musing here, but – You know what, I've noticed that I'm – I'm wasting your time, aren't I? [*laughter*] You lot are all staring at me, going, 'He's got some great beetle stuff coming up, I'm sure he has,' but no, [*laughter*] I'm just – That'd be so sad, wouldn't it, if I said to the stagehand,

'Let the beetle on now, I can do me beetle stuff!'
[*laughter*]'[15]

Shortly afterwards he moves into a prepared routine. He's filled up more than a minute of stage time and got at least eleven laughs by taking the audience with him on his flight of fancy, creating an imaginary scenario, acting it out, pulling back from it, replacing it with another, commenting on what he's doing and reflecting on the process of improvisation in stand-up.

In some ways, Lamarr is modest about his ability to improvise, saying that being able to do it in the high-pressure environment of a video shoot is a 'bare minimum' for him. On the other hand, he's aware that to be able to pull off a bit like this is something that's hard won by experience: 'People have said to me, "Oh, you were lucky there, weren't you," and I [say], "No, what's lucky? What, lucky I worked my arse off to be good at doing this?"' He explains exactly how experience can help: '[W]hen you're ad libbing, a lot of times it's not quite an ad lib, it's sort of just *remembering*, you know, and I've noticed I've got a lot better at it as the years go by, because someone'll say, you know, "Kentucky Fried Chicken," and you'll think, "Oh, I was working on a bit about that about ten, fifteen years ago," and something'll come out of it, often something you've never used before, but . . . thought you had. And a lot of it, it is obviously immediate spur of the moment, but a lot of it comes with experience.'

Jonathan Winters works with his audience

Improvisation is so central to the work of some stand-ups that it becomes what they are best known for. Jonathan Winters, part of the generation of sick comedians, is a classic example. Winters started working as a comic in New York in the early 1950s, playing at venues like the Blue Angel and Le Ruban Bleu, and became well known when he was picked up by TV, appearing on shows hosted by Jack

Paar, Garry Moore and Steve Allen. He was a major influence on Robin Williams, and would later go on to play the part of Mork's son in Williams's breakthrough sitcom *Mork and Mindy*. This was part of an eclectic career, which has included voiceover work for animated films, his own syndicated TV show, live performances and a series of comedy albums.

The format of his performances is simple. His routines are based on responding to requests. Audience members suggest scenes for him to act out, like, 'I wonder if you could characterise a male elephant wrapping a present for his girlfriend?'; or ask him questions like, 'Whaddya think about hippies?' He repeats the request or question, a vital part of the grammar of stand-up, ensuring that everyone in the audience has heard it. Then he either answers the question, making a few witty comments, or more typically he acts out the requested scene.

A woman asks him to do his impression of a doctor carrying out his first heart transplant, and Winters conjures up a surprisingly rich sketch, with a large and varied cast of characters. A stiff-voiced doctor talks to a gibbering patient before his operation, telling him they've had trouble finding a suitable heart, but assuring him, 'We do wanna get you a goodie!' A wobbling anaesthetist makes an appearance, turning out to be unashamedly drunk. A flirtatious nurse comes in ('I'm twen'y-three!'), and informs the doctor that all she has managed to get is a fox terrier's heart. When the patient comes round, in front of the eager cameras of the world's press, he is asked for a comment. 'Arf! Arf!' he replies.

In some cases, merely giving flesh to the suggestion given is enough. A man asks, 'Could you do a sergeant in the marine corps that is interviewing a gorilla that has been drafted by mistake?' Winters takes on the gruff, gravel voice of a drill sergeant, and shows him running through the list of names: 'Here's a guy – I guess he's tryin'a be some kinda clown. [*laughter*] 'S just puddown "gorilla". [*laughter*] That you, fella? [*laughter*]' Realising there's been a mistake, the sergeant tells the gorilla: 'You don't have to go to the rifle range today. [*laughter*] But I would shave. [*laughter and applause*]'

The fact that the audience collaborate in the creation of the show means that, as well as giving it great immediacy, it is also one of the most intense forms of sharing that exists in stand-up. Winters has a warm and generous relationship with his audience. Sometimes, their requests get laughs in themselves, and there's no hint that he is jealous of the punters when this happens. Indeed, he sometimes laughs along. He's enthusiastic when he gets a particularly appealing request, saying, 'Oh, yes!' or 'God bless your heart!' which gets a laugh in itself.

Occasionally the warm rapport breaks out into flirtation. Before starting to improvise a routine, he asks the woman who made the request how old she is. She tells him she's twenty-three. 'Perfect!' he replies, getting a laugh. He goes on to chat her up a little, finishing the conversation by saying, 'We'll talk about that later!' thus getting another laugh. On another occasion, the flirtation is initiated by the woman making the request, who says, 'I'd like you to do an imitation of you asking me for a date.'

Questions have been raised about how much Winters's live shows are prepared in advance, and while he is reasonably cagey about his methodology, he does admit to sketching out his ideas beforehand. However, the range and quirkiness of audience requests which kick off his routines mean that however much he prepares, he must have to improvise a great deal. Having said this, Winters act is not pure free-form, and there's plenty to ensure that it has shape. To start with, there's the basic call-and-response format of request and improvised bit, which automatically gives structure and rhythm to the show.

Winters also comes prepared with a whole set of tricks up his sleeve. He has a repertoire of running characters, like the crazy old lady Maude Frickert, and a six-and-a-half-year-old boy called Chester Honeyhugger, and audiences often ask to see these characters in a given situation. Then there are the sound effects he produces himself. Using just his mouth, he can produced a rapid series of wet clicks to imitate a squirrel storing nuts in its cheeks, the *ffffffffftkk!!* of an arrow being fired into a tree, or the deep, slow, drunken mechanical voice of a talking toy. The sound effects are an important crutch. When asked to do a piece with a motorcycle, he chides himself for not having the relevant sound effect in his repertoire.[16] The characters and the sound effects give him a series of comic readymades which he can pull out of the bag to fit together spontaneously during a show.

Ross Noble and the giant platform shoe

Improvisational stand-ups vary as much as any other kind of comedian, and Ross Noble is a very different kettle of fish from Winters. I first came across Noble in the early 1990s, when he played the comedy club I compèred, the Last Laugh in Sheffield. At the time, the club was being run by someone else, so the acts always came as a surprise to me. Noble seemed like a very ordinary sort of act, distinguished only by the fact that he juggled as well as doing gags.

A couple of years later, control of the Last Laugh had reverted back to Roger Monkhouse and me, and we started a short-lived second venue. The idea was that it would be a place to try out newer acts to see if they were ready for the Last Laugh, so we put them on in another pub on a Monday night, charged a pound to get in, and called it Cheap Laughs. Noble headlined one of the shows and he was extraordinary. He looked different, the T-shirt replaced by a suit, and the longer hair making him bear a slight resemblance to Steve Coogan. But the real change was in his comedy.

His material was fresh and offbeat. He talked about listening to what he thought was a really hardcore rave station for ten minutes before he realised he was actually listening to a badly tuned in BBC Radio 2. There was a new fluidity to the act, allowing him to move easily from material to playing the situation. Conversations with punters led to bizarre flights of fancy, which were interwoven and incorporated into existing material. One of the frosted glass dividers which separated the side of the stage from one of the tables became the window of an all-night garage, and every so often he would try to buy a Mars Bar from the person sitting on the other side of it. Crucially, he was much, much funnier, filling the small pub room with so much laughter and applause that it nearly burst. As we watched him work, Roger and I kept exchanging glances. After the show, I was astounded when Roger told me that Ross was only eighteen years old. That would have made him just sixteen when I'd seen him do his juggling act.

Having started performing stand-up at the age of fifteen, he has now been doing it for nearly half of his life, and his improvisation seems effortless. The simplest things can spontaneously take him down the strangest paths. At the Komedia in Brighton in 2001, a man wearing a flat cap backwards is complimented on a 'fantastic hat decision'. 'Yer like the coolest old man in the world,' says Noble, getting a laugh. To expand the idea, he adopts an old man's sandpapery voice and imitates Eminem: 'I'm Slim Shady!' Another laugh. He imagines the advantages of the hat: 'Cos you've got the two options, you can be down with the kids, or, you know, you can whizz it around and yer inta bingo half price! [*laughter*]'

He asks the man what he does for a living. He's a musician. 'I'm suspectin' one-man band?' asks Noble. In trying to argue the audience down for laughing at this, he starts defending one-man bands, which gets him into a quandary about the plural of this type of musician: 'one-men band' or 'bandy men'. Imagining the flat-capped man turning bandy evokes for him the image of 'a Victorian child with rickets'.[17]

190

At the Leeds City Varieties in February 2003, he notices that the theatre lights are in cages, and concludes that 'there must be a bit of thievery goin' on'. Running with the idea, he turns to a man with his feet on the steps: 'He's gonna nick these stairs, he's gonna pretend it's a giant platform shoe. [*laughter*]' This leads him to the idea that in case of a fire the man would be able to allow the audience to escape to safety, climbing up his staircase shoe. In fact, the man would be a superhero, his first task to provide something for Thora Hird to attach her Stannah stairlift to while filming an advert: 'Sounds like a job fer – Stairway Man! [*laughter*] Go on, Thora, clip yerself on there! [*laughter*]'[18]

At the Garrick Theatre in September 2003, a man making a particular hand gesture inspires the comment that perhaps he's fighting off a tiny vole, leading to a detailed fantasy about the vole (who has done 'a little bit of fringe theatre work') being bitter, having been rejected at the last minute from the supporting cast of *Wind in the Willows*, partly due to sexual tension between him and the badger.[19]

Noble has fewer safety nets than Winters when he lets his imagination fly. Rather than using the fixed request–response format, his ad libbed routines arrive more spontaneously, inspired by something in the venue, some-body's clothes, a heckle, some casual banter with an individual punter. He also lacks the handy bag of running characters and vocal sound effects. On the other hand, the spontaneous moments can be mixed with pre-planned routines: 'If I want to, I can do a whole show of prepared material or improvise a whole show. It all boils down to what's happening on the night. As soon as you say, "I'm going to do 40 per cent impro and 60 per cent prepared material," you're just making it hard for yourself. You need to feel it.'[20]

Noble explains that achieving the smooth blend of the improvised and the prepared was difficult: 'It used to be really clunky. It used to be the sort of thing where I'd be improvising and people go, "Wurr, he's improvising this," and then it'd be a real sort of clunky kind of gear change, of like, "Oh, he's not making this up any more." ' The answer was to make even the prepared material flexible and changeable: 'A lot of the time, I take stuff that I've improvised and then sort of play around with the idea. And . . . even an idea that I've used the night before, rather than just doing it . . . I'll keep playing with it . . . I just try and keep it as fluid as possible, in terms of like, halfway through I might start talking about something else . . . So it never becomes set . . . you never go, "I'm gonna say this, this and this," you go, "I might say that, but I might do that." . . . And that way, then, there's never a line between this-is-improvised, this-is-scripted, because then your scripted stuff, just, it's not, it's kind of like it's sort of scripted but it isn't, you know.'

What Noble does share with Winters is a warm rapport with the audience. When he makes fun of somebody, it's gentle and playful, and there's a distinct lack of hostility. Getting a laugh by drawing attention to the shirt and pullover worn by a 'relaxed kind of respectable-looking' man at the front, Noble starts defending him from the audience's laughter: 'I mean, I like it, I think it's a good look, [*laughter*] but er – No, yer wrong ta laugh, [*laughter*] no, I think –'[21]

Even a potentially bothersome heckler is treated gently. At the Orchard Theatre, Dartford, in June 2004, a strange woman in the front row tries to hijack the show from the start, turning round to address the rest of the audience directly. She says she works for the Communist Party, she gets upset and offended, she shouts bizarre comments.

Noble handles her with consummate ease, mugging to the audience to suggest he thinks she's potty, allowing her comments to lead him into strange imagery, pretending he's afraid she's a serial killer, calming her down when she gets cross, and sporadically coming back to her to pre-empt her tendency to grab some attention. He never allows her to become a scapegoat, never brings the full contempt of the audience down upon her as he so easily could. He comes up with the perfect description of what's going on, saying it's like returning to a lit firework, not knowing whether it'll blow up in his face. He has good reason to handle audience members gently: 'I just think it's just better to kind of create than it is to destroy, you know. Especially when you're improvising, just to let it go, you know, to let it kind of fly. If you go, if you talk to somebody and then go, "HWWUURR!!" instantly they clam up, and then the next time you talk to them they're not gonna be as friendly, you know?'

Heckling

When cousins marry

Nothing brings stand-up comedy as inescapably into the present tense as heckling. Exchanges with hecklers give substance and solidity to the illusion of spontaneity. When somebody shouts something, whether hostile or supportive, the comedian is under an obligation to respond. Heckling is not exclusive to stand-up. It happened in music hall, and can even be traced back to Elizabethan theatre, where clowns like Tarlton would respond to hecklers in rhyme.[22] Heckling is strongly associated with key features of stand-up: it brings any underlying hostility to the surface, it makes the directness of communication even more intense and it involves spontaneity.

In reality, the way comics deal with hecklers is not always as spontaneous as it seems. There are a number of standard lines which are used in response to hecklers, and even on the British alternative comedy circuit, in which stealing material from other acts is a taboo, these are seen as common property. Standard anti-heckle lines include:

'Isn't it a shame when cousins marry?'
'I remember *my* first pint.'
'Never drink on an empty head.'

'Sorry? [*the heckler repeats what he or she said*] No, I heard you the first time, I'm just sorry.'
'Just to think, out of millions of sperm, you had to get there first.'

In some cases, comics may invent anti-heckle lines of their own, perhaps designed to fit their style. Whether standard or original, a pre-planned line is not spontaneous, even though the comedian doesn't know in advance when or if it will have to be used. More experienced acts tend to avoid such lines, preferring to react to hecklers in the moment. For Mark Lamarr, this is a matter of principle: 'Again, the other I thing I did, was I never ever used stock putdowns. And I hated that . . . it would never be cousins marrying and all that business cos I always found that fucking agonising (after the first time you've seen it, when it's like the greatest thing you've ever seen in your life).'

Dealing with a heckle is a test of the comedian's ability. To ignore it is seriously to undermine the audience's faith, and if the comic ploughs on relentlessly with material rather than responding, the illusion of spontaneity is broken. On the other hand, to see a comedian deal brilliantly with a heckler can seem like magic, and can win over an audience that was cold or hostile before the heckle happened. This effect certainly existed in music hall. In 1892, Jerome K. Jerome recalled how the singer Bessie Bellwood dealt with a heckle from 'a hefty-looking coalheaver':

For over five minutes she let fly, leaving him gasping, dazed and speechless. At the end, she gathered herself together for one supreme effort, and hurled at him an insult so bitter with scorn, so sharp with insight into his career and character, so heavy with prophetic curse, that strong men drew and held their breath while it passed over them, and women hid their faces and shivered. Then she folded her arms and stood silent, and the house, from floor to ceiling, rose and cheered her until there was no more breath left in its lungs.[23]

It's not possible to read this description without wondering exactly what it was she said to the offending coalheaver to get such an extraordinary reaction. Presumably, you just had to be there.

Sometimes heckling is about hostility, and might involve more than just a personal antipathy towards a particular comedian. For black comedians like Dick Gregory in the early 1960s, playing to white audiences inevitably meant the risk of racist heckles, and dealing with them was hazardous in that knife-edge context. Gregory found his own way of coming back at racists. If somebody shouted 'nigger', he would tell them that there was a clause in his contract which gave him fifty dollars more every time he heard the word. Then he'd ask the whole audience to yell it.

Heckling used to pose a problem for Harry Hill, because responding with naked hostility would not suit his style: 'I always suffered with hecklers when I started off, because I didn't really have a kind of way of dealing with them. Because you can't just say, "Fuck off," you know.' With experience, though, he found suitably surreal ways of answering hecklers, like telling them, 'You heckle me now, but I'm safe in the knowledge that when I get home, I've got a nice chicken in the oven.'

Heckling isn't always about hostility, as Phill Jupitus points out: 'I think . . . a heckle says a lot more about what they're trying to say to the people they're with than about your act. They are establishing themselves within their social group . . . And drunk girls on hen nights, you know, who just are like car alarms. Quite often, you don't need a putdown so much as a mute button.'

Some hecklers simply join in for the fun of it, even positively contributing to the show. James Campbell has to treat the children who come to see him carefully, but he rarely encounters a dangerous heckle: '[W]hen adults start heckling, it's either a constructive heckle or a destructive heckle. It's either "Get off, you're shit", or it's "How about this?" With kids, they very, very rarely say anything sort of anti, it's usually "What about a sieve and a banana?" or something, it's usually something constructive. So you don't really have to put them down harshly. Sometimes you get one that just starts irritating the rest of the audience, and then I will put them down, but not that hard at all. You know, just ask them . . . "Is it the first time you've been out of the house for a while?" or something like that, you know, just something which is still quite whimsical. You do it with a smile, really.'

Kenneth Williams steals the attention by laughing

In a sense, comedians and hecklers are motivated by the same thing: a craving for attention. An exchange with a heckler is a battle for the attention of the audience, and there's a delicious example of this kind of tussle on the recording of Frankie Howerd's act at the Establishment. Kenneth Williams, another camp comic of the same generation as Howerd, is in the audience, and draws attention to himself using an unusual heckling technique: conspicuous laughter.

Williams was famous for his dirty laugh, and it is unmistakable as it blasts out like an effeminate machine gun with a blocked-up nose. On and on he laughs, for twenty seconds. The audience quickly tune into his laugh, and as it goes on they respond with two strong laughs of their own. Howerd is left floundering, saying things like, 'Oo, Gawd 'elp us!' to try and win the attention back to himself. Just when it seems like he's succeeding, Williams pushes his laugh up into a higher register and gets another laugh from the audience. Finally Howerd asserts himself, and very effectively at that: 'Ladies and gentlemen, I want you to watch this sight, of one comedian laughing at another one, [*laughter*] it's very rare. Very rare. [*some clapping*]

And of course, writing it down at the same time. [*laughter*]'

A couple of minutes later, Williams is at it again, inspiring the following exchange:

> Williams: *Hahahahahahahaha!!*
> Howerd: Shuuut up, you! [*laughter*] Anyway listen. Listen –
> Williams: Yeees.
> Howerd: Yeees. [*laughter and clapping*] Is 'e trying to steal the act? Is 'e trying to steal the limelight, do you think? [*laughter*][24]

Listening to the recording, it seems perfectly clear that Williams is trying to steal the limelight, but he makes no mention of this in his diary, simply remarking that Howerd's act was 'v. good' and complaining about 'an awful woman who kept shouting and interrupting him'. However, Williams's diaries do suggest that there was some rivalry between the two men after this incident. They competed over parts in the *Carry On* films, and after lunch with Howerd, Williams wrote: 'He is undoubtedly a very boring man.'

Heckling to kill

When I first started doing stand-up, I lived in fear of the heckler, believing that he (and it often was a he) was always lurking somewhere at the back of every gig, waiting to strike. With experience, I realised that hostile heckling is relatively rare, that dealing with it was largely a matter of showing the audience I was unruffled by it, and, most of the time, it was reasonably easy to cope with. As a result, I rarely worried or even thought about being heckled. However, the one thing that did unsettle me deep down was that, because I knew what heckling felt like from my side of the fence, I also knew how easy it would be for a determined heckler to destroy me.

A funny heckle can be a dangerous thing. I once saw a

comic valiantly struggling to win over a small, cold audience in a cellar bar in Manchester. As he started to look desperate, somebody shouted, 'Have you got any albums out?' On another occasion, a female comic at the Last Laugh was trying to use the standard anti-heckle line, 'What do you use for contraception? Your personality?' Sadly, she didn't get to the end of it. When she said, 'What do you use for contraception?' the punter answered, 'Your jokes.' If a heckler gets a bigger laugh than anything the comedian has got all evening, the comic's authority will often be badly dented. It is possible to share the audience's enjoyment of a funny heckle by laughing along or applauding it, but if the heckler comes off best in a battle of wits, it's very difficult for the comic to recover.

On the other hand, heckles don't have to be funny to be destructive. 'Say something funny' and 'Boring' are neither funny nor original, but they're so blunt, predictable and damning that it's difficult to come back at them inventively or positively. Eddie Izzard says these two are the worst you can get. The key to making an unfunny heckle really hurt is persistence, timing or a combination of the two. I once saw a comedian blowing routines through poor concentration and repeatedly putting down an apparently harmless punter sitting at the front, much to the audience's bemusement. Asking him about it afterwards, he explained that the punter had given him a non-stop barrage of insults too quiet for anybody else to hear. The malevolent persistence of the hushed-voice heckler was what broke the comic's nerve. I've faced audiences where a persistent unfunny heckler is supported by a table full of cheering friends. However much I put him down, he kept coming back for more, to the point where the rest of the audience was simply bored with it. By that point, I'd lost.

Timing is also crucial to effective heckling. The most destructive time to heckle is towards the end of a long routine. Even if the comedian puts the heckler down well, the chances are that the end of the routine will have to be abandoned. As Jeremy Hardy puts it, '[I]f you are trying to take someone into a world of your own, somebody at the back shouting, "Show us your tits," kind of breaks the moment.'[25] A steady series of well-timed heckles can destroy an act. The fact that this kind of determined, destructive heckling is so rare shows the extent to which most stand-up audiences have at least a modicum of good-will. The real point of heckling is not hostility, but to add the sparkle of spontaneity to the show.

7. Delivery

Timing

The secret of great comedy is – wait for it – timing. Ask anybody what you need to be a good stand-up comic, and the chances are that they will mention timing. The problem is that nobody seems very clear exactly what they mean by the word. Definitions of 'timing' come in all shapes and sizes.

Variety performer Valantyne Napier wrote a reference book of showbusiness jargon, in which she calls timing 'the most misused and misunderstood term'. For her, it means 'being able to anticipate the audience reaction to a line . . . and wait to deliver the next laugh . . . until just the right time when the laughter or applause starts to fade . . . The laughter . . . is often lost when cut off by the next line. On the other hand there should not be any discernible pause.'[1]

Lupino Lane, who also worked in variety, defines the term by describing bad timing:

> The use of too many words, taking too long to get to the point, making a bad entrance or exit, a gag too much, and too many choruses to a song, all help to put the timing wrong . . . Jumping in and interrupting before the sense of the line has been got over, is another fault; being too late with the interruption will also spoil the tempo. Speed

is important, not necessarily speaking too fast, but getting to the big laugh.[2]

Tony Allen's definition is more lyrical and succinct, describing timing as 'an intuitive state of grace that has to be discovered, an elusive abstract lubricant that exists in the eternal now'.[3]

Neal R. Norrick is drier and more academic: 'The overall tempo of the performance, the ebb and flow of given and new information highlighted by repetition and formulaic phrasing along with rhythms of hesitation and more fluent passages all co-determine timing.'[4]

Clearly timing means different things to different people. Various themes run through these diverse definitions. First, there's structure. As Lane points out, individual jokes and the act as a whole must not be cluttered up with the unnecessary. Second, there's pace and tempo, which both Lane and Norrick identify. Third, there's a sense of being responsive to the audience. For Napier, timing is the straightforward matter of waiting to deliver the line just before the previous laugh finishes. For both Lane and Norrick, control of information is important, and the comedian must have a sense of when the audience have understood enough. Finally, there's the idea that timing is a state of mind in the performer, a point which Allen makes so eloquently.

Joan Rivers describes the timing which she had, even as a child, as 'the right moment to pause, the instant to hit a line like punching a button to detonate laughter'.[5] Although she's talking about an instinctive, almost magical ability, this suggests the most basic, literal definition of timing: that it is, as the word implies, a simple matter of time. If a pause is exactly the right number of milliseconds long, and the punchline is delivered at exactly the right number of milliseconds afterwards, it will get the optimum amount of laughter.

I've always disliked the simplistic argument that stand-up

is entirely based on timing. I think timing has become such a popular explanation because people see something extraordinary happening when they watch a comedian at work. The comic seems to talk like a normal person, and laughter appears as if by magic, sparked off by a simple word or even a pause. It's easier to attribute the laughs to some kind of mysterious atomic comic clock in the comedian's head than to make sense of the whole complex process of what's going on behind that word or pause to make it funny.

I may have been unusual, but when I did stand-up I was never, ever aware of timing, and was always puzzled by what it was supposed to mean. I didn't consciously adjust pauses or wait to strike with the punchline to ensure it came in at exactly the right moment. When I was at my best, I was no more conscious of time or tempo than in everyday conversation. In fact, at my best, I was generally less self-conscious than usual. Of course, I had some understanding of rhythm. As I broke new material in, I would learn the best way of pacing and phrasing a key line, and this would become fixed so it was roughly the same at every gig. However, in the act of performing this practised phrasing, I would be thinking more about the content of the line than the minutiae of timing and rhythm.

What's so great about Bob Newhart's timing?

The problem with timing as a concept is not that it has no bearing on how stand-up works, but that it is such a loose, ill-defined term. It refers to several things, not just one, and not all of them are even connected to time. To illustrate the point, take Bob Newhart, who has been widely praised for his timing. There are a number of aspects of his performance which might have inspired this praise.

First, there's his beautifully relaxed manner. The old-fashioned term for this is 'stage repose', which means a quality of ease, assurance and control, and an avoidance of telltale signs of lack of confidence such as unnecessary

202

fidgeting. Johnny Carson has a neat definition: 'When you stand there doing nothing and it's funny, that's repose.'[6]

Second, there's the tempo. Newhart's delivery is slow and unhurried, something which undoubtedly enhances his stage repose.

Third, there's the careful way he unfolds the information in his routines. He subtly gives the audience enough clues to understand each gag, but leaves them a bit of work to do. For example, in the famous driving instructor routine from his first album, he plays the instructor who remains calm almost all of the time, no matter what dangers he faces. All of the other characters, including the dangerously inept woman he is instructing, are implied by what the instructor says. At one point, the woman has driven the wrong way down a one-way street, and after a pause filled by the audience's laughter from the previous joke, he says: 'Er – same – same to you, fella! [*extended laughter*]'[7] The joke works by what Newhart doesn't say. The audience don't hear the man in another car shouting an angry insult, they infer it from the instructor's response. This brings them the pleasure of solving a puzzle, as well as popping a mental cartoon of the altercation into their heads.

There's a similar example in a routine about Sir Walter Raleigh introducing tobacco to civilisation. The basic conceit is that Raleigh keeps sending his discoveries from the New World back to England, but the people back home don't appreciate their importance. Newhart plays somebody back in England, who talks to Raleigh on the telephone and, as in the driving instructor routine, Raleigh's contributions to the conversation are merely implied. Newhart's character nicknames Raleigh 'Nutty Walt', and can hardly conceal his amusement at what he sees as his crazy ideas. He is puzzled why Nutty Walt is sending him eighty tons of leaves: 'This er – this may come as kind of a surprise to you, Walt, but er – come fall in England here, we're kind of up to our, er – [*laughter and applause*]'[8]

Again, the joke is in the gap. Newhart stops before

finishing the sentence, making the audience fill in the blanks for themselves ('up to our necks/eyes/asses in leaves'). Both jokes involve pauses, so their success might be attributed simply to timing. However, in both cases, the pause is built into the structure of the joke, so that it's as much about writing as it is about delivery.

Having said that, the way the line is delivered is exquisite, and this leads to a fourth aspect of Newhart's performance that might come under the category of timing: his acting. Most of his routines, including these two, are performed in character, and although normally his characterisations are fairly close to the stage persona he uses in the introductions to his routines, there are fine nuances of tone, pace and punctuation which not only bring the situations he evokes to life, but also show the character's reactions to these situations without spelling them out in words. The 'same to you, fella' in the first example has the same mild, calm tone as the most of the rest of the routine, but there's the merest whiff of the exasperation he must be feeling in there too.

Sometimes, Newhart's acting is so delicious that the particular way that he says a word is all that's needed to bring out the flavour of the joke. In one routine, he plays a policeman trying to talk somebody down off a ledge, by following the advice of a new manual on the subject. In the introduction, Newhart summarises the manual, which advises the police to wear plain clothes in such situations, and talk casually to the potential jumper. The policeman, he says, 'slips into his sports jacket', lights a cigarette, and walks out on to the ledge. There's a pause as he lights up to play the policeman, then he says his first line in character: 'Oh, hi!'[9]

There's a huge, uproarious laugh, which is enhanced by a little clapping. It goes on for more than ten seconds, and individual laughs can be picked out: barking male guffaws, female shrieks. What makes these two simple, innocuous words so funny is the way he says them. He manages to fill them with the forced brightness of fake surprise. It suggests somebody trying to pretend they have just casually wandered out on to the ledge of a skyscraper to enjoy a cigarette, and being pleasantly surprised to find somebody else up there with him. He captures all of this perfectly in his tone of voice, and by doing so highlights the absurdity of the situation in one powerful comic flash.

Bob Newhart's performance makes it absolutely clear that timing is not one thing but many. The fact is that stand-up performance is infinitely subtle and multifaceted and, all too often, words are inadequate at explaining why a particular moment of delivery is so wonderful. As a result, trying to fit all of its many aspects under the leaky umbrella term of 'timing' is probably not a good idea.

Duh-d-d-dum-d-dum-d-durr

Rhythm is probably as important to comedy as it is to music, but in comedy it's much harder to identify and notate. Stand-up's backbeat pulses to and fro between performer and punter, the comedian's line followed by the audience's response, a joke–laugh–joke–laugh–joke–laugh rhythm that speeds and slows throughout the show. This is a beat that can be easily dulled by background noise. When I compèred the Last Laugh, sometimes I would forget to turn off the air-conditioning fans before I went on at the beginning. Although I'm sure the audience weren't consciously aware of this, my opening routine would feel like wading through blancmange, and I couldn't get the joke–laugh rhythm crisp and clear. One time I realised what was happening while I was onstage, and asked for the fans to be turned off. Suddenly, the blancmange was gone, and the joke–laugh beat started ringing out more clearly straight away. I'm not the only one who has experienced this effect. Shelley Berman once found himself distracted onstage by the noise of a refrigerator motor.

Comic rhythm can work almost like magic. Milton Berle once swapped the punchline of a joke for an unfunny one that didn't even make sense. The insistent rhythm of the gags was such that when he threw in the nonsensical, unfunny punchline, the audience laughed anyway. Mort Sahl's delivery has been compared to a drum solo. Similarly, Lenny Bruce had a routine in which he rhythmically spills out the things people say to each other after sex, which he compares to 'a big drum solo'. To make the point more audible, a drummer plays behind him, following the rhythms of his speech on his drums and cymbals. Harry Hill has a drummer and a keyboard player onstage with him, and as well as accompanying him in songs, they often chip in to routines, adding sound effects, particular during bits of physical business.

Sometimes comic rhythm is about repetition. In a routine about childhood, Jerry Seinfeld sums up his main motivation as a child as: 'Get candy, get candy, get candy, get candy, get candy, get candy.' He goes on to imagine a candy-obsessed child in an encounter with a candy-proffering stranger, and each moment of the child's reasoning is punctuated with the phrase, 'Get candy, get candy, get candy'. The insistent repetition of the three syllables gives the routine a relentless forward momentum, as well as capturing the feeling of obsession.

For Harry Hill, repetition goes hand in hand with economy: 'When writing gags, I think you should use the least number of words. Even though you can repeat the first line over and over again, which is so often what I do.' Hill laughs, and admits a more prosaic reason for the repetition: 'To fill it out!' In some of his jokes, though, there is a more practical reason to repeat something: '[I]f you have got a gag which is a bit obscure, or is not immediately obvious, it is useful to spell it out a couple of times. So I mean I had this gag which was, "You know the white plastic doll's house garden furniture that you get free with the home-delivery pizzas?" Right, that is a real mouthful, right? There's a lot of things in there, contained in there. That's the minimum amount of words you can use to say this gag. "I keep getting the table." That's the punchline. "I keep getting the table."

So what I do is, I say, "You know the white plastic doll's house garden furniture? That you get free with the home-delivery pizzas?" . . . You say it a few times. And then they're really kind of keen to know what the answer is. You know, so you can do the next bit, and you know they're all sort of going to be on top of it, pretty much.'

Hill also sees the myriad running jokes which punctuate his act as a kind of rhythm, and it's the feel of this rhythm, rather than a fixed running order, which allows him to structure his act.

Perhaps the subtlest rhythms at work in stand-up are those contained in the sound of the words that make up key lines. The music made by the patterns of vowels and consonants which a spoken sentence can contain often holds the key to why it gets a laugh. For Milton Jones, this music is crucial: '[Y]ou must have the duh-d-d-dum-d-dum-d-durr rhythm worked out, even if means including an extra word that's grammatically questionable. The rhythm is more important.' However, knowing this is not the same as knowing exactly how rhythm works, which is instinctive and does not yield easily to cold analysis. Jones doesn't claim to understand fully this kind of rhythm, but he has some interesting ideas: 'I dunno what rhythm does, it must be some deep subconscious thing. I mean, obviously, it's to do with timing, and I guess facial stuff as well. Because it's not unconnected to what you're doing with your face. You can even move from vocal to physical rhythm, the last face being the last beat of the rhythm, if you see what I mean.'

The rule of three

By contrast, the simplest rhythm in stand-up is the rule of three. The classic version of the three-part list joke has been defined as 'Establish, Reinforce, Surprise!'[11] A lot of comedy works by deviating from an expected pattern. The first part of the list establishes the pattern, the second reinforces it and the third subverts it. Jo Brand's early work provides a couple of fine examples, which I've laid out so as to emphasise their tripartite shape. At the beginning of her act, she apologises for looking 'a bit shit', and explains:

> I've 'ad flu recently,
> and I forgot to wash my T-shirt, and er – [*quiet laughter*]
> my parents weren't very attractive, so er – [*laughter*][12]

In another performance, she's talking about how she's been thinking a lot about body image:

> I read that book *Fat Is a Feminist Issue*. [*quiet laughter*]
> Got a bit desperate halfway through.
> And ate it. [*laughter*][13]

In the first gag, she gives two legitimate reasons why she's looking 'shit' at this particular moment, and a third one which is so permanent and self-deprecating that it doesn't really follow. In the second gag, she has two sentences which set up the simple narrative about reading a classic feminist text, and a third which gives the story a surprise ending.

Not all three-part gags work like this, though. Omid Djalili has a joke which goes: 'Also, I know that some of you, you associate the Middle East, er, with, er, oil. And phlegm, and halitosis, er – [*laughter and clapping*]'[14] In this three-part list (oil, phlegm, halitosis), the normal structure is inverted because the expectation is subverted after the first item.

In some cases, the three-part rhythm isn't integral to the structure of the joke at all. In other cases, separate jokes may be grouped together in threes. One reason for this might be that the rhythm of three is intrinsically pleasing in public speaking. In his book on political oratory, Max Atkinson shows how politicians use three-part lists to elicit applause from their audiences, and provides plentiful examples to prove his case. He points out that they have 'an air of unity or completeness about them'.[15]

208

Those terrible syllables 'er' and 'um'

While most of the tips Lupino Lane gives in his 1945 book *How to Become a Comedian* would be of little use to anyone starting out as a stand-up today, he does give a useful snapshot of stage practice in British theatres in the mid-twentieth century. The advice he gives on delivery suggests a very formal approach. He advises comedians to undertake 'a short study of elocution', warns against 'the continual use of phrases such as: "You see?", "You know!", "Of course", etc.', and commands, 'Avoid those terrible syllables, "ER" and "UM".' Although he suggests that front-cloth comedians should appear to be 'speaking in ordinary conversation', he actually makes it clear that they should speak much more crisply than this:

> Patter doesn't come all at once. Go into an empty room and practise on your own, listening to the sound of your own voice . . . Watch your inflections and see that you do not drop your voice at the end of a sentence or the audience will lose interest. You must learn to speak with clear diction, always see that you pitch your voice so that the people who are farthest away in the audience can hear you.[16]

Listen to recordings of the comics of this era, and you'll tend to hear diction that's clear as a bell. Ted Ray may have worn an ordinary lounge suit onstage to make it look as if he was just one of the audience, but his delivery was polished and formal. He grew up in Liverpool, but there's no trace of a Scouse accent. The northern *u* sound is gone, so that 'umbrella' is pronounced 'ambrella', not 'oombrella'. The *a* sound is rather affected, so that 'chap' becomes 'chep'. The consonants are sharp and punchy, and there's none of the mess of ordinary conversation.[17]

In contrast to this, Mort Sahl's delivery was so much like ordinary conversation that, as Woody Allen observes, 'you thought he was just talking'. Sahl's comedy is often misrepresented. In 1960, *Time* magazine did a piece on him which quotes some of his finest one-liners, and this is often reproduced as a way of giving a flavour of his style. One-liners suggest a honed, minimalist delivery, but Sahl's is nothing like this, and the killer lines which *Time* quotes often emerge from a swamp of conversational messiness.

Sahl is no stranger to the terrible syllable 'ER'. He is perfectly comfortable with using fragmented sentences as he tries to find the best way of explaining something, or to go off at a tangent, and return to the original theme by way of a quick 'Anyway –'. His speech is punctuated with the kind of phrases Lane warns against: 'You know?'; 'See?'; So, now –'; and 'What else?' Sometimes, he punches a gag home with a staccato 'Ha ha!' Arguably, Sahl's greatest achievement, in a whole series of great achievements, is that he showed that everyday speech could be just as effective as elocuted stage speech, if not more so. Certainly, when I listen to recordings of his act from forty years ago, I can't get most of the topical jokes or pick up a lot of the cultural references, but the 'UM's and 'ER's make it sound fresh and immediate.

The range of expression

The mask of deadpan

Today, many stand-ups follow Sahl's example, and adopt everyday rhythms of speech, but there are still many who adopt a more stylised approach. Deadpan comedians are a classic example. The word 'deadpan' suggests an impassive, expressionless manner, with body, voice and face giving very little away. Many stand-ups start their careers by adopting a deadpan delivery, because it offers something to hide behind. Jo Brand, for example, says: 'The way it evolved was just because I was very nervous, and that's how it naturally came out, I didn't plan it like that, it was just the first few kind of open spots that I did, I found myself talking like that. And I didn't really even notice it until people started taking the piss out of it, you know. I got all this stuff about reading the football scores and all that kind of thing.'

Dave Gorman took a similar approach, for similar reasons: 'I was very deadpan when I first started. Which was largely a defence mechanism . . . I've seen so many other people starting in the same way since, where you think, "If I appear not to care, then if it doesn't go very well, it hasn't hurt me. But if I appear to care about this, and it doesn't go very well, then I'm fucked."'

Shazia Mirza was the same, being 'very deadpan' because she was 'very scared'. All three comedians realised the limitations of the style they had adopted. Brand says: 'If you do a series of very deadpan one-liners . . . it's impossible to keep that up for any longer than about twenty minutes without the audience getting bored shitless, to be honest. Because there's something about that rhythm that's slightly sort of narcoleptic.'

Gorman agrees, saying, 'Deadpan acts find it hard to get beyond the forty minutes.' He slowly realised that 'caring about it makes it go better anyway . . . showing them you care about it means you're less likely to die'. Mirza changed her delivery because she felt it was inauthentic: 'The deadpan wasn't me, the gags weren't me and the material wasn't personal. Now that I'm very relaxed onstage and I'm more myself . . . how I am offstage is exactly how I am onstage. And that's exactly how I think it should be.'

For Brand, dropping the deadpan was an important move, and she took concrete actions to achieve it: 'I just felt that I had to loosen up a bit and be a bit more conversational and have a few more strings to my bow, rather than just going de-der-de-der-de-der at people. So the way I did that was I deliberately asked people to put me in as a compère. So that I knew that I would have to sort of talk to the audience, and I would have to kind of be more spontaneous than just doing my set.'

Harry Hill, on the other hand, liked deadpan comedy but found he was incapable of doing it. When he started on the

London comedy circuit, he admired deadpan comics like Stewart Lee, Jack Dee, Norman Lovett, Arnold Brown and Jo Brand: '[T]here's something I do love about that, because it is so dependent on the kind of delivery and the quality of the gags, you know, there's no kind of frills – moving around, you know, pulling funny faces, none of that. So when I started off, I wanted to be like that.' In an endearing admission, he explains why he never achieved the deadpan style: 'I mean, my problem with being a deadpan comedian was I used to smile a lot. I'm a bit too pleased with myself, so, you know, I would laugh at my own jokes.'

Different kinds of deadpan
For some comics, deadpan is more than a mask to hide behind, and it becomes the style they adopt for their whole career. Jack Dee is widely known as a deadpan comedian, but, having said this, his delivery is by no means expressionless. He's probably been given the label because of his miserable, surly, cynical persona. Unlike many stand-ups, he never seems to be making an effort, and rarely shows any obvious sign of warmth towards his audience. His delivery is calm, slow and quiet. His eyes seem cold, his lids slightly lowered. When his face is in repose, the corners of his mouth turn down. But this is only his neutral state onstage; he often moves out of it. Sometimes, his eyes will gleam, or he will smile or even laugh. He screws his face up, or impersonates other people. The laughter he gets from the way he says 'Are you?' in his *Gladiators* routine gives a strong indication of the range and skill of his expression. The subtlety of Dee's performance suggests that, for him, deadpan hasn't been adopted as an artificial style, but is a natural form of expression extending out of his offstage self.

Steven Wright is a very different deadpan. He started performing in American comedy clubs in the late 1970s, and has perfected possibly the most minimalist style in the whole of stand-up comedy. One after another, he delivers a series of short jokes which give a jarringly bizarre view of reality, such as: 'I got up the other day and everything in my apartment had been stolen and replaced with an exact replica. [*laughter*]' Or: 'It's a small world, but I wouldn't wanna paint it. [*laughter*]'[18]

His voice is deep, slightly croaky, and sounds as if overwhelming weariness has robbed it of all expression. There is none of Dee's range, but even here there is still inflection and rhythm, albeit incredibly subtle. He points out that because he is so deadpan, 'everything is magnified', so that even the way he takes a sip of water, or the exact moment he puts his glass back on the stool can make a difference: 'You can take the pause in jokes right to the edge – almost of boredom, and in doing so you create a tension which is palpable.'[19]

Hand puppets and hair squirrels

In reducing expression to a minimum, Wright highlights how much of it other comedians use. It's difficult to describe a moment of stand-up because so much is going on, more than any formal system of transcription could take in, no matter how scientific or precise. There are infinite subtleties of tone of voice, pace of delivery, facial expression, hand gesture and whole body movement. Pretty much the whole of a joke's funniness can be contained in the merest gleam of an eye or the quirky way a particular word is pronounced.

Some comics really explore the full range of human expression. In a performance in the late 1990s, Bill Bailey suddenly forms his hands into beak-like mouths, turning them into puppets. His hands engage in a quickfire argument, the right apparently a dog, the left a cat: 'Rruff! Mew! Rruff! Mew! Rruff! Mew! Rruff! Mew!' The right hand starts slightly higher than the left and, as the argument continues, he forces the left further down. Bailey takes it all in, staring with eyes wide.

Suddenly, the left hand leaps up and springs open, fingers splayed, and the voice Bailey gives it changes from a squeaky 'Mew!' to a loud, guttural 'BLUUUURGGHH!!! YUURGGH!!' The dog hand mutters a muffled, 'Oh, my gawd!' and bounces off, apparently terrified. The cat hand reverts to its normal shape with a 'Bip! Zzhhhhh!', and chuckles to itself. Bailey lowers his hand, and looks at the audience. His eyes gleam with satisfaction and expectation, as if to say, 'Well, that's given you plenty to think about – what did you think of it?'

There are small waves of laughter as the sequence starts and these build as the argument between the hands heats up. There's a full laugh when the dog hand runs away, and another when the left hand transforms back from a monster to a cat. When Bailey looks at the audience at the end, there's a big round of applause. It's amazing how effective a naked hand-puppet show can be.[20]

In his Dartford show, Ross Noble generates a huge amount of energy onstage, sweating through his shirt by the end. He demonstrates what it would be like to be a puppet, being controlled by someone else. Putting his whole body to work, he flops about the stage, and while he may lack a formal training in mime, he's surprisingly convincing in suggesting that he's being manipulated by an external force. In another routine, he starts punching and karate kicking an imaginary panda with real gusto. In yet another he flops his long, curly hair over to one side of his head, and pretends it's a squirrel.

All of this might seem silly, but hand-based puppet shows and hair-based squirrel mimes show that stand-up comedians can do so much more than just stand there and talk.

When comedians laugh

When I was a kid, I remember being told that only bad comedians laugh at their own jokes. I don't know what the thinking behind this was. Maybe the idea was that it makes the comic look conceited. Or perhaps it was seen as a sign of desperation. Certainly, it was a ridiculous thing to say, given the number and variety of highly skilled, successful comedians who do actually laugh at their own jokes, including Gladys Morgan, Tommy Cooper, Ken Goodwin, Billy Connolly, Phyllis Diller, Eddie Murphy and Bill Hicks. In fact, the phenomenon predates stand-up. In music hall, performers like Billy Williams and Randolph Sutton would use a kind of laugh–singing technique, chuckling in a slightly forced way between the verses and even while they sang the lines.

There are plenty of good reasons why stand-ups laugh onstage, but conceit and desperation aren't among them. When the comedian laughs, it signals that something is particularly funny. Billy Connolly often laughs in anticipation of what he's going to say, and this creates expectation in the audience. After all, if Connolly's laughing, it must be pretty funny. When the comic laughs after the punchline, it creates a lovely moment of sharing. Performer and audience are united in their enjoyment of a funny idea.

Laughing onstage also suggests authenticity. It implies a moment where the comedian loses control and seems to allow us a glimpse of the real person. I was never a habitual laugher when I was a stand-up, but there were times when I cracked up onstage, and they were among the most glorious moments I experienced. Laughing is always a pleasure, but to experience that moment of joy and unselfconsciousness in such a public context, and for my laughter to boost the audience's, felt like a very special kind of acceptance.

Particular comedians put their own laughter to more particular uses. Phyllis Diller, for example, has an amazing laugh that can veer from an uncontrolled gurgle to a raucous bark. For her, the laugh is part of her eccentricity, something which glues together the gags and the persona. Her comedy revels in grotesqueness, both her own and that of the world around her, and the laughter is outrageous enough to fit in perfectly. Its sonic properties are such that sometimes simply hearing her go, '*Ah ha ha ha ha ha!!*' is all that's needed to make the audience laugh. She also uses the laugh as punctuation, adding beats to get the rhythm of a line perfect: 'But we still have a lot of fun in here every night, one woman nearly died laughing, *ha ha!* But I'm all right now. [*laughter*]' The 'ha ha!' adds an extra clause to the set-up, giving the sentence a three-part structure. It also cements the idea that Diller is celebrating her own success, thus sharpening the contrast with the downbeat delivery of the punchline.[21]

Eddie Murphy's laugh is a kind of catchphrase. By the time he made his 1983 concert film *Delirious*, his laugh had become his trademark, thanks to appearances on *Saturday Night Live* and a starring role in the previous year's movie *48 Hours*. At the end of a long routine in which Murphy plays a man drunkenly accusing a female relative of being a Bigfoot, there's a big response from the audience and as the cheering, whistling and applause dies down, somebody shouts something. Murphy replies, 'Do that shit again?' and does the laugh. It's a salvo of deep, rasping inhalations, bringing to mind an asthmatic walrus. Just hearing this familiar sound makes the audience laugh, cheer and whistle.

Bill Hicks has a very different kind of laugh: a thin, bitter ironic laugh. Whereas most stand-ups use laughter to highlight how funny something is, Hicks uses it to emphasise how unfunny something is. Sometimes it's a way of demonstrating his bitterness, like when he recalls his girlfriend leaving him and taking the TV, the bed and the VCR with her. Other times it's a way of introducing apparently unpromising subject matter, like abortion. 'Let's talk about mass murder of young, unborn children, see if we can't coalesce into one big, healthy gut laugh,' he says, and lets out a chuckle so mirthless it's almost demonic.[22]

What he says might suggest he opposes abortion, but in fact he goes on to make a scathing comic attack on so-called pro-lifers. The point of talking about 'mass murder of young, unborn children' is to really ram home how unsuitable the subject is for stand-up. By laughing at the very idea of this, Hicks does the opposite of sharing

216

amusement with the audience. When his laugh finishes, there's just silence. It's as if he's emphasising how different he is from the people he's playing to, showing that what he finds funny is very different from what they find funny. Or it could be a joyless admission of how unfunny the world can be. Either way, it's a very unusual strategy for a comedian.

Instant character

There's something that occurs so regularly in stand-up that anybody who has spent any time watching it will recognise it. The comic is telling a gag, recalling an anecdote, talking about a particular person, or describing a fantasy, and in the course of this, he or she lapses into acting it out. This is different from a formal character piece signalled by a change of costume, like Victoria Wood's yellow-bereted Lancashire girl or Stacy Leanne Payne, her hilariously savage parody of cruise singer turned celebrity Jane McDonald. The kind of acting out I'm talking about involves an instant transition from narrator to character, achieved through tone of voice, posture or facial expression. There's a huge variety of characters a stand-up can momentarily become, from the stereotyped Irishman of the formulaic gag, to a celebrity or a politician or just a particular type of person. Even animals and inanimate objects can be characterised.

This is a common mode of performance in stand-up, and most comedians use it in their acts. Eddie Izzard calls it 'the motherlode'. Yet it has so rarely been discussed that it doesn't even have a standard word or phrase to describe it. American comedian Judy Carter calls it 'mimicking'. Tony Allen has labelled it 'snapshot characterisation'. The phrase I coined myself, when working on stand-up with students, is 'instant character'.

The roots of instant character can be found in the kind of acting that takes place in everyday conversation. A book published in the 1920s notes how shop girls often amuse each other by imitating the customers, in a way which 'would delight the heart of a vaudeville audience'.[23] In his classic essay 'The Street Scene', Brecht discusses how witnesses to a traffic accident act out what they saw to explain it more clearly, and sees this as a 'basic model' for his epic theatre. In a footnote, he also talks about comical instant character in everyday conversation, for example when a next-door neighbour takes off 'the rapacious nature of our common landlord'. He notes how this kind of characterisation is inflected with the performer's attitude: 'The imitation is summary or selective, deliberately leaving out those occasions where the landlord strikes our neighbour as "perfectly sensible", though such occasions of course occur. He is far from giving a rounded picture; for that would have no comic impact at all.'[24]

He also notes that such characterisations can be linked together with 'some form of commentary', a description which could equally be applied to a stand-up routine. Some comedians have directly cited such everyday performance as an influence. George Carlin, for example, recalls how his mother would act things out: 'She'd come home from the bus and tell a story about something that just happened, and she could do all five characters.'[25]

Instant character with attitude
Instant character is extremely varied, and can work in a number of different ways. Sometimes, the comedian's attitude is made perfectly clear in the way he or she performs a characterisation. In a routine from the early 1990s, Jack Dee imitates his politically correct neighbour, who wears a badge which says, 'You smoke – I choke.' Dee uses the neighbour's voice to say the words on the badge. He makes the voice infantile and slightly croaky. When he's said the words, to make the point more clearly, he characterises the neighbour's face. The eyes become exaggeratedly sincere, the brow wrinkles with concern, the mouth turns further down at the corners, and he moves his head about slightly

to suggest excessive earnestness. It gets a laugh. He continues: "'You smoke, I choke. [*laughter*] 'S my cause, that is. [*laughter*] You smoke, I go *ahcuh hugh huh huh!*" [*laughter*]' This last bit is Dee's impression of his neighbour's coughing. He curls up his upper lip, screws up his eyes, and emits a pathetic, squeaky cough which sounds like crying. The whole characterisation is shot through with the contempt which Dee feels for this person. It's reminiscent of a school bully imitating somebody to make fun of them, generating a hilarity born of cruelty.

In this case, the attitude encapsulated in the characterisation is a kind of personal, disgruntled cynicism, but in other cases it's more political. In his 2001 *Dambusters* show, Mark Thomas chronicles the successful prank-laden campaign he helped to run against the Ilisu Dam project, which would have wreaked environmental havoc in Turkey and devastated the local Kurdish population. One of the characters whom Thomas brings to life in the story is Lord Weir, the chairman of Balfour Beatty plc, the company which would have built the dam. Weir is introduced with a compact verbal sketch: 'He reeks of alcohol, he carries a stick, he is a ball of gout with a mouth. [*laughter*]' When he makes Weir speak, he gives him the stereotyped voice of a patronising aristocrat. A few jokes down the line, he cranks the characterisation up a few notches into the realm of pure caricature:

> That man should just be followed by a bloke playing the organ, everywhere. [*laughter*] 'Hello, my name's Lord Weir!' *bam-bam-bam-baaaam!* [*laughter*] 'Hurr ha ha harr! I'm a little bit camp, but I'm *very frightening!*' *bam-bam-bam-baaaam!* [*laughter*] 'My name's Lord Weir, I was touched as a boy, it hurt me, but I liked it!' *bam-bam-bam-baaaam!* [*laughter*]

It's a cartoon melodrama, with Thomas imitating both the villain and the *bam-bam-bam-baaaam!* of the organ. The

Lord Weir voice has become irresistibly funny, with a gleeful, gloating tone and a fabulously evil laugh. Thomas points out that his characterisation of Weir is based on actual meetings with the man, but acknowledges his own bias: 'You know, both him and I would see each other in very, very strict cartoon terms . . . Actually I think I said . . . you couldn't have got better if you'd put him in a top hat and given him a cigar, you know. When you say that, you're not only describing him, but you're also making an admission of actually how you're seeing him.'

Both Dee and Thomas do what Brecht's next-door neighbour did when imitating the landlord: they present a selective characterisation which shows their particular view of the people they are imitating. Interestingly, Thomas admits: 'It's fucking rather pretentious, but I was hugely influenced by Brecht.'

Real people
While Dee's neighbour could well be a generic, fictional liberal do-gooder, Thomas's Lord Weir is a real person, and this takes us back to the ethical question of how stand-ups deal with the real world onstage, and particularly how they represent other people. *Dambusters* also features Thomas's friends and colleagues: Nick Hildyard of the campaigning organisation Corner House, and Kerim Yildiz, a Kurdish human rights campaigner and former prisoner of conscience. Unsurprisingly, Thomas's characterisation of these people is far more sympathetic than his sizzling cartoon of Lord Weir. He acknowledges onstage that representing people he loves and finds inspirational is 'really fucking odd'. However, as Thomas points out, even Nick and Kerim are not characterised with literal exactitude: 'They were very funny, because they'd bring along their friends, and their friends were the most interesting things, because they'd say, "Oh – that *was* Nick!" Do you know what I mean, even though Nick said, "It doesn't *sound* like me!" I said, "Well, your accent's quite hard, Nick, but you know,

it's actually not about *sounding* like you. It's about getting what you're like and what you're like in that moment and conveying it. And it doesn't *matter* that I don't enunciate the words *exactly* the same as you. It's a thumbnail sketch that's there to kind of quickly show people roughly what you're like."'

Thomas's version of Kerim bears a slight resemblance to Harry Enfield's 1980s Greek Cypriot kebab shop character Stavros, and comes complete with a catchphrase, 'Was hilarious!' This is liberally deployed in Kerim's anecdotes about his abuse at the hands of the Turkish authorities, his cunning attempts to outwit them, and the problems he experiences with British immigration officials who keep mistaking him for Saddam Hussein. At the end of the first half of the show, Thomas describes how nervous he felt when the real Kerim first saw the impersonation, asking, 'What right have I got to tell his stories?' He brings the moment to a head by giving Kerim's reaction: 'Was hilarious!'

In fact, Thomas's portrayal of Kerim is steeped in affection and respect which he transmits to the audience: 'We did a couple of gigs in Edinburgh, to raise money for Kurdish human rights. And we did a panel afterwards and I introduced Kerim, and he got this amazing round of applause, you know, because they knew him, they felt they knew him, and in many ways they did.'

Richard Pryor fills the stage with his imagination

As various comedians have acknowledged, instant character works not by literally representing people, animals or objects, but by doing just enough with the face, voice and body to paint a picture in the mind of the audience. This makes the stage extraordinarily pliable, capable of being filled with a whole universe of characters, events and sound effects which can be conjured up at the comic's command. Some stand-ups act out whole scenes, which can be extremely rich.

221

In a 1968 routine, Richard Pryor acts out a scene showing a theatre company visiting a prison. He becomes a gruff-voiced guard introducing the company to the prisoners, then a pretentious actor with a pseudo-English accent who explains that the play is about 'a young, Southern girl who falls in love with a black'. Hearing this, the prison guard tries to stop the play, complaining it is 'a little too controversial', but the actor explains, 'It's quite all right, the nigger gets killed.' Then Pryor enacts a play-within-a-routine, playing all the characters: a white patriarch; his son; his daughter; and Ben the blacksmith, an outrageous stereotype of a subservient Southern black man. The play ends with Ben telling the son that he is going to marry his sister, but instead of the expected lynching, the son accepts Ben as his future brother-in-law, explaining, 'We'll be the first in the South to know true freedom and true love.' Outraged at this, the prison guard interrupts the play, demanding the ending he was promised: 'Nobody leave, I wanna dead nigger out here!'[26]

There's an amazing complexity in the levels of fiction in this routine, and the fact that Pryor can become a whole cast of identifiable characters shows his outstanding technical excellence as a performer. His instant character work is simply superb. In a later routine, he talks about hunting in the woods, creating a set of images which range from the delicate to the slapstick. Observing that snakes are so frightening that they make you run into trees, he brings this to life, by quickly turning his body and walking into his hand, which he has raised to head height to indicate the tree trunk. 'Pah!' he says, voicing the impact of face against wood, and the audience laugh at the knockabout image he's created so simply.

Later, he shows a deer drinking water, by bending his body forward, side on from the audience, and lapping with his mouth. For an instant, he becomes the hunter again, making the leaves crunch as he steps forward. Then he's the deer again, snapping upright, facing the audience and staying absolutely still. His frightened eyes move from left to right, and there's a big laugh and some applause at the accuracy of the image. He extends the moment, getting waves of laughter by making the deer narrow its eyes suspiciously, look behind itself and tip its head to one side with a suspicious look on its face.[27] What makes this so effective is that he does so little to create such a vivid comic image. Just as in the acting that Brecht envisaged, the performer is just as clearly present as the character he is representing, with the picture of the deer superimposed on Pryor's body.

Cinematic technique

The scope of the scenes which comedians act out in their stand-up acts is increased by the fact that modern audiences are familiar with cinematic convention. This means they are easily able to cope with a sudden scene change. Lenny Bruce would directly refer to the language of cinema when acting out his routines. In his appearance on *The Steve Allen Show*, 5 April 1959, Bruce performs a routine about a boy building a model aeroplane and getting high on the glue. He exclaims, 'I'm the Louis Pasteur of junkiedom!' and plans to exploit his discovery. Then Bruce changes the scene: 'Cut to the toy store.' In the toy store, we see another child asking for various items before getting to what he's really come to buy: two thousand tubes of airplane glue. The simple device of using the cinema term 'cut to' allows an easy transition. His next routine is a parody of a Hollywood issue movie, and he uses a similar device, switching between scenes with the phrase, 'Now we dissolve to the exterior of the schoolyard.'

Today, audiences are so familiar with the idea of instant-character scenes in stand-up that such obvious devices are no longer necessary to effect a transition. Ross Noble describes how he works when he's acting something out: '[Y]ou're actually making people visualise what's happening, obviously with your own physicality . . . Setting up things on the stage, and then obviously sort of playing around with people's perspective of what's happening . . . Like when I was doing . . . the Jesus thing . . . One minute, Jesus is on the ground, looking right up . . . to that guy up the top there . . . and then by just standing and, like, looking down, instantly the people watching the stage go from there, all of a sudden . . . the camera's gone up there.'

Running characters

Sometimes, stand-ups create instant characters which take on a life of their own, reappearing in show after show. In Richard Pryor's 1983 concert film *Here and Now*, he finishes a routine, then wanders over to the microphone stand and stool. The expression on his face changes, and he starts to talk in a different voice: 'You know – when I first –' He pauses, chewing imaginary tobacco. The audience applaud cheer and whistle.

This response might mystify anybody unfamiliar with Pryor's earlier work, but the audience are showing their recognition of a familiar character. Mudbone, an old Southern black man with a penchant for tall tales, was brought into Pryor's act in the 1970s, and unlike, say, Victoria Wood's running characters, he is conjured up without the aid of a costume change. A hesitant, barking voice, an infirm posture, and a chewing motion with the mouth is all that it takes, and by the time *Here and Now* is filmed, the audience can recognise him from the smallest cues.

Similarly, Jim Davidson has a named running character which he produces with just a change of voice. Davidson's character is also supposed to be black, but unlike Mudbone, Chalkie is very much a white person's crude stereotype. His voice is instantly recognisable: a cartoonish West Indian accent, in a strangulated tone, with a pitch slightly higher than that of Davidson's normal voice. As well as cropping up regularly in Davidson's act, Chalkie may have had a life beyond it. Certainly, Jimmy Jones, another comic who emerged from the working-men's clubs, used exactly the same Chalkie voice when he imitated West Indians in the 1970s; and Tony Allen remembers seeing many acts doing similar characters when he made forays into the club scene at the end of that decade.[28]

Voicing the audience

One very useful function of instant character is to allow the comic to comment on how he or she is being received by the audience. Bill Hicks does this in his savage routine in which he asks people who work in advertising and marketing to kill themselves. He takes on the character of the ad men he imagines are in the audience, and voices their responses to his suggestion. Ben Elton uses a similar technique. After a rude word or an obscene reference, he puts on an uptight voice with a poshed-up northern accent which vaguely resembles that of Mary Whitehouse, and protests: 'Well, Mr Elton, frankly that was a lovely observed piece of satire and suddenly you had to bring your penis into it, [*laughter*] I don't know why!'[29] Mark Thomas does much the same thing after a brief reference to 'fistfucking', but in this case, he imagines different kinds of reaction, using first a posh, uptight voice, then a shaky, slightly seedy one: 'Ha ha, there's some of you out there, just going, "I, I didn't know it was going to be like *this*, darling, I really – [*laughter*] Fistfucking in the first two minutes? Marvellous!" [*laughter*] And then there's half a dozen of you in there going, "I've got a website that I need to tell 'im about," [*laughter*] so the, um –'[30]

Voicing the audience's thoughts is a common technique, and it's useful in various ways. It allows comedians to anticipate and neutralise any potential bad reactions to what they're saying. It's another way of drawing attention to their own performance processes, which is an effective trick in stand-up. Also, by showing that the comedian understands how the audience might be reacting, he or she demonstrates control of the situation, as well as strengthening the rapport between stage and auditorium.

Another useful function of instant character is simply to allow the comic to show off. Acting out different scenes, performing simple mime, and demonstrating a range of voices and vocal sound effects allow comedians to show the range of performance they're capable of. If a particular characterisation is performed with enough energy and panache, it can get a round of applause in its own right, regardless of the gag or comic idea it is tied to.

Examples of this range from African-American comedian Jimmy Walker demonstrating for the white punters the way the MC at the Harlem Apollo would introduce him; to Lenny Henry doing a full verse and chorus of Prince's 'Kiss' on the slender pretext of this being what he felt like doing when he played the Mandela concert at Wembley Stadium; to Al Murray's crazed impression of a Frenchman repeatedly shouting, 'I call myself Marcel!' In each case, while there are laughs along the way, it is the sheer chutzpah that has the biggest impact. The comic pushes and pushes the characterisation, driving the energy up, and when the piece ends, the audience explode into applause.

Emotional depth

Perhaps the most extraordinary use of instant character is when comedians act a scene to show us the most terrifying, painful experiences they have been through. Billy Connolly re-enacts an incident from his childhood, on holiday in Rothesay. Connolly becomes his father, instructing his younger self to take a family photograph on the Box Brownie camera. Then he becomes himself as a child, small and vulnerable, but canny enough to know what will happen if he messes it up. Frozen by the pressure, the young Connolly struggles until his father beats him around the head.

It's a brilliant piece of performance. The father is a rounded character, not a two-dimensional monster. His first words are kind and paternal, and the bad temper and violence emerge bit by bit. Connolly's re-creation of his own childish wailing is a hilarious yodel, which gets gales of laughter in its own right. As he gets more upset, this changes to 'Buddhist chanting mode', a guttural, rhythmic grunt: '*Mm-nm-ng-mn-mn-nm-ningh-nun-yun-nggh-nn-naiyayyyy-deewaydutt!!*' This draws out more big laughs. It's the detail of the acting which does most of the work. The scene Connolly paints with his voice and body is vivid and upsetting, and it's a testament to his skill that he transforms it into something which the audience can laugh at.[31]

Richard Pryor effects a similar transformation by re-enacting his heart attack. Twisting his right fist in the centre of his chest, he makes his heart talk in a fierce, threatening voice: 'Thinkin' 'bout dyin' now, aintcha?' His own voice is a frantic, panic-stricken falsetto: 'Yeah, I'm thinkin' 'bout dyin', I'm thinkin' 'bout dyin'!! [*laughter*]' The angry heart replies: 'You didn't think about it when you was eatin' all that *pork*! [*laughter*]'

'Pork' is emphasised with another twist of the fist, and Pryor keels over from his knees to his back, writhing on the floor, his eyes wrinkled hard shut, his mouth wide open in a silent scream. It's a truly amazing moment, because while Pryor recreates his agony across the floor of the stage, the audience's laughter erupts into a storm of applause and whistling. A man is reliving a physical trauma that could easily have killed him, and the audience is ecstatic.[32]

The ability of comics like Connolly and Pryor to present something so naked and raw, to act it out so well, and to turn it into something funny is truly remarkable. Stand-up comedy is thought of as merely popular entertainment, but I defy anybody to find anything more daring and profound in the realm of theatre and performance than in routines like these.

Clearly, stand-up can have an emotional range that goes far beyond just getting laughs. Sometimes comedians can provoke unexpected responses. Phill Jupitus has a bit where he talks about his fear of spiders. Obviously, this is not in the same league of trauma as being beaten as a child or having a heart attack, but Jupitus still conjures up an evocative scene. He talks about helping to move some furniture in the cellar with his father-in-law and encountering an enormous arachnid. At one point, the father-in-law picks it up. Slowing the pace for dramatic effect, Jupitus says: 'The *legs* of this spider –' Then he splays the fingers of both hands, and slowly intertwines them, staring intently at what he's doing. There's an audible groan, as the audience anticipate the unpleasant image he's going to create. He clenches the fingers of his left hand, and wiggles the fingers of his right. The audience laugh, acknowledging how vividly his simple mime is showing the wriggling legs of the spider emerging from his father-in-law's fist. Then he finishes his sentence: '– stickin' out from 'is knuckles.'[33] The groan is as interesting as the laugh, because it shows that Jupitus is doing more than just amusing his audience. He remembers: 'I did have a woman burst into tears and run out of the show in Edinburgh when I did that bit.'

One of the things Mark Thomas likes about doing shows such as *Dambusters* is that it allows him to explore a bigger emotional range: 'I've found the nice thing about doing kind of longer shows, like two-hour shows, is that you get a chance to go through all sorts of different moods. You can take audiences into places they didn't expect to go.'

The end of that show certainly takes the audience to such a place. He talks about going to a restaurant in Turkey while he was working on the campaign against the dam. On the next table are a judge, a prosecutor and an intelligence officer, all of whom he knows are important in helping to carry out the Turkish state's persecution of the Kurds, even though they are dressed like golfers. He realises that he can't confront these people without endangering the people he's with. This makes him start to remember all of the Kurds he's spoken to, and the stories they have told him. It's an urgent, furious rant, detailing appalling human rights abuses:

Each and every one! From the mothers of the disappeared who sit there in Ankara – *Women* – who have, all their crime – is to stand on the street, with photographs of their loved ones, who have been disappeared – as in Chile, as in Argentina, as in El Salvador – and they will tell you – how the police *beat* them – *each* and *every* week when they stand there with their photograph. And you sit there, and you go, 'Fuck, that's incredible!' and they lift their shawl, and you can *see* – their necks and their shoulders *are black and blue*!

The list continues, going through torture techniques, Kurds forced to walk across a minefield by the Turkish authorities, and women raped by the military. It's a terrible, gut-wrenching experience hearing the real stories Thomas has been told, and his anger takes him to the verge of tears as he gets to the end. 'And I wanted to kill those golfers!!' he shouts. 'I'm fuckin' pacifist and I wanted to kill those golfers!' He briefly describes a revenge fantasy with a woman emerging from the fountain in the middle of the restaurant and shooting them dead. Then his anger is spent. In the aftermath, he is quiet and shaken. The show ends with him imagining the woman from the restaurant telling him to go back to Britain and 'tell them everything'. 'And I haven't even really touched the surface,' he admits, his voice aching with regret. Throughout this whole sequence, there's a taut silence in the audience, which stretches across the long, long pauses he takes.[34]

Achieving this level of anger at the end of the show was important to Thomas: 'Just from a performance point of view, every night, there are two things that I did. And one of them was to rejig that kind of long list of atrocities. So I'd remind myself of things that I might not've mentioned the night before, and kind of include them, and just kind of put them in my mind, that they would be there.'

Crucially, there is nothing to relieve the anger. There is no gag to let the audience off the hook, to release the tension in a huge laugh. The only relief comes from the resounding applause. When I saw the show in Canterbury, the people pouring out of the theatre at the end looked subdued and shaken. The political effect of choosing to end the show in this way is clear: the issue is left burning in the minds of the audience, making it difficult to forget. The artistic effect is to prove once again how elastic the boundaries of stand-up comedy are, and show how far it can go beyond its basic remit of getting a laugh.

8. *How It's Done*

Magic

Stand-up comedy happens by magic. Comedians are born with a fully developed comic talent, and the first time they ever perform in front of an audience, they are greeted with gales of laughter. There are different theories to explain this. Some people believe that the comic emits psychic beams which cause involuntary laughter in anybody they pass through; others think that stand-ups have a symbiotic relationship with miniature, invisible beings, or 'Comedy Pixies', which fly around the auditorium tickling the entire audience.

Perhaps I have somewhat overstated the case?

What certainly is true is that many comedians believe they are born with their talent. Woody Allen says he learnt the basics of stand-up very quickly because of instincts he was born with. Jerry Seinfeld believes he was born with the ability to find potential material in his everyday experiences. Dan Aykroyd has argued that Richard Pryor was born with his talent, that it is in his chemistry, in his blood. Ken Dodd has implied that his own comic ability is a gift from God, and his career as a comedian part of a divine mission: 'I get absolutely wonderful reactions from people, you get some marvellous feedback from the people you've entertained, and you think, "Good God", and I mean *Good God*, "Did I really, was I really able to help that person?" . . . that makes me feel . . . perhaps I've got a reason then, I've got a purpose in life, I'm not just a dot, not just a speck.'[1]

Alexei Sayle has fun with the idea that comedy comes from a magical ability in his 1987 graphic novel *Geoffrey the Tube Train and the Fat Comedian*. There's a footnote about a fictional music-hall comic called Albert 'Oo wants to see me luvverley cockles' Magoogle, who lost his ability during a performance at the Bristol Hippodrome, when 'a small pink light was seen to exit from his right ear'. In spite of this, though, Sayle still believes there is 'something which is indefinable' about comic ability, and argues that some comedians have 'funny bones' and others don't.

Superstition

It's also true that comedians tend to be superstitious, and the phenomenon of lucky clothes seems to be very common. Bill Bailey says he has done all his best gigs in the same black shirt: 'It's falling to bits, but I'm loath to let it go. It's got my superpowers in it.' When he first started, Mark Thomas used to wear a 'crap suit' in a 'subconscious homage to Alexei Sayle . . . And it was really rank, it was really bad. But I couldn't do the gig unless I was wearing the suit.' Rhona Cameron still likes to wear suits, which is the latest stage of an ongoing relationship with lucky clothes: 'I used to have certain clothes I could never deviate from in the early years. I've never been able to, lately, ever go onstage without a suit. I would find that unbearable. I've only just progressed to a different type of shoe. I used to have, in all the years of the circuit I had, like, the one pair of socks I'd wear, I'd rinse them out at night and wear them again the next night. And the same with pants as well.'

For Andre Vincent, it's more a question of what he must avoid wearing: 'I'm a bit anti-green. I went through a point where I seemed to really stink a room up if I wore green. Yeah. I had like, years ago, really early stages . . . I had these really lovely green silk trousers . . . really lovely Italian pleated green trousers, and they looked great. I did two gigs in 'em. Just died on my hole. And I got a bit sort of like, "It's green, it's green, it's gotta be green." And I'm still slightly, every now and again, you know, if I'm wearing green, if I've got green in there, and something doesn't get a laugh, that's where my head goes. My head goes, "It's cos you got green on." And it's ridiculous. It's absolutely ridiculous.'

Superstitions can be attached to anything. I once died horribly when I was on with a particular comedian, and I was never at my best whenever I shared a bill with him after that. I thought of him as a jinx. Rhona Cameron used to always write out her set list before every show, even though the material hadn't changed, and keep it in her pocket as a 'security blanket': 'And [I] would often even set out the page in a certain way and I would rarely deviate from it, because I think you do think you end up being attached to kind of mini-forms of compulsive disorder, and ritualistic stuff, because it's comforting.'

The most superstitious comedian I've talked to is Jo Brand, who impressed me with the number of superstitions she's had (including touching wood, an obsession with numbers and lucky socks), and the specificity of one of her rituals: '[W]hen I first started, I had a really storming gig one night, and I just happened to have a bit of green toilet paper in my pocket, and of course after that I just thought that I've got to have some wherever I go. And then of course if I couldn't find any green, it was like, "Arrgh! . . . I'm gonna die. It's gonna be awful." . . . it was green toilet paper, there were nine bits, right, like nine sections, so I thought that's what I had to have, so I did that for *ages*, you know. Probably for a couple of years. Always had some in my pocket. Religiously. And then I think one night, there was just no way of getting any green, so I used white, and it seemed to work all right.'

Brand realised that this kind of behaviour was 'irrational' and that she had to wean herself off it. She eventually succeeded: 'I have to say . . . now it's become more like a

job, I don't feel quite so much that I have the need to . . .
cling on to those sort of magical crutches in the way that I
used to.' Rhona Cameron came to a similar realisation
about her clothing ritual: '[T]he one time you break it, you
realise it's nothing to do with that.' Shazia Mirza, who
started her career having to wear the same pair of trousers,
was another who weaned herself off such superstitions: 'I
thought, "No, it's silly," and I had to throw them away, and
I'm glad I've thrown them away, because I thought to
myself, "Oh, maybe I won't be funny if I stop wearing these
trousers," which is silly really, because I should be funny
whatever I wear. And so I threw them away and I realised I
don't need things like that.'

Why the rituals?
Stand-up comedy seems to work almost like magic, so,
naturally, many performers become attached to rituals and
superstitions. What gives the idea of comedy-as-magic
weight is that funniness is not an inherent property; it's
elusive, slippery, difficult to pin down. While we can
identify certain structures in a joke that make it work,
ultimately it's only funny if you find it funny. The thing that
transforms an ordinary incongruity into a joke is faith. The
audience must *believe* it is funny. Given that laughter is
driven by something as invisible and delicate as faith, it is
not surprising that those who have to get laughs for a living
surround themselves in mystique, and are seen as pos-
sessing a mysterious genetic or God-given power.

However, there is a counter-argument. Tony Allen has
called the 'natural gift' behind the comedian's art a 'myth'.
For Jeremy Hardy, successful stand-up is based on learned
techniques: 'I do think stand-up is excessively revered. I
think it's just talking. I think it's part of the oral tradition,
it's the same skills as a Hyde Park ranter or a barrister or a
teacher, lecturer, priest, *seanchai* as it's called in Irish. It's
platform speaking, and that's a skill, but it's a skill that's
needed in lots of occupations. There's all kinds of tricks in

stand-up, but I don't particularly respect them because they are tricks.'

Lupino Lane was making a similar argument, as early as 1945, in *How to Become a Comedian*:

> If there is such a thing as a born comedian, why, for instance, does a brilliant person like Leslie Henson have to spend hours creating comic ideas and gags? Why does my old boyhood friend Charles Chaplin take months to make a picture? . . . Surely, if these were naturally born comedians, they wouldn't have to worry: it would just happen to them.

Arguments against the idea of comedy-as-magic reveal something important that often tends to get lost in the mystique: that there is some kind of process behind what we see onstage in a stand-up comedy act. While it may be true that what distinguishes a great comedian from a competent one is indefinable, and there must be an element of native talent involved, there is also a methodology at work, which has been learned by experience. This chapter is a whistle-stop tour through the processes that lie behind a stand-up comedy act.

Creating material

Bob Hope's joke factory

Very rarely does a comedian deliver a whole act off the top of his or her head. Some preparation is involved, and the jokes have to come from somewhere. Once upon a time, there was no real expectation for comedians to write their own material. Those who could afford to employed writers; those who could not would beg, borrow or steal their gags. In both vaudeville and variety, small-time comics would steal material from each other, from the better-known acts, or from humorous magazines and joke books. Once the material was assembled into an act, the same act could be performed for decades. Indeed, vaudeville managements were fearful about comedians trying out new gags, preferring them to stick to tried and tested routines guaranteed to get laughs. On the other hand, in Britain, George Black, who did so much to prolong the life of the variety circuit, took comedians to task for stealing jokes or refusing to spend money on new material.

Some comics did pay scriptwriters. At the bottom end of the market were writers who provided books or sheets of jokes. Further up, there were small-time comedy writers like Bill McDonnell, a Scots maths teacher who between 1941 and 1953 sold 725 items to acts such as Alec Finlay and Suzette Tarri. The items he sold included complete acts with song and patter, or sets of gags for ad lib use, and the rights for these would differ according to whether they were to be used on radio or for live performances. In America, top comedians like Bob Hope would employ teams of writers. Over the years, he employed eighty-eight of them, keeping as many as thirteen in his team at any one time. Towards the end of his life, his staff writers earned between $150,000 and $250,000 a year, but the terms of employment were such that the gags they produced became Hope's intellectual property. He continued to employ a couple of writers even when age and infirmity stopped him from performing, and he has left behind a massive archive, containing about a million jokes.

When the sick comedians started breaking through in the 1950s, they promoted the idea that comics should create their own material. For Lenny Bruce, performers whose material was provided by writers were 'fine comedy actors', but only those who wrote their own gags could be called comedians. Today, there are still acts who work with writers, but it has become much more normal for comedians to come up with their own jokes and routines. The way they go about doing this differs from comic to comic.

Writing it down

Some stand-ups literally write their acts. For them, jokes do not arrive in the moment, while performing for an audience, but are written in advance. Jenny Éclair, for example, says, 'Every word is totally scripted.' Woody Allen would sit and write his act on a typewriter, based on ideas for gags which he noted down on scraps of paper. Ben Elton says: 'To me, performing is an extension of writing. Everything for me starts with the words, the writing. I write my act just as I write a novel, or . . . sitcoms . . . or whatever.' He writes his material, learns it and performs it, even seeing the improvisation which is an essential part of stand-up as 'sort of writing on the spur of the moment'.[2]

In other cases, comedians work with something looser than this. Lenny Bruce would note down ideas on match-book covers, napkins or memos pads. The notes he kept suggest a neater, more clipped style than the free-flowing routines he specialised in. A set of notes for performances in St Louis and Chicago in September 1959 is largely made up of short jokes or one-liners, some of them apparently only partly formed, like: 'No use for H in Italian alphabet.' Or: 'Chicago people have a strange way of talking – they're always looking for someone who isn't there.'[3]

Rhona Cameron says: 'I'd have a list, like a shopping list. A lot of comedians are list-based.' This seems to be the case. Eddie Izzard's script takes the form of a 'set list': 'It just says "European History" and I go into it. And sometimes, on different nights, I'll do totally different material on the same idea.'[4] For Omid Djalili, planning a routine is 'almost like theatre blocking', and it's written out as a set of bullet points: 'When I have a bullet point, I have a general ball-park idea that has to be put across before a joke.'

Billy Connolly says he has 'really fought the idea of coming on as an act. You know, having an act.' Instead, he writes down a series of headlines on a piece of paper. At his Hammersmith Apollo show, he has his notes on a stool, next to his glass of water. He makes no attempt to hide them, and indeed, they become part of the act. At one point, he knocks over the water, and gets laughs by playing on the idea that this is a disaster, making the ink run so that he can't read what he's written. He also plays up struggling to remember what the notes are supposed to mean. '"Sex"?' he says. 'What have I got to tell you about that?'

This illustrates just how flimsy the existence of stand-up material can be, outside the actual moment of performance. That's why the notebooks which comedians keep are so important to them. Bob Monkhouse kept his material in two loose-leaf files. When they disappeared from his car in 1995, there was significant press coverage, and he offered £10,000 for their safe return. They had been stolen by someone who eventually approached Monkhouse's agent demanding money, and were recovered by undercover police in a sting operation. Monkhouse was mystified as to why they had been stolen, saying that the files were 'of little use to anyone else but me', presumably because the information they contained would have made sense only to him. However, what the culprits had realised was that even if these files of raw comic material were valuable only to Monkhouse, to him their value was immense.[5]

The way that the notebook or gag file fits into the comedian's overall methodology varies. For Alexei Sayle, it was something in which to deposit raw ideas: 'The way I worked was that I never scripted it as such . . . I would think of a gag, and then I would make a note of it. I would make a note of it in me notebook.' Material from the notebook would then be put into a list which he would have onstage with him: 'I always had a running order. I had, like, a little box with me props in on the floor, which was sort of vaguely built to look like a sound monitor, and taped to the top of it was always me running order.'

Harry Hill has a more involved relationship with the 'books and books' of notes he generates: 'What I used to do was, I always used to try and spend the first hour of the day doing it [writing notes]. You know, get up, sit down, do it for an hour, cos I think it's the best time. Then gradually, as I've had kids and all the rest of it, that's all gone out the window, but I try to do it every day, really.' He acknowledges that most of what he writes in the books is 'just rubbish, utter rubbish', so he has a process of sifting through it. Over the course of a year, he generates three or four notebooks, and to prepare for a tour he goes through them making notes of the ideas he thinks are 'worth trying'. He will then take these and try them out in a low-key gig. The ones that go down well become the material of the show.

Off the top of the head

At the other end of the spectrum are those comedians who come up with material while they are actually performing. This method was popular among the sick comedians. Mort Sahl, for example, remembers: 'If they'd laughed at something, I would extend it from night to night. In other words I'd write it in front of them. The joke'd grow, like a house, but you couldn't write it by yourself, you had to be there with them.'[6] Shelley Berman says that of all the routines he recorded, only one was written down on paper. The rest are 'stuff that happened on the spur of the moment, and maybe had gone through some refinement in the repeating, but they began purely as improv'.

There are still many comedians who work in this way. Adam Bloom says: 'I go onstage with a rough idea of what I'm gonna say and then it evolves onstage. I never, ever write it down.' Similarly, James Campbel: 'Almost all of my material comes about through mucking about on the stage. And the stuff that works is the stuff that sticks, and goes on to the next day, basically . . . I never write anything down beforehand.'

Phill Jupitus gives a detailed account of exactly how he grows his material onstage: 'I think that there's the nut of the joke. I think the joke is one idea, it's like the joke is the punchline, and it's the route there that you let unfold onstage, really. And when you first do it, the route's very short. And then if it goes really well, you make the route longer, and you find more. You just find a longer and longer way to get to the end of a joke. So it's like the *Star Wars* show that I did in Edinburgh started out as me saying to [fellow comedian] Kevin Day in the dressing room, "I will do some stuff about *Star Wars*." . . . And I think I had a Wookiee impression and a joke about Darth Vader. And then the next week, because you've thought about it a bit more, you have a few more bits, and if they're good and they work, I would just remember them . . . It would grow very organically . . . so within three months, that couple of one-liners is a whole twenty minutes.'

Some comics use a mixture of techniques to generate material, some routines being scripted in advance, others developed in front of a live audience. Mark Thomas, for example, says: 'Some stuff, I'll write. And you sit down and . . . you worry about it and you kind of try it one way and then you try it another way and what have you. Other stuff, because it's based around events that actually happened, and people who are there who are real . . . it's like telling a story to your mates or to people who don't know. And quite a large section of stuff is busked . . . you just kind of tell the story, and in the process of telling it, bits drop out, or bits add in, and you play around with things.'

For Milton Jones, the particular form his material takes is crucial: 'The stuff that I tend to do tends to be very honed. And even an intonation can mess it up.' He gets it to a honed state by taking it through 'lots of incarnations' before he finds the words he wants. The final part of the process falls somewhere between scripting and improvisation: 'What I tend to do is write what I think the exact wording should be, and then not take that to the show, and see what it comes out like. So I've rehearsed it as I think it should be, but there's something about facing an audience that suddenly means you turn it round, or use fewer words, or you see it from the audience's point of view, because of the adrenalin, for some reason.'

The dangers of roll-over

When comedians reach a certain level, they stop playing short sets in comedy clubs, and start touring their own show. This adds an extra dimension to the process of generating material, because when a new tour starts, rather than having to come up with a new routine or a few new gags, the comic has to put together an entirely new full-length show. One way of approaching this problem is to use what Eddie Izzard calls 'this roll-over thing'. This involves starting a tour with the old show, then gradually changing it bit by bit. For Victoria Wood, this means replacing old bits with new twenty-minute sections week by week until the new show is complete.

Jo Brand likes the security of keeping a bit of old material in the show: 'I always have to have an overlap, a sort of, a bit of old stuff to make me feel safe, that I know's gonna work, you know. And then build on that. So most shows I do tend to be, like, three-quarters new stuff, eventually, and a quarter of an hour of old stuff which I've just kind of clung on to, really. Like a drowning man.'

Ross Noble achieves a smooth transition from one show to the next by constantly touring. In a twelve-month period between 2003 and 2004, he took in the Edinburgh Fringe, a month in a West End theatre, a UK tour, a few months in Australia, and finished in New Zealand. His improvisational technique means that by the end of this process, the show is completely different from when it started: 'Obviously, it's just evolving all the time . . . I just made sure that while it was in New Zealand, I just changed the show completely, so that . . . basically, no one in England had seen . . . any of the [material]. So you just bring it back and you go, "Right – here it is!" In this way, he avoids the danger of the roll-over method: presenting an audience with material they have already seen.

Calling this a 'danger' might seem a bit strong but, in 1999, the consumer programme *Weekend Watchdog* was contacted by punters complaining that Eddie Izzard's *Circle* show largely consisted of material they had seen on the previous year's *Dress to Kill* video. His promoter admitted that 80 per cent of the material was the same as in the video, but said that by the end of the tour this should be reduced to 25 per cent. Later, his tour manager claimed that Izzard had received a warning letter from the Office of Fair Trading over the complaints. Clearly, stand-up has come a long way from the era of variety and vaudeville, when comedians could get away with touring the same act for years.

The show

Planning a show

Jo Brand plans her shows section by section: '[F]or a longer show which is an hour, I roughly kind of divide it in my head into twelve five-minute chunks. And I think, "Well, if I can write . . . six of those, and then that's kind of half an hour." Then hopefully I can expand on a couple of them and they'll expand into seven or eight minutes, maybe, and then I'll see how I'm doing.'

Although Ross Noble's material is more fluid and improvisational, he also tends to build his shows from separate chunks, albeit fewer of them: 'What tends to happen is, I've noticed that when I've looked back at previous notebooks, each kind of two-hour, two-and-a-half-hour show I've done seems to always consist of eight words.'

For some comics, the fluidity is part of the structure of the show. In Billy Connolly's Hammersmith Apollo show, he starts telling an anecdote about something that happened to him in Dunedin, New Zealand. He strikes off on a number of lengthy tangents, and each time he returns to the story ('So, we're in Dunedin . . .'), the audience laugh and sometimes clap. It's a technique he shares with a number of other performers, from Eddie Izzard to Henry Rollins, and it's difficult to say why it's so pleasing. Perhaps it's the incongruity of having drifted so far from the story. Perhaps it makes the audience feel clever at being able to tune back into the anecdote so easily. Perhaps the tangents are seen as part of the comedian's endearingly chaotic way of thinking. Whatever it is, although it might seem like sloppiness, the ability to dip in and out of a routine in this way shows an impressive mastery of the material.

Steven Wright uses a different kind of fluidity. His act is made up of a large number of short jokes. It is structured not by having a fixed running order, but by having a set of jokes which are brought out in the order he sees fit, depending on how the audience are reacting. Dividing the gags up into three categories, A, B and C, according to quality, he alternates between the different categories in response to the laughter he gets.[7] Milton Jones has a different way of categorising his jokes: 'If I do ABC, it tends to be more in terms of formula. Because, you know, some stuff I do, it's either a pun or a reversal or a concept, but if you do too many of the same formula in a row, the crowd find it easier to guess what's coming . . . suddenly the scaffolding is there, and you see how the thing is put together.'

Rehearsing

When I used to compère the Last Laugh comedy club, I would always spend half an hour going through my material out loud to myself. This would allow me to finalise the structure of the gags I was going to start the show with, to get an idea of the actual words I would use, and to fix them in my memory. It was a deeply unpleasant, enervating process, bringing down upon me an almost irresistible urge to collapse in a heap. Although I was alone in the room, I would always imagine someone was outside, listening, finding what I was saying the unfunniest thing they had heard in their life. Preparing to perform my twenty-minute set at another venue would be less unpleasant. I would write out a running order and, later, I'd run through it in my head while driving to the gig. I had no idea if I was the only comedian who rehearsed in this way, as I never really discussed the matter with other performers.

The front-cloth comics of the variety era would certainly have rehearsed. In spite of his aim of coming across as being as natural and unaffected as if he was one of the audience who had climbed on to the stage from the front stalls, Ted Ray prepared meticulously for performance: 'Every night, hour after hour, I would stand in front of the mirror in my bedroom, grimacing, smiling and winking with the idea of getting the most effective expression for putting over a joke . . . Every inflection of voice and every shade of emotion as reflected in a comedian's voice do count tremendously and I was determined that if hard work and ceaseless rehearsal would help, no trouble on my part would be too great.'[8]

Frankie Howerd, who, like Ray, strove for a greater naturalness of delivery, also rehearsed meticulously. A 1990 documentary shows him wandering through fields near his home, obsessively going through pages of script, while surrounded by grazing cows. This seems somewhat at odds with the apparent spontaneity of his stammering style of delivery.

Many present-day comedians do some form of rehearsal outside the performance. In its subtlest form, this is a purely mental process. Jeremy Hardy, for instance, says, 'I try and run through things in my head, but I don't rehearse saying things.' Adam Bloom takes the same approach: '[I]t's all in my head. I have an idea, I think of it to myself. It bounces round in my head. So I'm hearing my voice in my head.' For Rhona Cameron, rehearsal is simply a matter of getting the material to stick in her memory: 'I would have the list a few days before the gig on a huge piece of paper, poster size, at the end of my bed or when I'm lying in the bath, Blu-tacked to the wall, because you have to memorise the list.'

Other comics rehearse by talking the material through. This is how Omid Djalili gets new jokes ready: 'I write them out then perform it to myself. Never in a mirror, but just say it out to myself and just visualise myself onstage.' Milton

Jones takes a similar approach: 'I rehearse in so far as I sit at my desk and I go through the words. But I don't stand with a microphone at a mirror, as it were . . . But I do feel like I need . . . the *muscle memory* of going through the words.' Both Djalili and Jones mention not using a mirror, implying that their process of rehearsal is less involved than Ted Ray's was.

When Alexei Sayle was doing stand-up regularly, he would primarily work on new material with an audience, improvising and working in new routines as he went along. Later in his career, he would only perform in big tours, and this meant having to rehearse offstage: 'The last few tours . . . I'd rehearse in front of my wife. We'd be sitting there, in the conservatory, you know, in the front room or something, and I'd do the show for her . . . Her and the cat would sit there, and I'd do the act, you know.'

This conjures up a pleasingly bizarre image, given Sayle's unique performance style: all that surreal comic fury raining down on his wife and cat in the conservatory. It also raises an important point. Whereas most actors are guided through the process of creation by a director, stand-ups nearly always have to find their own way. In some cases, they look for informal direction from someone close to them acting as an outside eye. Sayle is careful to explain just how important his wife was in this respect: 'I've always said my wife Linda is as responsible for my career as I am . . . because it's very difficult to find somebody who knows . . . what works, and also will be honest with you.' She was helpful not just in the rehearsal process, but also in performance: 'When I came offstage, for my first encore, she would remember the whole show, and she would tell me anything I'd left out . . . We never actually . . . discussed it, it's just she fell into doing that . . . She would say, "You haven't done that bit" . . . and I'd go out and do it in the first encore.'

Similarly, Omid Djalili uses his wife as a sounding board for new material: 'I try it to my wife. I tell my wife, "What do you think of this?" and she often finds a better word. I think it's good to collaborate with other people where you can find a correct word, a funny-sounding word.' He credits her with coming up with the word 'halitosis' for the joke about associating people from the Middle East with oil, phlegm and halitosis. Originally, he had used 'bad breath'.

Test gigs

Other comics rehearse by performing small-scale, low-key test gigs. Mark Thomas developed the material for *Dambusters* during a ten-week run at the Soho Theatre: '[O]ver the ten weeks, the stories just changed and developed and tweeted. But the essential ingredients of it, the big changes happened within the first three weeks . . . and then the rest was refining it. And I'd write it literally onstage, so you'd write it in those gigs and you'd say to people, "This is the trial gig." '

In order to be effective, the test gig has to be carefully set up. Harry Hill used to make appearances around the London comedy circuit, but found it 'quite difficult to try stuff out' because 'really they want you to storm it', something that's hard to do with untested material. He now tends to try out new jokes and routines supporting fellow comedian Ivor Dembina at the Hampstead Comedy Club: 'I can do forty minutes, and, basically, the rules of engagement are that the audience know I'm floundering around trying to find out what's funny, so they give me a lot more rope. You know, a lot more leeway. And I can really get a lot out of it quite quickly.'

The 'rules of engagement' are established by making the process of trying out material completely open. At a test gig for a TV series in May 2004, Jack Dee tells the audience at the Stag Theatre in Sevenoaks exactly why he's there, explaining that they shouldn't think that his career is on the skids just because he's playing in a small, out-of-the-way venue like this. He has a big sheet of notes with him. It's placed on a stool on the stage, but he doesn't refer to it much. However, when a routine gets slightly less response than he'd hoped for, he goes over to the paper and makes a note of it, saying aloud what he's writing: 'Never do that bit onstage again. In Sevenoaks.'

In a show at the Battersea Arts Centre, a rehearsal for the filming of *An Audience with Harry Hill* on the following Sunday, Hill has his set list taped to the monitor at the front of the stage. When he forgets where he's going, he makes a joke of it. 'Where was I?' he asks, then very obviously leans forward, making it clear he's looking at the list. 'Oh, yes. I've remembered now,' he says. At one point, he comes out with the word 'fucking', then gets a laugh by saying, 'We won't be doing *that* on Sunday night.'

Before the show

Having generated the material, and possibly rehearsed it, the next step the comedian faces is to prepare for actually going onstage and performing. Pre-show rituals vary from doing things which seem like common sense to the strange and quirky. At the sensible end of the spectrum are comics like Omid Djalili: 'I have my set list written out and I find that if I don't really study it a good hour before, for a good twenty, thirty minutes, and go over it, and go over things in my head, the gig suffers, really. Especially when I'm doing touring, but even [doing] twenty minutes. I remember back in '97, '98, I always had my computer printout of all the bullet points and going through it over and over again in my head.'

Because he performs for children, James Campbell's shows tend to start in the early afternoon. This means making sure he is properly prepared to perform at this comparatively early time of day: 'I mean, I do sensible things now, like make sure I get up early enough to be awake for the show. And I'm currently always walking on with a cup of coffee. I couldn't walk on without my cup of coffee.'

Even apparently rational pre-show rituals can have an obsessive element to them. Alex Horne stretches his mouth and moves his tongue around to prepare himself for speaking clearly, but he also engages in more compulsive behaviour: 'And I'll always go through just my opening line, over and over again. I don't know why, but I guess that's a superstitious thing. To make sure I know exactly what I'm gonna say straight away.'

For some comics, the pre-show ritual is there to get them in the right mood, or to generate performance energy. Phill Jupitus says: 'I had to listen to very loud rock music before I went on, I would like the sort of physical psyching up.'

At one stage, Mark Lamarr's pre-show ritual was to avoid doing anything special to prepare: '[F]or years I would've literally been sat chatting in the dressing room and someone'd go, "You're on," and you get up and walk on. Not that it meant little to me, but that's always been very, very important to me, to be natural. And so I think it was that, maybe that's my process, is not preparing.' However, he also finds it necessary to generate performance energy before going on: 'Because I don't have a process . . . for sort of five or ten minutes before I go on, I'll probably start pacing up and down, just to work myself up. Because otherwise, I'm just a bloke. D'you know what I mean? Yeah, otherwise, I'm just . . . not gonna put any effort into it. That's the only thing, probably, and that's not a super-stitious thing, that's purely for performance . . . I try and get some kind of adrenalin going, cos otherwise, I wouldn't really be that interested in talking to a roomful of strangers.'

Getting into the right state of mind to perform can involve pre-show rituals which seem to veer towards the metaphysical. Of the nineteen comics I interviewed for this book, three revealed that they pray before going onstage. Yes, Milton Jones is a Christian, but, for him, the prayer is more about his performance than faith: 'I do pray before I go on each time. I mean, sort of, a general sort of focusing and just clearing my head. It's always tricky in a dressing room. I try and just have some time on my own before I go on. And that's not even really a superstition, that's probably a drama school thing.'

Shelley Berman is emphatic that, for him, prayer is not motivated by religion: 'I don't want people to go off thinking that I'm some sort of religious fanatic, but at least for the first ten years, fifteen years of my work, I never went on without a little prayer. That was to myself, and it had nothing to do with anybody else.' Only the agnostic Adam Bloom acknowledges that pre-show prayer might have a religious aspect: 'I say a little prayer. Despite not being religious. When I first started, I was fascinated with the whole concept of "Is there a God?" which is surely the biggest question there possibly is to ask. So . . . because I was kind of dabbling in the idea that He was there and you could talk to Him and He can hear your thoughts, I thought I'd have a little prayer . . . I still say a little prayer. Also, it's talking to someone inside yourself, you know? If man invented God, it still wouldn't be a bad thing to talk to the person you invented in your head, because it's bringing yourself together, isn't it? It's no different to just going, "Come on, Adam," you know, it's the same thing. Whether God's, you know, outside of you or in you, it's still something that helps you get through your gig. And the thing is, in a particularly rough situation, you know, very late show, crowd are tired, it helps you focus, so that's 50 per cent superstition and 50 per cent . . . some kind of mental strategy.'

Beyond prayer are those pre-show strategies we've already seen which veer off into pure irrationality, whether these be wearing a particular pair of trousers or putting nine sections of green toilet paper in your pocket.

Doing it onstage

The actual moment of being onstage is all that really counts in stand-up comedy. The process which leads up to it may be important, but only if it makes that moment right. As I discussed earlier, most comedians use a mixture of prepared material and improvisation, and the moment of performance requires them to juggle these different elements, putting them together in the moment to make them work in the best possible way for that particular show.

Mark Lamarr tried to contain as much of the creation of his act as possible within the performance itself, believing that 'doing it onstage' was 'the organic way': 'I would tell a bit, and each night it would grow or diminish, you know, as it deserved to, and I never, ever wrote any of it down . . . even then I always sort of thought, "If you don't write it down, it looks like you're making it up." . . . And it would make me laugh myself, you know, cos there'd be a bit, you'd think, "God, I forgot that line, that's a fucking killer line, I haven't done that for three months!" And you'll suddenly be talking, and it's like ad libbing it even though you've done it before, because . . . it just comes out, you know. And, yeah, that was very important to me, to make sure I didn't do it as a written piece, you know, after those first few years of being really tied to words.'

Many experienced comics share this fluidity of material, cutting routines together in response to the audience. Alexei Sayle says: 'To edit, I threw a lot of stuff out, did a lot of new stuff, you know. A two-hour show or something . . . that I edited on the fly, you know, while at the same time still working to an audience.'

To be able effortlessly to piece a show together while performing it suggests that comedians achieve a very sophisticated mental state while onstage. Eddie Izzard says that when he's performing, his brain is 'almost like a split screen', so that he can play to the audience and 'work things out at the same time'. Other comics share this ability to analyse what is going on at the same time as actually doing it. Victoria Wood says: 'While one side of your head is performing, the other half is thinking, "Oh, that didn't go so well, I'm going to miss out the next bit," or, "I'd better speed up, some quick laughs are needed!" Alan Davies gives a similar description of the mental process: 'You're rarely thinking about what you're actually doing . . . it's the next thing and the next thing. That line didn't work, so the other one in twenty minutes probably isn't going to go down too well either . . . Why's that person not laughing?'[9]

Paradoxically, the other side of this detached, analytical state is instinctive and often ecstatic. Victoria Wood describes the feeling when a show is going well as being 'like flying'. The tendency of comedians to forget material they have improvised may be connected with this more instinctive side of the mental process. Certainly, in my own experience of performing, I found that good shows, where I felt happy to improvise, were almost trancelike. I felt confident, free, fluid, engulfed by my train of thought but just aware enough to react if something unexpected happened. I completely lacked uncomfortable self-consciousness. Time seemed to go very quickly. Sometimes somebody would come up to me after shows like this and tell me about something I'd said onstage. It would be a pleasant surprise, because I'd have forgotten saying it.

Bad shows create a different state of mind. I'd feel trapped and exposed, and time would seem to go more slowly, allowing me to take in every horrible detail. Ironically, this kind of extreme self-consciousness improves the memory. I had no trouble remembering the stupid, unfunny things I'd said to hecklers after a bad show.

Phill Jupitus shares this perception: 'The funny thing is, I bet most people you talk to could tell you, like, the temperature in the room, what they heard when they died . . . You can't capture moments from a good gig . . . I think good stand-ups' brains switch off. Conscious thought abandons you . . . whereas you are nothing but conscious brain when you're dying, it is all conscious, absorbing every fact, facet, you know. It's all front brain when you're dying.'

Trial and error

The forgetfulness that follows a good gig is inconvenient, because part of the experience of performing is seeing what works so that it can be reused in future shows. Most comedians seem to agree that developing a stand-up act is simply a question of trying things out. Phill Jupitus says: '[W]ith stand-up you throw anything at the wall and see what sticks . . . It's just when something works, you know it works and you do more of it.' Adam Bloom makes a similar point: 'Honing [material] in is the *best* way to get something, because it evolves through trial and error.'

This suck-it-and-see methodology is yet another thing that links stand-up with the music hall. Max Beerbohm describes how Dan Leno would work in a new routine:

> A new performance by Dan Leno was almost always a dull thing in itself. He was unable to do himself justice until he had, as it were, collaborated for many nights with the public. He selected and rejected according to how his jokes, and his expression of them 'went'; and his best things came to him always in the course of an actual performance, to be incorporated in all subsequent performances. When, at last, the whole thing had been built up, how perfect a whole it was![10]

The material isn't the only thing that can develop by trial and error. As I discussed earlier, many comedians find their trademark costume simply by trying things out and seeing what works. For Shelley Berman, the distinctive overall style of his whole act came about by accident rather than design: 'It's a style that just happened. It was never something I thought of. It was just something that happened.' Even the trademark barstool came about more through a particular set of circumstances than being a carefully thought-out strategy. His earliest stand-up routines were one-sided telephone conversations which he'd originally done with the pioneering improvisational group the Compass Players. Performing them in a stand-up environment meant making certain adjustments: 'I sat on a chair when I first did these things, and then I realised that some of the nightclubs that I was working in, the audience couldn't see me in the back if I sat down on a chair. So I asked to borrow a barstool. So I've been sitting on a barstool ever since.'

Getting it taped

The essential element of trial and error means that the final stage of a stand-up's methodology is to think back over how the act has gone once the show is over. In many cases, though, genuinely spontaneous moments in stand-up disappear into thin air as soon as the show is over. Phill Jupitus says: 'I've lost two Edinburgh shows of spontaneous thought that just happened on the night and I didn't write down.' Jeremy Hardy agrees: 'I can never remember when I come offstage. I might improvise something really good, and I'll have forgotten it. And I lose quite a lot of stuff because I write things down in note form and often things are never actually properly written out in full, so I forget the end of things, and I can never get it back again, which is annoying.'

Ken Dodd used to keep detailed notebooks, filling in details on every show. A particular entry might include information on the length of the act, the size and character of the audience, even the weather outside. Then there would be two columns, one listing each joke that was told, the other containing notes on how well each of these had gone down.

A more common method is to make an audio recording of the show. This dates to at least as far back as Lenny Bruce, who bought a reel-to-reel tape recorder when such items were still relatively uncommon. Recordings allow the comic to assess the performance objectively, check the exact wording of a strong new joke, notice mistakes and consider different ways of arranging a routine. Harry Hill regularly makes audio or video recordings of his act: '[S]ometimes watching things back . . . at the time I haven't thought they're very funny, then sometimes watching them back you think, "Oh, well, yeah, no, that *is* quite funny," or, you know, "Here's something you could do . . ." exaggerate it, or do something extra on it.'

Recordings are useful, given that many comedians keep minimal notes, or avoid writing down anything at all. Phill Jupitus says: 'I used to do the Square [a venue in Harlow, Essex], cos they had an A/V set-up and so you could record your act, and I'd keep the Square videos and would watch them back, and would remember pieces.'

Similarly, Jeremy Hardy says: 'If I haven't gigged for, like, three or four months, then I have to do quite a lot of work trying to remember [it], and sometimes I will find a tape of a gig I've done and listen to it through. If I'm doing gigs reasonably regularly, there's enough in my head that I can choose from.' Listening back to recordings of the act is not necessarily a pleasant process. Jeremy Hardy says it's 'unbearable . . . it's just so tedious to listen to, for me'. Then he laughs, adding, 'I hope not for the audience, but –' Mark Lamarr found recording his act unhelpful, precisely because listening back to it made him uncomfortable: '[I]t sort of made me too self-conscious, and again, because I want it to be as natural as possible, and that's always been, like, the overriding thing for me, I didn't think it did any good, really.'

Some comedians use the commercial recordings of their acts to revise for a gig. A documentary from 2000 sees Alan Davies travelling to a show in a van, going over routines by listening to his audio cassette *Urban Trauma* on a personal stereo. 'It's been a while since I've done a gig and I don't have any scripts. Nothing's scripted. So the only way to remember routines is to listen to tapes,' he explains, noting down gags in a list. Later in the same programme, Eddie Izzard admits to listening to CDs of his act for the same reason.

Laziness
Talking to stand-ups about how they work, an interesting tendency emerges. As they become experienced, their

254

preparation becomes more and more minimal and the job starts to involve little more than the actual act of performance. Dave Gorman says: 'It used to be very written. At the beginning, when I was deadpan, there were a lot of one-liners, which would be very precisely worded. There was one way of telling them. But then as it got more storytelling and stuff towards the end . . . I never wrote them down.'

Jo Brand gives a more detailed account of how her preparation has decreased: 'How I generate material's kind of changed over the years. I have to be honest, I was a lot more conscientious when I started. I would sit down and I'd write it all down, sort of word for word, and I would learn it, you know, almost like a poem, really. And kind of over the years . . . I, personally, have just found I've got a lot lazier about it . . . I'll have an idea in my head, and think, "Well, that might be a funny punchline," and I'll just try it out. And if it works sort of 50 per cent, then I'll just keep trying it and refining it until it does, really. And I'll have it on a bit of paper as just one word, whereas before I would have kind of had five sheets of paper very neatly typed out with the whole thing, you know.'

Words like 'conscientious' and 'lazier' suggest Brand feels a twinge of guilt about having to spend less time preparing. It's a twinge which is shared by Andre Vincent, who accuses himself of laziness although he has never written material down. He tends to generate new jokes by going through the *Evening Standard* and circling stories, then taking the newspaper on with him and busking routines from it. He says of this method: '[I]t is really bad of me, really lazy. I'm *so* lazy. That's the worst thing.'

Harry Hill shows a similar pang of guilt about his aversion to rehearsal: 'I don't rehearse, I can't bear rehearsing, I can't rehearse really, no. I mean, normally on the way to a gig I would do it in the car, you know. I'd have a sort of list on the passenger seat, and run through it like that. But I think probably I should rehearse, I think probably, you know, it wouldn't do you any harm, would it?'

While some comedians may feel guilty about their apparent laziness, others realise that, with experience, preparation becomes unnecessary, even counterproductive. The very idea of rehearsing stand-up is rejected. Eddie Izzard says: 'You can't rehearse it. This is the terrible and brilliant thing of stand-up . . . I think you rehearse in front of paying audiences.' Dave Gorman puts his argument beautifully: 'It's impossible to rehearse. It's like a guitarist rehearsing by playing air guitar. The audience are actually the instrument.'

The fact that comedians can reduce the amount of preparation they do and still perform as effectively (or possibly even better) when they are faced with an audience, is a testament to the skills they have acquired. The idea of sketching down a few notes, going through it in your head, then going onstage might make stand-up seem like the ideal job for the lazy person, especially with working hours of between twenty minutes and two hours a night. However, in most cases it only becomes a slacker's profession after years of experience, and the learning process is usually a long, hard slog.

9. Why Bother?

As somebody who teaches stand-up comedy, I'm faced with a nagging question: Why bother? After all, *The Stage* is undoubtedly right when it points out that '[G]raduates of an academic comedy course who believe they will make an instant impact on the stand-up world are in for a big shock'. The comedy circuit is purely market-driven, and people who run comedy clubs will only book acts they can be sure will please the punters. It's now more difficult than ever to get established in British comedy clubs, and the only way to avoid months or even years spent slogging away in the amateur open-mike clubs is to have the luck to win a competition or be spotted by an agent. Given this, a degree certificate is not likely to cut much ice.

There's also the possibility that trying to teach somebody how to do stand-up might do more harm than good. As Jo Brand puts it: 'I think it's a very bad idea to have training. I think being able to do stand-up is a very natural thing, helped along by age or experience . . . Having been to workshops for stand-up comedians, I personally don't think they're a good idea. I think they tend to bland everyone out a bit by making the stand-ups uniform in the way that they approach the job. All the best stand-ups I've seen have developed on their own.'[1]

This taps into a commonly held idea about teaching: that it is something the teacher does to the learner. The teacher is active, the learner is passive. This idea is implicit in the current tendency to depersonalise teaching in higher education. Learning outcomes are published in advance, and ticked off one by one. Marks are neatly divided up between the assessment tasks. Essays are anonymously marked, feedback written without any idea of who will be reading it. Somehow, not knowing the students is supposed to improve their learning; they are customers who should be given a standardised slice of the education salami.

It may be true that comedy workshops 'bland everyone out', but it doesn't have to be like that. I see my job as helping the students to learn and develop for themselves, to find their own way of becoming a comedian. This doesn't fit the impersonal model of modern higher education. I have to understand the students and get to know them as individuals, because their personalities and the lives they lead are the raw materials they'll be working with. Their work couldn't be anonymously assessed unless they disguised their voices and did the act with bags on their heads.

I do what happens in the professional world. I watch them work and give them advice. I play Max Miller to their Bob Monkhouse, Jack Rollins to their Woody Allen. I have to try and understand who they are, and what makes them tick. I have to spot what they're doing that's brilliant, interesting or quirky, and encourage them to develop it further. I have to notice where they're struggling and try and help them get through it. Each one of the first four students on my year-long course has different strengths and weaknesses, and needs nurturing in a different way.

Charlie is a nervous performer, and sometimes her act falls apart because fear causes ideas to leave her head by the nearest exit and she's left floundering. In spite of this, she's gutsy, and early on in the term she decides she wants to try something controversial and political. She's got the idea of talking about September 11, but she's not sure. I encourage her to give it a try. Exactly a month after the terrorist atrocities, she goes out and talks about them. She's nervous, but she has a point to make: other disasters killed more people and didn't get the same attention. She points out that the English are more stoical about these things, turning the Black Death and the Great Fire of London into nursery rhymes: 'I mean, imagine how insulted the Americans would be if we started making up nursery rhymes about their disaster. [*laughter*]' She gets a piece of paper out of her pocket. 'I refer to my piece of paper. "Bin Laden had two little planes / Their wings were long and shiny / He drove them into World Trade towers / And now they're very tiny." [*laughter and applause*]'

Jimmy is great at anecdotes, structuring them well, and always acting them out evocatively, with great characterisation. I encourage him to follow this line, touching on as many areas of his life as possible. He fills the stage with stories about bullying at school, a trip to the GU clinic, and what his mum thought when she found a can of butane gas under his bed. He talks about his military father co-ordinating a group of animal rights protestors ('Right – Mingey, Manky, Swampy, Crusty and Fuck – you go all the way round the back and break in. And I'll stay in the Renault Espace operations room'). One day, Jimmy comes into the workshop and tells us about an incident with an aggressive drunk in the bar where he works. The next night, he does it onstage. It's an effective, colourful routine, and it gets plenty of laughs.

Katie has some great lines, such as 'I was voted child least likely to heal properly on the children's ward', and 'I do sleep around a bit – bloody narcolepsy'. Her geeky, swotty persona is refreshing and quite original, but being a true swot by nature, she likes to write out her entire script in advance, then learn it and polish it. This makes her seem a bit stilted and theatrical. I encourage her to improvise more, and work from a looser script. She's reluctant, and does it only occasionally. However, by the time she does her twenty-minute set in a local pub, she's finally found the confidence to let loose. She has eighteen minutes of material, but she spins it out to twenty-eight, and her biggest laughs come from improvising and playing the moment. She's on first, and in her introduction, I call her 'sweet and charming'. After a rude gag, she says: 'See, you're starting to ask for your money back now Olly said I'm sweet and charming, aren't you?' There's a small laugh. She takes on the character of an outraged audience member, hands on hips, head wobbling with annoyance: ' "She's not sweet and charming, what are the others like?" ' There's another small laugh. Then she slips back into her own voice, and says, with uncharacteristic self-confidence: 'Not as funny.' There's a big laugh and a round of applause.

One day, Gav is not giving his full attention to what we're doing in the workshop. He's doodling. I ask him to show us what he's been drawing. It's silly and puerile, and it makes us laugh. I suggest he should draw it again on a big piece of paper, take it onstage with him and explain to the audience what he's drawn. He does, and it gets a great response. Later, he does it in a small theatre in Whitstable, to an audience dominated by rather reserved middle-aged amateur theatre people. They're hard to please, but they like this routine.

Saying that he's a contemporary artist, he tells them that Damien Hirst has suggested he show them one of his paintings. 'It's a bit avant-garde, I don't know if you'll like it,' he explains. Then he unfolds a piece of A2 paper on which he's redrawn the childish cartoon he first drew in class. As the audience take it in, they start to laugh. He tells them what he's drawn in a slow, deadpan voice. 'That's me,' he says, pointing to a crudely drawn figure in the middle, an arrow pointing towards it with the word 'ME' at the other end. 'And that – that's a knife,' he says, pointing to the dripping knife in the figure's hand, 'there.' He moves on to two figures lying on the floor, both of which are cut in half, with pools of blood trickling out. 'Just down here,' he says, pointing to each in turn, 'are, are the Chuckle Brothers.' There's a big, long laugh and a smattering of applause.

He get a few more laughs by explaining some of the details he's drawn on the figures labelled 'PAUL' and 'BARRY', then says that his art teacher always used to tell him, 'Gav – don't leave anywhere blank on the page, try not to leave any white spaces.' He draws the audience's attention to what he's drawn to fill the space, a figure nailed to a flaming cross:

So up here – I've put Jamie Oliver. [*laughter and a few claps*] Thank you, thank you. On, on a crucifix. Flames just licking at his feet. [*laughter*] Now I don't know if anyone else has tried to draw Jamie Oliver, but it's quite tricky – erm, I can't really capture his smug cunt face, so – [*laughter*] I've got him saying, "Pukka." [*laughter*]

A pair of working-class children's entertainers and a celebrity chef are not exactly dangerous targets, but the charm of the routine is in the puerility of the drawing and the way this contrasts with Gav's quiet pride as he explains his work. It's like a twelve-year-old boy explaining his revenge fantasy on his teacher, and it's really odd as part of a stand-up act.

Most comics begin their careers on the open-mike circuit and many of them start out by copying techniques or even material from more established acts. I've seen a greenhorn comic doing Bill Hicks routines not just word for word, but inflection for inflection. There were only two things that distinguished him from the original: an English accent and an almost total lack of funniness.

What's nice about teaching stand-up is that I can help students express themselves as individuals. It's a joy to see them facing an audience with their own quirks, anecdotes, conspiracy theories, even their own stupid doodles, and to hear the audience laughing in reply. The course may not help them get bookings, but as well as giving them some stage experience and material to face the open-mike circuit with, it should certainly stop them pretending to be Bill

Hicks. For those who don't want to go on to become comedians, it should also teach them things which could be useful in any career or, indeed, any other area of life. They have to organise their own time, take risks, cope with stress, think through their attitudes, play with ideas and see the world through different eyes. After doing a year of stand-up, addressing a meeting, presenting an award or giving a best man's speech will be easy by comparison.

Ultimately I would answer the question 'Why study stand-up comedy at university?' by saying 'Why not?' It seems wacky only because it's a comparatively new idea. The idea of formalised training for actors would have seemed bizarre two hundred years ago, when most of them learned their skills as Lupino Lane did, through teaching carried out within theatrical families. RADA was founded only in 1904, and it wasn't until 1947 that Bristol became the first British university to establish a drama department.

Stand-up comedy is a vibrant, popular form, which attracts far bigger audiences than many of the playwrights and performers who are routinely studied in universities. At its best, it manages to balance popularity with cutting-edge inventiveness, daring and profundity. It can encompass an individual revealing intimate secrets to a group of strangers, a performer–audience relationship so intense that it can descend into violence, a challenging of taboos so serious that the authorities intervene, and the most painful moments being transformed into occasions for laughter. Surely, something that exciting is worth studying.

Appendix:
Exercises for Teaching
Stand-up Comedy

None of these exercises works if students try to be funny. Students are told to do the exercise as described, and if something funny happens, great, but not to worry if it doesn't. Paradoxically, this significantly increases the chance of something funny actually happening.

Microphone Conversations

How it's done

This is a devilishly simple exercise. The students arrange their seating so that they form a small audience. The microphone stand is placed in front of them, to form a stage area. One of the students then gets up behind the mike, and simply has a conversation with the audience. There's no requirement to be funny, or to assume any kind of formal stage attitude. This should be as much like a normal, everyday conversation as possible, in spite of the microphone. The student can ask questions of the audience, and vice versa. The entire group should acknowledge the reality of the situation, rather than pretending that this is a real stand-up gig. The subjects discussed can range from the banal (what the student had for breakfast) to the profound (the student's religious beliefs). The only potential hazard of the exercise is that sometimes members of the audience talk among themselves. If this happens, the teacher should step in.

What it's for
Microphone Conversations is the best way I have found of getting students used to the feeling of being onstage and addressing the audience directly, without the crutch of a fixed script. Their confidence increases, and they start to define who they are in relation to the audience. Because the exercise is so easy, the students relax and often manage to make the rest of the group laugh. There are also times when a tangible sense of excitement is generated and something comes up in conversation that can form the nugget of a gag or a routine.

Find the Link

How it's done
The students sit in a circle, and the sequence moves clockwise round it. Person 1 starts by suggesting a subject, say, cornflakes. Person 2 (to the left of Person 1) then suggests a second, completely unrelated subject, say, lawnmowers. Person 3 then has to find a link between the two subjects. This can be anything:

- a simple, factual link (e.g. cornflakes are made from corn, which is harvested using machinery which is essentially like a giant lawnmower)
- a personal association (cornflakes and lawnmowers are both things I remember from when I was a kid, classic items of traditional family life)
- a tortuous imaginary connection (they make the yellow dust at the bottom of the packet of cornflakes by running over the cornflakes with a lawnmower)

Then the sequence starts again, with the person to the left of Person 3 suggesting a new first subject. The game continues until it runs out of steam. There is absolutely no requirement to make the links funny; if they are, it's a bonus. It's best if the students come up with subjects and find the links as quickly as possible, because thinking too much about it robs it of spontaneity. There's no way anybody can lose, because no link can ever be wrong. Sometimes the sequence is broken, for example, if the second person gives a subject which is clearly related to the first (Person 1: 'Satan'/Person 2: 'George Bush'). This doesn't matter: a lot of comedy is made by breaking sequences. In fact, it's good to vary the format. Let anyone come up with a link, even when it's not their turn, if they think they've got a better one than the first one suggested. Make everyone except the two people who suggested the subjects come up with a link. Try taking the sequences anti-clockwise round the circle for a change.

What it's for
Find the Link is designed to encourage the kind of associative, lateral thinking that happens when comedians work on ideas for material. It encourages reversals, incongruities and jarring contrasts. It helps the students to start to see the world through a comedian's eyes. They enjoy playing it, so it creates the right atmosphere: relaxed and playful. It also starts to suggest rhythm and structure. The basic three-part sequence mirrors the rule of three, on which many jokes are based.

Here and Now

How it's done
The basic set-up is exactly the same as in Microphone Conversations. This time the student behind the mike does all the talking, and may talk only about things that are happening in the here and now: the decor; the things people are wearing; somebody breathing heavily or sneezing; the thoughts and feelings passing through his or her head. The

tendency is to veer off into the past tense: 'I'm wearing grey trousers [good] . . . I got them from Next last week [oops!].' Sometimes they slip up on the future tense: 'Look at that Fire Exit sign [good] . . . I'm gonna nick that one day [oops!].' When the player strays from the here and now, the audience has to shout 'Here and now!' and the first person to do so takes up the position behind the mike, becoming the next player.

What it's for
Here and Now is designed to encourage players to work in the present tense. It forces them to pay attention to and comment on the particular circumstances in which they're working, and allows them to externalise their inner thought processes. There are clear rules and it's easy to make mistakes, so it forces the students to think on their feet. They find it quite a difficult game, and sometimes they dislike it. It's at its best when they have fun with it, playing with the possibilities of what they're allowed to say, and even bending the rules.

Compulsory Lying

How it's done
Another variant of Microphone Conversations. This time the student behind the mike can say anything as long as it isn't true. The audience can ask questions to try and catch the player out. As in Here and Now, the fun starts when the students start playing with the possibilities. Someone in the audience might come out with a particularly confusing question ('James – is it not true that your name isn't not James?'). The player might use the idea that everybody knows that whatever they say is a lie ('Thanks for that brilliant question – I'm truly impressed with your intellect'). When the player clearly says something which is true, the first person to spot this takes up the position behind the mike and becomes the next player.

What it's for

Compulsory Lying is another game about thinking on one's feet. It encourages lateral thinking, and because it's a battle of wits with the audience, it gives a hint of what it's like to take on a heckler.

The Attitudes Game

How it's done

Again, the basic set-up is a student behind the mike facing the rest of the group arranged as an audience. The player is given a series of subjects, and has to give his or her honest opinion of that subject. As always, there is no requirement to be funny. The key thing is for the player to think about the subject and try to work out how it makes him or her feel. The reactions can encompass deeply held political beliefs, prejudices, pet hates, relevant anecdotes, even the admission that the student has no strong feelings on the subject. The subjects given should be as varied as possible, and move between the trivial and the serious. Some examples: cheese; your insecurities; your favourite TV show; facial hair on women; zoos; shopping; sexual attraction; adulthood; your greatest fear; dreams; embarrassing situations; boy bands.

What it's for

The Attitudes Game makes students think about who they are and the relationship they have to the rest of the world. If modern stand-up is often about sharing a worldview with the audience, it helps to know what your opinions are. This exercise can help a student to define who they want to be onstage. It's also another game which can generate basic ideas for gags and routines.

Instant Character

How it's done

This time, the student behind the mike has to tell a short anecdote, or even just describe someone he or she knows. This has to involve an instant character, so that the student has to act at least one other person, and practise switching between character(s) and narrator.

What it's for

Instant Character is about practising a basic performance skill common to most stand-ups. It might reveal a hidden talent for voices and impressions, or the characterisation might be imbued with the student's attitude to the person, as in Jack Dee's 'You smoke – I choke' routine.

Glossary of Comedians

This glossary helps you to keep track of who I'm talking about when you read the book. It's not meant to be a definitive list, and not every comic mentioned in the book appears here. I've only included people who are mentioned more than once in a reasonably substantial way. The length of entry in no way reflects the importance, status or longevity of the comedian it describes.

Tony Allen (1945–) UK
The founder member of Alternative Cabaret, and one of the original alternative comedians, Allen started doing stand-up comedy in the late 1970s, after working with Rough Theatre. His comedy was daring, often dealt with difficult subject matter, and was informed by his anarchist politics. He no longer does much stand-up; instead, he runs the Performance Club, appears at Speakers' Corner, and teaches and writes about stand-up and similar subjects.

Woody Allen (1935–) USA
Originally a successful comedy writer, in the early 1960s Allen started performing clever, surreal and very funny stand-up routines, initially in small venues in Greenwich Village. By the middle of the decade he was a well-known comedian, and released a series of comedy albums, before moving into the movie business and becoming the legendary film director he is today.

Bill Bailey (1964–) UK

Bailey started in London comedy clubs in the 1980s as part of musical double act, the Rubber Bishops. He went solo in the early 1990s, and now performs surreal, cerebral, spaced-out stand-up dressed up in rock and roll stagecraft, drawing heavily on his musical virtuosity: he plays guitar, keyboards and even theramin in his shows. He's also a team captain in the comedy pop music quiz *Never Mind the Buzzcocks*.

Milton Berle (1908–2002) USA

After performing in vaudeville as a child, Berle found fame as a monologist. When the vaudeville circuit died, he performed in nightclubs and appeared in films and on radio, and became massively famous in the early days of television in the late 1940s and early 50s as the star of the shows *Texaco Star Theatre* and *The Buick-Berle Show*, where he became known as 'Uncle Miltie'.

Shelley Berman (1926–) USA

Berman became a stand-up in 1957 after training as an actor and working with improvisational theatre group the Compass Players. He performs his act seated on a barstool, and many of his early routines took the form of imaginary telephone conversations, although he also did a nice line in observational comedy. One of the sick comedians, he has had huge success with a series of comedy albums, starting in 1959 with *Inside Shelley Berman*. He still performs stand-up, and works as an actor.

Adam Bloom (1970–) UK

Bloom has pursued a very successful stand-up career in British comedy clubs since the early 1990s. His delivery is frenetic, his jokes often clever and offbeat. Two series of his show *The Problem with Adam Bloom* have been broadcast on BBC Radio 4. He's known on the circuit for being almost obsessively analytical about his comedy (and comedy in general).

Jo Brand (1957–) UK

After a career as a psychiatric nurse, Brand moved into stand-up in the 1980s, originally working under the stage name 'the Sea Monster'. Much of her early comedy dealt with her physical size, and she has been unfairly criticised for basing all her comedy on this one subject, as well as being regularly vilified by the right-wing press for her feminist politics and left-wing sympathies. In fact, her comedy is based on a gleeful outrageousness which takes in a broad range of targets, and both her live act and her TV work have deservedly made her a big star, and earned her a devoted following.

Arnold Brown (1936–) UK

This Jewish Glaswegian former accountant started performing stand-up on the first night of London's Comedy Store in 1979, before working with the likes of Rik Mayall and French & Saunders at the Comic Strip in Soho. He has a charming, laid-back style of delivery and quirky, tangential material. He won the Perrier Award at the Edinburgh Fringe in 1987, for the show *Brown Blues* (with Jungr and Parker)

Roy 'Chubby' Brown (1945–) UK

Brown originally started as a drummer in the working-men's clubs in the 1950s before turning to stand-up. He has enjoyed much success by doing 'blue' (i.e. sexually explicit) material, touring big theatres and selling shedloads of videos. His trademark costume is a garish, multicoloured suit and a leather flying helmet.

Lenny Bruce (1925–66) USA

A legendary stand-up, Bruce's act was extraordinary for a number of reasons: he improvised, dealt with obscene subjects, used expletives, talked about illegal drugs, and attacked racism and hypocrisy. His willingness to delve into taboo areas in his comedy – and, it must be said, his drug use – led to legal difficulties which destroyed his career, and probably contributed to his early death from a drug overdose.

Rhona Cameron (1965–) UK
A Scots comedian who started in the early 1990s, Cameron's delivery is assured, her material observational and autobiographical and, as she puts it, 'my lesbianism show[s] itself in a comedic way'. She moved out of the comedy clubs into touring her own show, and has also worked on TV, e.g. as a presenter of *Gaytime TV* and a contestant on the first series of *I'm a Celebrity, Get Me out of Here!*.

James Campbell (1973–) UK
Having started his career as a storyteller in schools in the mid-1990s, Campbell gradually found that the stories were disappearing in favour of more tangential material until he realised he was performing stand-up comedy for kids. Although he has performed for adult audiences in comedy clubs, he now mainly works in theatres, touring internationally to audiences of children and parents.

George Carlin (1937–) USA
After some success as half of the clean-cut double act Burns and Carlin, he reinvented himself in the early 1970s, adopting a hippie image, aligning himself with the politics of the counterculture and talking about drugs. Still a prolific stand-up, he has also set up Laugh.com, an excellent website that sells comedy merchandise and reissues classic comedy albums on CD.

Jimmy Carr (1973–) UK
Carr started on the comedy circuit in the 1990s, and has enjoyed much success with a middle-class persona, deadpan delivery and a series of short, well-crafted gags which are often calculatedly offensive. He also hosts the Channel 4 game show *Distraction*.

Jasper Carrott (1945–) UK

Originally a folk singer, Carrott ran a folk club called the Boggery in his native Birmingham. Gradually, his act mutated into stand-up comedy, and he's enjoyed much success with his live act, various TV projects and a series of successful comedy albums starting with *Rabbitts on and on and on . . .* in 1975. His classic routines include 'Car Insurance', 'The Mole' and 'Nutter on the Bus'.

Billy Connolly (1942–) UK

A Glasgow-born comedian who was a shipyard worker and a folk singer before his act slid into stand-up comedy. Connolly built up a huge following, originally in Scotland and subsequently in the rest of the UK, thanks to a series of interviews on *Parkinson* in the 1970s. As well as various TV projects and film-acting roles, he continues to tour internationally to big audiences, and constantly produces high-quality new material. A consummate performer, his act can be angry, tender, wistful, sick, scatological and joyful.

Steve Coogan (1965–) UK

A successful impressionist on the comedy circuit in the late 1980s, Coogan moved into character comedy in the early 90s, winning the Perrier Award (with John Thomson) at the Edinburgh Fringe in 1992. His characters, who appear in various TV shows as well as in his live act, include drunken Mancunian lad Paul Calf, minor TV personality Alan Partridge and no-hope comedian Duncan Thickett.

Bill Cosby (1937–) USA

Probably best known for starring in the highly successful 1980s sitcom *The Cosby Show*, Cosby has also pursued a successful stand-up career dating back to the early 1960s. At that time, he was unique in being an African-American who didn't deal with race in his act. Instead, with a gentle, anecdotal style, he told stories about his childhood and early manhood.

Rhys Darby (1974–) NZ
Darby started out on the nascent New Zealand alternative comedy scene in the second half of the 1990s, regularly appearing in and helping to run Christchurch's first comedy club, touring his own shows, and starting to work on TV. He moved to the UK, feeling that the Kiwi comedy scene was a bit limiting, and is now a regular in British clubs.

Jim Davidson (1953–) UK
After various childhood forays into show business, Davidson began performing stand-up in pubs and working-men's clubs in London, and became well known nationally after winning *New Faces* in 1976. His mainstream TV work on shows like *The Generation Game* contrasts with his live stand-up act, featuring 'blue' material and racial gags which many would find offensive.

Jack Dee (1964–) UK
Dee is a highly skilled deadpan comedian who started in the London comedy clubs in the late 1980s. His act transferred extremely well on to TV in two series of *The Jack Dee Show* in the early 1990s, and since then he has continued to work as a live act, on TV and in various acting roles. His image is that of a sophisticated, besuited entertainer with shades of the Rat Pack, and his comedy is based on a kind of weary, sometimes scathing cynicism.

Phyllis Diller (1917–) USA
Diller was thirty-seven when she first started in the 1950s, and was the first female stand-up to become a big star. Her act was based on the premise that she was the opposite of society's image of womanhood, and she joked about her looks and lack of domestic skills. Her delivery was dominated by her extraordinary laugh, her material made up of a string of short gags.

Omid Djalili (1965–) UK

A British-Iranian comedian, Djalili threw himself in at the deep end in 1995 by taking a show called *Short Fat Kebab Shop Owner's Son* to the Edinburgh Fringe despite having no previous experience of doing stand-up. Subsequently, Djalili has built up a successful career as a live act, initially in the comedy clubs, then touring his own show. He also works as a character actor, with cameos in such movies as *The Mummy* and *Gladiator*.

Ken Dodd (1927–) UK

An eccentric Liverpudlian comedian who started in the latter days of the British variety circuit, Dodd's act encompasses comedy songs, sentimental ballads, ventriloquism and quickfire gags ranging from the whimsical to the surreal. He has an extraordinary image, with spiked-up hair and prominent teeth, and uses a feather duster known as a 'tickling stick' in his shows. Still a hard-working touring comic, his shows are famous for being extremely long.

Ben Elton (1959–) UK

Starting on the alternative comedy circuit of the early 1980s, by the end of that decade Elton had become well known as a motormouthed comedian in a spangly suit and glasses, mixing observational and scatological routines with satirical jibes against the Thatcher government. Once quite a controversial figure, in recent years he's moved into the mainstream, although he has not jettisoned his leftish political beliefs.

Dave Gorman (1971–) UK

After working as a clever deadpan stand-up and comedy writer, in the late 1990s Gorman moved into autobiographical one-man shows in which he chronicles a series of challenges, like finding a given number of people who share his name (*Are You Dave Gorman?*) or using the Internet to find ten Googlewhacks in a row (*Dave Gorman's Googlewhack Adventure*).

Dick Gregory (1932–) USA

A groundbreaking African-American comedian, his big break was a highly successful appearance at the Playboy Club in Chicago in 1961 in front of a predominantly white audience. Before this, Gregory had worked only in black venues. With a cool, relaxed style, his stand-up act aimed sharp satirical barbs against racism and hypocrisy, and as the 1960s progressed he became increasingly involved in the civil rights movement, as well as running for President in 1968.

Jeremy Hardy (1961–) UK

Starting on the alternative comedy circuit in the early 1980s, Hardy won the Perrier Award in 1988. His satirical stand-up act is superbly written and performed. Originally, his acerbic left-wing views were nicely counterbalanced with a tweedy, slightly cuddly middle-class image, but more recently he has tended to play on being grumpy and out of touch with modernity, which works equally well. He also writes newspaper columns and appears regularly in such radio shows as *The News Quiz* and *Jeremy Hardy Speaks to the Nation*.

Lenny Henry (1958–) UK

In 1975, at the tender age of sixteen, Henry won the TV talent show *New Faces* with an act based on comedy impressions. With very little experience of performance (or life), he was launched into a comedy career playing working-men's clubs and summer seasons, becoming the only genuinely black person to appear on *The Black and White Minstrels*. In the early 1980s, seeing acts like Alexei Sayle at the Comic Strip led him to change his act, rejecting the self-deprecating racial gags in favour of a more positive style. Since then, he has become one of Britain's most popular entertainers.

Bill Hicks (1961–94) USA

After growing up in Houston, Texas, and starting to perform stand-up while still in his teens, Hicks forged a career by working hard and pushing at the boundaries of what it was possible to do with the form. His act took in spirituality, smoking, rock and roll, conspiracy theories, the evils of American God-fearing capitalism and UFOs, among other things, veering between the sick, the tender and the thought-provoking. He worked in the UK as well as the States, and received more recognition in the former than in his native country.

Harry Hill (1964–) UK

Doctor Matthew Hall gave up his job in 1990 to pursue a stand-up career in London comedy clubs, after performing in medical revues. Originally taking the stage name Harry Hall, he then became Harry Hill, a surreal comedian with a unique style involving quirky catchphrases, running jokes, non-sequiturs, pop songs quoted out of context, and a distinctive costume with beetle-crusher shoes, an enormous collar and pens protruding from his jacket pocket. As well as his various TV shows, he continues to tour his live show around large venues.

Bob Hope (1903–2003) USA

Although born in the UK, Hope was raised in the USA, and forged a phenomenally successful career as a comedian, originally in vaudeville and subsequently in radio, movies and TV. His persona was that of a wisecracking Everyman, his material provided by a team of writers, some of whom he kept on even when age stopped him from performing. A tireless entertainer of American troops abroad, his vocal support for the war in Vietnam led to difficulties with some of the soldiers while performing shows there.

Alex Horne (1978–) UK

A relative newcomer, Horne started doing comedy while

still a student at Cambridge University. Entering various stand-up competitions got him an agent and allowed him to break into the comedy club circuit. His 2003 Edinburgh Fringe show *Making Fish Laugh* recreated a 1970s scientific experiment which sought to determine what makes people laugh.

Frankie Howerd (1917–92) UK
After experience as an amateur entertainer before and during the Second World War, Howerd first toured the variety circuit in a show called *For the Fun of it* in 1946. By the end of that year he had started working on *Variety Bandbox*, the radio show which very quickly made him a huge star. His stammering, gossipy style was distinctly camp, as he reeled out far-fetched tales of woe, heavily laden with numerous catchphrases. He sprang back from a career lull in the early 1960s, largely due to a highly successful season at Peter Cook's venue, the Establishment, and continued to perform live stand-up throughout the rest of his life.

Eddie Izzard (1962–) UK
Izzard started doing stand-up in London comedy clubs in the late 1980s, after working in street theatre. His style is highly distinctive: tangential, surreal and improvisational (but not entirely improvised). His subject matter is eclectic, ranging from jam to European history, from cats to religion. His stage costumes are sensational, partly because he's a transvestite. He's built up a massive following through touring big venues in the UK and internationally (including performing his act in French in Paris), and his hugely successful live videos. His British shows now tend to take place in arenas.

Milton Jones (1964–) UK
Starting at the end of the 1980s, Jones has become very successful in British comedy clubs with a stand-up act based

on clever surreal jokes, with a quietly unhinged persona dressed in appalling pullovers, his hair alarmingly gelled. His radio work includes *The Very World of Milton Jones* and *The House of Milton Jones*. A Christian, he has done stand-up shows in churches. He was the very first act to headline at my old comedy club, the Last Laugh in Sheffield.

Phill Jupitus (1962–) UK
Jupitus first became established as Porky the Poet on the ranting poetry scene of the 1980s, then worked in the pop music business, before becoming a stand-up at the end of that decade. Physically large, the laddishness of his act was nicely balanced by a more delicate side, skilfully acting out his ideas. His *Jedi, Steady, Go* show in 1998 focused exclusively on *Star Wars*, and was eventually almost as long as the film itself. He no longer performs stand-up, instead presenting the breakfast show on BBC Radio 6 and working on TV as a team captain on the comedy pop quiz *Never Mind the Buzzcocks*.

Daniel Kitson (1978–) UK
Bearded, bespectacled, lisping and stuttering, Kitson doesn't seem like an ideal candidate for a stand-up comedy, but he's a natural, improvising effortlessly, telling revealing stories, and criticising his own technique while being technically excellent. Starting in the mid-1990s, he's built up a big following in the comedy clubs and beyond. He won the Perrier Award at the Edinburgh Fringe in 2002.

Mark Lamarr (1967–) UK
Lamarr became a performance poet at the age of eighteen, having had a poem published in a Faber anthology, but he quickly abandoned the poetry in favour of stand-up and moved on to the London comedy circuit. Sharply dressed, with quiffed hair, he had an easy authority, playfully improvising around conversations with the audience and the whole situation of the gig, as well as having some strong

material. He no longer performs stand-up, instead concentrating on his long-running career in TV and radio, including appearing as the host of the comedy pop quiz *Never Mind the Buzzcocks*.

Dan Leno (1860–1904) UK
Probably the greatest and most popular music-hall comedian of his time, Leno's comic patter was more important than his singing, thus making his act a crucial evolutionary step in the development of stand-up comedy. He was also the most successful pantomime dame of his generation.

Little Tich (1868–1928) UK
A highly successful music-hall comedian, Little Tich was only 4 foot 6 inches tall, and the word 'titch', meaning somebody who is very small, originates from his stage name. Most famous for his big-boot dance, he was also very skilled in performing songs and patter routines.

Bernard Manning (1930–) UK
This rotund Mancunian progressed from singing to stand-up comedy on the working-men's club circuit, as well as running his own venue, the Embassy Club. Achieving national recognition on *The Comedians* in the early 1970s, he has established a fearsome reputation by working hard in his live shows and liberally dispensing gags which are offensive on the grounds of race, obscenity or just pure abrasiveness.

Steve Martin (1945–) USA
Martin's stand-up act was clever, wacky and stylistically subversive, and he built up a following so huge that by the late 1970s, he became one of the first comedians to perform in arenas. He found the rock and roll atmosphere of these big venues unconducive to the subtleties of his art and moved into starring in such films as *The Jerk* and *Roxanne*.

Max Miller (1894–1963) UK

Wearing a white trilby and an outrageous multicoloured suit, with an irresistibly cheeky persona and a penchant for daring sexual innuendo, Miller was the most successful front-cloth comic in the heyday of the British variety circuit.

Shazia Mirza (1975–) UK

A Muslim stand-up most famous for the post-9/11 gag 'My name is Shazia Mirza – at least that's what it says on my pilot's licence', her act was originally characterised by short, clever jokes and a deadpan delivery. She's now breaking away from that, with a more expressive, anecdotal style.

Bob Monkhouse (1928–2003) UK

Starting as a comedian in the variety theatres, Monkhouse's career encompassed comedy writing and presenting numerous TV game shows as well as his stand-up act. He continued to perform stand-up throughout his career, but although he had plenty of efficient material, his 'smarmy' delivery was frequently criticised. In spite of this, he was a very popular light entertainer, and an intelligent one, writing insightfully about the craft of comedy.

Dylan Moran (1971–) Eire

One of the comedians who emerged from Dublin's Comedy Cellar, Moran moved to London in the early 1990s and became a big name on the circuit with a charming, shambolic style and an intelligent, literary gift for imagery. He won the Perrier Award at the Edinburgh Fringe in 1996, and has gone on to co-write and star in the sitcom *Black Books*, as well as continuing to perform his live stand-up act.

Al Murray (1968–) UK

Murray performs his stand-up act in the irony-steeped guise of the Pub Landlord, a patriotic, pub-loving bar-room philosopher who takes common sense to the point of bigotry and nurses a particular hatred of the French. The character originated in Harry Hill's 1994 Perrier-nominated show *Pub Internationale*, and Murray went on to win the Perrier Award for his own show in 1999.

Bob Newhart (1929–) USA
Having written some great material, Newhart's record company set up a gig for him to record his first album, in spite of the fact that he'd never performed stand-up before. The success of his comedy albums, starting with 1960's *The Button Down Mind of Bob Newhart*, allowed him to pursue a career as a live comic, with an act made up of a series of separate, individual routines introduced as if they were songs. He has starred in sitcoms, appeared in movies and still tours with his live show.

Rob[ert] Newman (1964–) UK
Originally an impressionist on the comedy circuit, Newman became a big star thanks to the TV show *The Mary Whitehouse Experience*, in 1993 becoming (with David Baddiel) one of the first stand-ups to play the Wembley Arena. In the late 1990s, he stepped away from the superstar comedian role, instead pursuing a career as a serious novelist, and a much more low-key approach to performing. His current stand-up is intelligent, thought-provoking and politically radical.

Ross Noble (1976–) UK
After starting as a juggling comedian at the age of fifteen, Noble progressed through the comedy clubs to the point where he now tours big venues with his own show. He has become well known primarily by working hard with his brilliant live stand-up act, which is energetic, highly improvisational and surreal, often building ideas based on conversations with members of the audience.

Tom O'Connor (1939–) UK
Before becoming well known as a TV quizmaster,

O'Connor was a stand-up on the Merseyside working-men's club circuit, and was unusual because rather than simply telling a series of pre-existing gags, he would do observational routines and material about his upbringing in working-class Liverpool. He still works as a live comedian.

Richard Pryor (1940–) USA
Starting in the 1960s as an African-American comedian in the Bill Cosby mould, by the end of that decade, Pryor's stand-up started taking a more militant approach to racial matters as well as encompassing obscene language and subject matter. His work was exquisitely performed and searingly honest, dealing frankly with events in his turbulent personal life, tackling difficult topics and acting out scenes with a rare delicacy. In America, he's widely regarded as the greatest stand-up comedian of all time, and he's at his peak in the film *Live in Concert*. He gave up performing in the early 1990s, due to the effects of multiple sclerosis.

Ted Ray (1906–77) UK
After starting as Nedlo the Gypsy Violinist in the late 1920s, Ray made an important innovation, rejecting theatrical costumes in favour of an ordinary lounge suit, and becoming possibly the first front-cloth comic to perform as an ordinary bloke, just like one of the audience. In addition to his live act on the variety circuit, he also enjoyed success with the long-running radio series *Ray's a Laugh* and a variety of TV and film work.

Joan Rivers (1933–) USA
Emerging from the Borscht Belt hotels and small clubs in Greenwich Village, Rivers gained national recognition through a series of TV appearances starting with the Carson show in 1965. She went on to enjoy a successful stand-up career, with a style based on calculated bitchiness and a look based on plastic-surgery-style glamour.

Chris Rock (1965–) USA

Probably the most important African-American comedian since Richard Pryor, Rock started in American comedy clubs, released his first album in 1991, and had appeared in movies and on TV by the time of his 1996 HBO special, *Bring the Pain*, which made him a stand-up superstar. His material deals fearlessly and controversially with racial and sexual matters, and his delivery is loud, impassioned and sometimes angry.

Mort Sahl (1927–) USA

Sahl gave his first performance at a beatnik club called the hungry i in San Francisco in 1953, and there developed a style which would revolutionise comedy and lay the ground for the modern stand-up style. His delivery was conversational, his material intellectual and satirical, sometimes daringly so. Although his career was damaged when he got caught up in the investigation of the assassination of JFK, he continues to perform stand-up to this day.

Alexei Sayle (1952–) UK

The original compère of London's Comedy Store in 1979, Sayle was one of the first alternative comedians. His act was silly, surreal and satirical, with a manic, sometimes furious delivery, his fat figure stuffed into a tight suit, his skinhead haircut sometimes hidden under a porkpie hat. Although he called himself a Marxist, the jibes at Thatcherism were interspersed with vicious gags at the expense of his left-wing audience. He last toured in 1995, and has now given up performing for a career as a writer.

Frank Skinner (1957–) UK

Skinner cut his teeth as compère of the 4X cabarets in his native Birmingham in the late 1980s, and made a name for himself in comedy clubs nationally, before winning the Perrier Award at the Edinburgh Fringe in 1991. With a laddish charm, he enjoys a warm rapport with his audience, and is extremely deft with explicit sexual and scatological material. TV vehicles like *Fantasy Football League* and *The Frank Skinner Show*, as well as his live stand-up shows, have made him a big star.

Mark Thomas (1963–) UK
First taking the stage at the White Lion in Putney on 19 November 1985, Thomas made a name for himself on the London comedy circuit for his biting political comedy. In 1996, the first of several series of *The Mark Thomas Comedy Product* was broadcast on Channel 4, containing a brilliant mix of his stand-up act and pranks played on politicians and other worthy targets. Recently, his live shows have reflected his creative activism, like 2001's *Dambusters*, which chronicled his role in the successful campaign to stop the controversial Ilisu Dam project in Turkey.

Andre Vincent (1964–) UK
After training at the Fratellini Circus School, doing a street-theatre act and working with Keith Johnstone's Loose Moose theatresports company, Vincent moved on to the London comedy circuit in the 1990s after some stand-up work in America. He established a name for himself as a hard-working circuit act, with a penchant for topical material and sick jokes. In 2002, he did an extraordinary show at the Edinburgh Fringe, *Andre Vincent is Unwell*, about the cancer he was suffering from at the time.

Jonathan Winters (1925–) USA
One of the sick comedians, Winters emerged from the New York clubs in the 1950s. His stand-up was largely made up of improvised scenes based on suggestions from the audience. He would act out all the parts himself, as well as providing the sound effects. He enjoyed a successful career with his own syndicated TV show, live performances and a series of comedy albums, and was a major influence on Robin Williams.

Victoria Wood (1953–) UK

Wood started out as a playwright and singer of cabaret songs after appearances on the TV talent show *New Faces* in 1974, and by the 1980s her live act had mutated into stand-up comedy. TV programmes like *Victoria Wood: As Seen on TV*, as well as her solo shows in big theatres, have made her the first British stand-up comedienne to become a huge star. She sold out a fifteen-night run at the Royal Albert Hall in 1993, another in 1996, and a twelve-night run in 2001.

Steven Wright (1955–) USA

At the age of twenty-three, Wright started performing in American comedy clubs, building a career on an act based on extraordinary comic minimalism. With a rigorously deadpan delivery, he dispenses a large number of short, bizarre, brain-frying jokes, offering little in the way of variety. In 1985, he released a comedy album, *I Have a Pony*, and his live work has been supplemented by cameos in numerous films and TV shows.

Henny Youngman (1906–98)

Known as 'The King of the One Liners', Youngman's act was a relentless stream of them. Starting in the Borscht Belt hotels while still in his twenties, Youngman spent nearly seventy years performing his stand-up act. His short gags were conventional, his delivery an old-fashioned quickfire bark. He's widely believed to be the originator of the gag, 'Take my wife – please!'

Notes

1. Born not Made

1. Kingston, 'King of Comedy', *Guardian*, 10 August 1999
2. See 'Comedy Goes on the Curriculum', *Sunday Times*, 11 July 1999; and Wilson, 'New degrees of Comic Learning', *The Stage*, 23 September 1999
3. Spanton, 'I've Got a Degree in Beckhamology', *Sun*, 14 August 2000
4. Hind, *The Comic Inquisition*, p. 32
5. See Louvish, *Monkey Business*, p. 391 (Groucho Marx and Woody Allen); and Berle (with Frankel), *Milton Berle – An Autobiography*, p. 130 (Milton Berle and Henny Youngman)
6. See Monkhouse, *Crying with Laughter*, pp. 56–9; Monkhouse, *Over the Limit*, p. 184
7. *Pillories of the State*, BBC Radio 4, 28 January 2001
8. Watkins, *On the Real Side*, p. 581
9. The routine in question is 'Grandpa Funk', which can be heard on Robin Williams, *Reality . . . What a Concept*
10. Bevan, *Top of the Bill*, p. 81
11. Bobby Thompson, *The Little Waster*
12. Nicolson, *Bobby Thompson*, pp. 104–8
13. See Carter, *Stand-Up Comedy*, pp. 3, 45 and 46
14. See Lane, *How to Become a Comedian*, pp. 55–6 and 61
15. See www.humourversity.com/frame.html (Pete Crofts' Humourversity); www.comedyworkshops.com (Judy

Carter's comedy workshops); www.comicstriplive.
com/class.asp 22/11/04 (the Comic Strip's comedy
workshops); and Ajaye, *Comic Insights*, p. 265 (Jamie
Masada's comedy workshops for kids)
16. Tony Allen offers a commentary on *Comedians in
Attitude*, pp. 123–6, and makes some insightful criticisms
of Eddie Waters's deficiencies as a teacher of stand-up
17. See www.thecomedyschool.com (on the Comedy
School); and www.newagenda.org.uk (on Tony Allen
and Den Levett's classes)
18. See Appendix for a description of some of the exercises
I have developed

2. A Beginner's Guide to Stand-up Comedy
1. 'Television and English', *Listener*, 11 August 1966. To
be honest, I didn't make the discovery by going to the
OED myself. It came up in a student essay, and even
then, the student hadn't got the information direct from
the *OED*, but via another book: Limon, *Stand-Up
Comedy in Theory*, pp. 7 and 126
2. The two sentences read 'People, she points out, who
appear before television cameras (apart from "stand-up
comics") never attempt to talk for more than two
minutes at a time' and 'In television complex sentences
need to be eschewed, especially by stand-up comics'.
Oddly, it is the second of these sentences which the
OED quotes
3. K. Bruce (ed.), *The Unpublished Lenny Bruce*, p. 16.
Interview broadcast 26 February 1959, WFMT,
Chicago
4. The claim about the term being coined on Carson's
show is made in Cook, 'Rising to the Joke', *Guardian*,
22 February 2003. However, the following website
reveals that although *The Tonight Show* actually started
in 1954, Carson didn't follow Steve Allen and Jack Paar
as host until 1962: (accessed www.johnnycarson.com/
carson/did_you_know/history/index.jsp 27/9/04). The

web discussion that followed can be found at www.pub122.ezboard.com/fwordoriginsorgfrm8.show Message?topicID=464.topic. The person who posted the message says that Berle claimed to have originated the term in 1942, although the claim was actually made in 1991. Sadly, the 1991 source of the supposed claim is not actually cited. That's the Internet for you, isn't it?

5. Double, *Stand-Up!*, p. 4. Other examples of laughter-based definitions include: Lenny Bruce, 'A comedian is one who performs words or actions of his own original creation, usually before a group of people in a place of assembly, and these words or actions should cause the people assembled to laugh at a minimum of . . . one laugh every 25 seconds for a period of not less than 45 minutes, and accomplish this feat with consistency 18 out of 20 shows' (K. Bruce [ed.], *The Unpublished Lenny Bruce*, pp. 41–2); John Limon, 'Your laughter is the single end of stand-up . . . Stand-up comedy does not require plot, closure, or point, and there need not be anything but jokes. Constant, unanimous laughter is the limit case' (*Stand-Up Comedy in Theory*, pp. 12–13); Mark Lamarr, 'defining stand-up in itself is very simple: a solo performer, usually a man, performing verbal comedy' (*Stand-Up America*, BBC2, 22 February 2003)

6. Quoted in Ajaye, *Comic Insights*, p. 65. Belzer's view is supported by an entry on 'Hispanic Humor' in Nilsen and Nilsen (eds), *Encyclopedia of 20th Century American Humor*, which refers to 'the American tradition of professional stand-up comedy' (p. 145) and 'the American custom of stand-up comedy' (p. 147)

7. Cook, 'Rising to the Joke', *Guardian*, 22 February 2003

8. Berle (with Frankel), *Milton Berle*, p. 86

9. Berle remembers swapping ad libs with the acts he introduced, admitting that they were actually pre-arranged and rehearsed

10. Berle interview with Vernon Scott, *United Press International*, 20 August 1991
11. Slide (ed.), *Selected Vaudeville criticism*, p. 20
12. Ibid., p. 1
13. Louvish, *Monkey Business*, p. 331
14. Quoted in Appignanesi, *Cabaret*, p. 175
15. Goldman, *Ladies and Gentlemen – Lenny Bruce!!*, p. 226
16. Quoted (or paraphrased?) by Paul Krassner in an interview with Lenny Bruce in K. Bruce (ed.), *The Unpublished Lenny Bruce*, p. 40
17. For reproductions of these programmes, see Honri, *Working the Halls*, pp. 28 and 54; and Wilmut, *Kindly Leave the Stage*, p. 12
18. Holborn Empire poster is reproduced on a facsimile postcard produced by the Badger Press, Westbury, Wiltshire (available from www.vaudeville-postcards.com)
19. Beerbohm, *The Bodley Head Max Beerbohm*, pp. 375
20. Various artists, *Music Hall Alive*
21. T. S. Eliot, 'Marie Lloyd', in Gross (ed.), *The Oxford Book of Essays*, p. 428
22. See Grenfell, *Joyce Grenfell Requests the Pleasure*, pp. 262 and 247
23. Various artists, *Fifty Years of Radio Comedy*
24. See Napier, *Glossary of Terms Used in Variety, Vaudeville, Revue & Pantomime*, pp. 7 and 27; and East, *Max Miller*, p. 66
25. Drobot, 'No Laughing Matter', *Descant*, vol. 18, 1987, pp. 162–3
26. 'Banksy' is the cult graffiti artist whose work is featured on the cover of the Blur album *Think Tank*
27. Googlewhacking is a game which involves putting two random search terms into the search engine Google, and getting just one website in the search results, subject to certain specific rules
28. Broadcast on BBC1, 20 April 1994. I hope nobody ever gets the clip of my act out of the archive – it's pretty dreadful. No, really

29. Zmuda (with Hansen), *Andy Kaufman Revealed!*, p. 91
30. 'A Stand-Up Life', *Funny Business*, BBC2, 29 November 1992
31. Kubernik, quoted in Parker, *Turned On*, p. 131
32. Mulholland, 'When Eddie Met Henry', *Time Out*, 2–9 December 1998
33. 'Language', on Henry Rollins, *A Rollins in the Wry*
34. See Zmuda (with Hansen), *Andy Kaufman Revealed!*, pp. 88–9 and 185. Even Kaufman's death is not 100 per cent certain. Although he died from a rare form of lung cancer in 1984, in May 2004, exactly twenty years after his death, somebody posted a website (www.andykaufmanreturns.blogspot.com/) claiming to be Kaufman, and it was announced that he would perform a show at Los Angeles' House of Blues (see Allan Wigley, 'Pulling Fast One on Death Never Works', *Ottawa Sun*, 22 May 2004). Needless to say, he didn't turn up for the show, but the fact that he successfully pulled off a number of hoaxes in his lifetime, and had told others of his intention to fake his own death, gives a certain limited credibility to the comeback claims

3. Personality

1. 'Copyright in Personality; VAF and Brussels Convention', *The Era*, 21 July 1938
2. See *Funny Business*, BBC2, 29 November 1992 (Milton Berle); Berger, *The Last Laugh*, p. 423 (Jack Rollins); and Nachman, *Seriously Funny*, p. 546 (Woody Allen)
3. *The South Bank Show*, ITV, 15 September 1996
4. *Stand-Up with Alan Davies*, BBC1, 19 June 2000
5. www.livejournal.com/community/eddieizzard/ (accessed 11/10/04)
6. See Nachman, *Seriously Funny*, p. 567 (Bill Cosby); Brandwood, *Victoria Wood*, p. viii (Victoria Wood); True, *American Scream*, p. xv (Sean Hughes); and

Mulholland, 'When Eddie Met Henry,' *Time Out*, 2–9 December 1998 (Eddie Izzard)

7. See Thompson, *Sunshine on Putty*, p. 137 (Jo Brand) and p. 139 (Jenny Éclair)

8. See Haddon, *The Story of Music Hall*, p. 91 (Archibald Haddon); Brandreth, *The Funniest Man on Earth*, p. 46 (Marie Lloyd); and *The Bodley Head Max Beerbohm*, p. 376 (Max Beerbohm)

9. Ripley, *Vaudeville Pattern*, p. 37

10. Sweeting, 'From Big Yin to Big Yank', *Guardian*, 2 December 1992

11. *The South Bank Show*, ITV, 4 September 1992

12. Gill, 'The Devil's Work', *Sunday Times*, 9 August 1998

13. Monkhouse quoted in Farndale, 'Insincerely Yours', *Sunday Telegraph Magazine*, 13 September 1998

14. Lee, 'All Present and Politically Correct', *Observer*, 25 August 2002

15. See Lahr, *Show and Tell*, pp. 210, 203 and 213; and Nachman, *Seriously Funny*, p. 22

16. Skinner, *Frank Skinner*, p. 80

17. Various artists, *Stand-Up Great Britain*

18. Enfield, *Harry Enfield and his Humorous Chums*, p. 6

19. Monkhouse, *Over the Limit*, pp. 38–9

20. Mare, *Comic Visions*, p. 13

21. Brandwood, *Victoria Wood*, p. 91

22. See Billen, 'I'd Die if My Parents Saw Potato Men', *The Times*, 16 March 2004; and Woods, '"Omega 3 Fatty Acids? Fantastic"', *Daily Telegraph*, 26 November 2003

23. Harrop, *Acting*, p. 5

24. Barker, 'The "Image" in Show Business', *Theatre Quarterly*, vol. VIII, no. 29, 1978, p. 8

25. Richard Pryor, *Live on Sunset Strip*, 1982

26. Jack Dee, *Live in London*

27. Duncan, 'Jack of All Tirades', *Radio Times*, 21–27 February 2004

28. Morecambe and Sterling, *Morecambe and Wise*, p. 177; also see p. 111
29. Bailey, 'Champagne Charlie: Performance and Ideology in the Music-Hall Swell Song', in Bratton (ed.), *Music Hall*, pp. 50–1
30. Duncan, 'Lenny's New Face', *Radio Times*, 12–18 April 2003
31. Dawson, *A Clown Too Many*, pp. 70–5
32. Allen, *Attitude*, p. 35
33. See Lahr, *Show and Tell*, pp. 177 (Eddie Izzard), 290 (Bert Lahr) and 128 (Roseanne Barr)
34. Ripley, *Vaudeville Pattern*, pp. 35–6
35. Thompson, *Sunshine on Putty*, p. 103
36. Ray, *Raising the Laughs*, p. 67
37. Howerd, *On the Way I Lost it*, pp. 67–8
38. Sahl on *Stand-Up America*, BBC2, 1 March 2003
39. *The South Bank Show*, ITV, 4 September 1992
40. In fact, Humperdinck was born Arnold George Dorsey. Gerry Dorsey was his first stage name
41. According to John Lahr, Dick Van Dyke was the original subject of Izzard's fake death announcement routine (see *Show and Tell*, p. 173)
42. I emailed Pryor as part of the research for this book, asking for any wisdom he could pass on to me. His reply read 'Always only tell the truth! love Richard' (received 2 July 2004)
43. Monkhouse, *Over the Limit*, p. 66
44. Track 3 on Shelley Berman, *Outside Shelley Berman*
45. Mark Lamarr, *Uncensored and Live*
46. Jo Brand on *Jack Dee Live at the Apollo*, BBC1, 27 September 2004
47. *Lenny Bruce: Swear to Tell the Truth*, BBC4, 3 June 2003
48. Phill Jupitus, *Live – Quadrophobia*
49. Cameron on *The Stand-Up Show*, BBC1, 18 November 1995

4. Working the Audience

1. *Face to Face*, BBC2, 12 January 1998
2. E.g., 'An electric shock shoots around the room when a comic is really cooking', Cook, *Ha Bloody Ha*, p. 181; and comedian Simon Evans: 'Laughter is like electricity', quoted in Cook, *The Comedy Store*, p. 110
3. Really
4. See Mackintosh, *Architecture, Actor and Audience*, pp. 172 and 128
5. *The South Bank Show*, ITV, 24 January 1991
6. Mikhail, 'Eddie Izzard, Comedian', *Observer Magazine*, 22 September 2002
7. 'The Robin', on Dan Leno, *Recorded 1901–1903*
8. 'Gladys Morgan', on various artists, *Great Radio Comedians*, BBC Records
9. *The Stand-Up Show*, BBC1, 18 March 1995
10. Track 8 on *Inside Shelley Berman*
11. Track 2 on various artists, *Stand-Up Great Britain*
12. 'Live and Lewd', extra feature on Steve Coogan, *Steve Coogan Live: The Man Who Thinks He's It*
13. 'Car Insurance', on Jasper Carrott, *A Pain in the Arm*
14. 'Arms and Asylum', on Mark Thomas, *Dambusters*
15. 'Kids', on Tom O'Connor, *Ace of Clubs*
16. 'Kindergarten', on Bill Cosby, *Why Is there Air?*
17. *Stand-Up with Alan Davies*, BBC1, 26 June 2000
18. 'Local Radio', on Jasper Carrott, *The Unrecorded Jasper Carrott*
19. Phil Kay, *That Philkay Video*
20. 'Our Text for Today', on Richard Pryor, . . . *Is it Something I Said?*
21. Henny Youngman, *Henny Youngman Himself*
22. 'Hong Kong', on Jasper Carrott, *The Stun (Carrott Tells All)*
23. 'Zits', on Jasper Carrott, *A Pain in the Arm*. According to Jonathon Green, the word has been in use since the 1950s, and was originally used by American teenagers (Green, *Cassell's Dictionary of Slang*, p. 1311)

24. *The South Bank Show*, ITV, 5 December 1993
25. 'Stoke Newington Calling', on Alexei Sayle, *Cak!*
26. 'Let's Get Small', on Steve Martin, *Let's Get Small*
27. Lenny Bruce, *The Carnegie Hall Concert*, disc 1

5. Challenging the Audience

1. Monkhouse, *Over the Limit*, p. 85
2. True, *American Scream*, p. 178
3. See 'Intro' and 'Worst audience ever', on Bill Hicks, *Flying Saucer Tour Vol. 1 Pittsburgh 6/20/91*
4. 'More about Smoking', on Bill Hicks, *Live at the Oxford Playhouse 11.11.92*. The gag is a reference to the famous incident at a 1960s festival when Bob Dylan was booed by folk purists for playing with an electric rock band
5. Frankie Howerd, *At the Establishment Club & at the BBC*
6. Jo Brand, Stag Theatre, Sevenoaks, 10 May 2004
7. Richard Pryor, *Live in Concert*
8. 'Revelations', on Bill Hicks, *Totally Bill Hicks*
9. Douglas, 'Jokes', in *Implicit Meanings*, pp. 150, 152 and 159
10. Hope, *Show and Tell*, p. 213
11. Jo Brand on *Jack Dee Live at the Apollo*, BBC1, 27 September 2004
12. Bill Hicks, *Revelations*
13. Thompson, *Sunshine on Putty*, p. 128
14. See Allen, *Attitude*, pp. 165–81 for a full transcript of his extraordinary act
15. Andre Vincent, *Hurrah for Cancer*, BBC3, 28 October 2004
16. *Stand-Up America*, BBC2, 1 March 2003
17. The claim that Joseph Kennedy put pressure on Banducci not to book Sahl was made by Banducci himself
18. See True, *American Scream*, pp. 93–5; and Hicks, 'Dear Bill', *Index on Censorship*, vol. 29, no. 6, 2000, pp. 68–77

19. 'I Just Do it and That's All', on Lenny Bruce, *To Is a Preposition; Come Is a Verb*
20. 'Commercials', on Lenny Bruce, *The Lenny Bruce Originals, Vol. 2*
21. 'A Pretty Bizarre Show', on Lenny Bruce, *To Is a Preposition; Come Is a Verb*
22. 'Blah Blah Blah', on ibid.
23. In *Ladies and Gentlemen – Lenny Bruce!!*, Albert Goldman says the show started at 12.30 a.m. on 6 December, but on the recording of the show, the compère can be clearly heard announcing the date as Tuesday 4 December
24. *Stand-Up America*, BBC2, 1 March 2003. Also see Watkins, *On the Real Side*, p. 372
25. Dick Gregory, *Talks Turkey*

6. The Present Tense

1. 'Muppets', on Jasper Carrott, *The Unrecorded Jasper Carrott*
2. Allen, *Attitude*, p. 28
3. Cantril and Allport, *The Psychology of Radio*, p. 100
4. The opening line of a poem about acting by Brecht starts: 'Show that you are showing!' ('Showing Has to Be Shown', in Brecht, *Poems 1913–1956*, p. 341
5. 'One Night Stands', on Richard Pryor, *Here and Now* in . . . *And It's Deep, Too! The Complete Warner Bros. Recordings (1968–1992)*
6. Priestley, *Particular Pleasures*, p. 190
7. Nathan, *The Laughtermakers*, pp. 228–9
8. Cook, *Ha Bloody Ha*, pp. 181–2
9. See Thompson, *Sunshine on Putty*, pp. 65, 94 and 107
10. 'Pussywhipped Satan', on Bill Hicks, *Arizona Bay*
11. Hicks, 'Vs. the Audience 2', on *Flying Saucer Tour, Vol. 1 Pittsburgh 6/20/91*
12. Harry Hill, *'First Class Scamp' Live at the London Palladium*

13. The story is related in a Pathé News interview (entitled 'Reg Dixon Hometown') dating from 1950–9, available via www.britishpathe.com, and in Wilmut, *Kindly Leave the Stage*, p. 169. In the Pathé interview, he claims the incident happened in his first radio broadcast in Blackpool. In Wilmut's book, he claims it happened at the Palace Theatre, Manchester. The quotes from Dixon are from the Pathé interview, the excerpt from the act being as remembered by Dixon. Also see Monkhouse, *Over the Limit*, p. 189 (on Roy Barbour)

14. See Felstead, *Stars who Made the Halls*, p. 106; and Hudd, *Roy Hudd's Book of Music-Hall, Variety and Showbiz Anecdotes*, p. 108

15. Lamarr, *Uncensored and Live*

16. All examples from Winters's act taken from Jonathan Winters, *Stuff'n Nonsense* (esp. see 'Male Elephant Wrapping a Present', 'Hippies', 'Heart Transplant', 'Gorilla Drafted into the Marine Corps', 'Astronauts Going to the Moon', 'Chester Honeyhugger as an Elevator Operator', 'Chester Honeyhugger Asking for a Date', 'Maude Frickert on a Motorcycle – Asking for a Date – Funshirt' and 'Unusual Sounds')

17. 'Excellent Hat', on Ross Noble, *The Official Bootlegs – Part 1*

18. 'Hello', on Ross Noble, *The Official Bootlegs – Part 2*

19. *Ross Noble – Unrealtime*, BBC2, 21 February 2004

20. *Guardian*, 8 August 2001

21. 'Hello', on Ross Noble, *The Official Bootlegs – Part 2*

22. It would be lovely to revive the idea of answering hecklers in rhyme: 'Thanks for that but let me be blunt / Your comment was rubbish and you're . . .'

23. Banks and Swift, *The Joke's on Us*, p. 15

24. Howerd, *At the Establishment Club & at the BBC*

25. *Metro*, 12 March 2002

7. Delivery

1. Napier, *Glossary of Terms Used in Variety, Vaudeville, Revue & Pantomime*, p. 54
2. Lane, *How to Become a Comedian*, p. 124
3. Allen, *Attitude*, p. 19
4. Norrick, 'On the Conversational Performance of Narrative Jokes', *Humor*, vol. 3, no. 14, 2001, p. 256
5. Rivers in Nachman, *Seriously Funny*, p. 596
6. See Lane, *How to Become a Comedian*, p. 15; and Monkhouse, *Over the Limit*, p. 107
7. 'Driving Instructor (Pilot for a New TV Series)', on Bob Newhart, *'Something Like this . . .' The Bob Newhart Anthology*
8. 'Introducing Tobacco to Civilisation', on ibid.
9. 'Ledge Psychology', on ibid.
10. 'Halloween', on Jerry Seinfeld, *I'm Telling You for the Last Time*
11. Allen, *Attitude*, p. 42
12. 'Tory MPs', on Jo Brand, *Jo Brand Live*
13. *Friday Night Live*, Channel 4, 26 February 1988
14. track 9 on *Stand-Up Great Britain*,
15. Atkinson, *Our Masters' Voices*, pp. 57–73
16. Lane, *How to Become a Comedian*, p. 71; also see pp. 14–15
17. This description comes from listening to the opening monologue of an episode of *Ray's a Laugh*, originally transmitted 8 November 1949, on Ted Ray, *Ray's a Laugh*
18. Both examples from '7's and Museums', on Steven Wright, *I Have a Pony*
19. Hind, *The Comic Inquisition*, p. 53
20. See *Bill Bailey Live*, Channel 4, 2 January 1998
21. See *The Best of Phyllis Diller* (esp. 'The Way I Dress' for an example of Diller's laugh making the audience laugh; and 'Don't Eat Here' for the quoted joke). Diller herself has acknowledged using her laugh as punctuation: Nachman, *Seriously Funny*, p. 231

22. See 'You Can't Get Bitter', on Bill Hicks, *LoveLaughterAndTruth*; and 'Pro Life', on Bill Hicks, *Rant in E-Minor*
23. Frances Donovan in *The Saleslady*, 1929, cited in Goffman, *The Presentation of Self in Everyday Life*, pp. 150–1
24. Willett (ed.), *Brecht on Theatre*, p. 123; also see p. 121
25. Carlin in *Comic Insights: the Art of Stand-Up Comedy*, p. 84
26. 'Prison Play', on *Richard Pryor* in . . . *And It's Deep, Too! The Complete Warner Bros. Recordings (1968–1992)*
27. Richard Pryor, *Live in Concert*
28. Jimmy Jones's West Indian accent can be heard in various routines on Jimmy Jones, *All the Breast: Best from Jimmy Jones*. Tony Allen mentions West Indian impressions on the working-men's club scene in *Attitude*, p. 83. In private conversations, he's told me that many of the comics who did the impressions would use the name Chalkie
29. Ben Elton, *Live 1989*
30. 'Farewell to Knobgags', on Mark Thomas, *Dambusters: Live 2001 Tour*
31. Billy Connolly, *Two Bites of Billy*
32. Richard Pryor, *Live in Concert*
33. Phill Jupitus, *Live – Quadrophobia*
34. 'Dinner with the Murder Machine', on Mark Thomas, *Dambusters: Live 2001 Tour*

8. How It's Done

1. *In the Psychiatrist's Chair*, BBC Radio 4, 19 August 1987
2. Ben Elton on *Face to Face*, BBC2, 12 January 1998
3. K. Bruce (ed.), *The Unpublished Lenny Bruce*, p. 22; also see Berger, *The Last Laugh*, p. 79
4. Mulholland, 'When Eddie Met Henry', *Time Out*, 2–9 December 1998
5. Monkhouse, *Over the Limit*, pp. 171–2 and 244
6. Mort Sahl in *Funny Business*, BBC2, 29 November 1992

7. Wright, in Hind, *The Comic Inquisition*, pp. 51–2
8. Ray, *Raising the Laughs*, p. 69
9. See Lahr, *Show and Tell*, p. 176 (Eddie Izzard); Hind, *The Comic Inquisition*, p. 98 (Victoria Wood); and Thompson, *Sunshine on Putty*, p. 109 fn (Alan Davies)
10. *The Bodley Head Max Beerbohm*, p. 377

9. Why Bother?

1. Oddey, *Performing Women*, pp. 108–9

Sources

Books

Ajaye, Franklyn, *Comic Insights: The Art of Stand-Up Comedy*, Los Angeles: Silman-James Press, 2002

Allen, Tony, *Attitude: Wanna Make Something of it? The Secret of Stand-Up Comedy*, Glastonbury: Gothic Image Publications, 2002

——, *A Summer in the Park: A Journal of Speakers' Corner*, London: Freedom Press, 2004

Appignanesi, Lisa, *Cabaret: The First Hundred Years*, London: Methuen, 1984

Atkinson, Max, *Our Masters' Voices: The Language and Body Language of Politics*, London and New York: Methuen, 1984

Banks, Morwenna, and Amanda Swift, *The Joke's on Us: Women in Comedy from Music Hall to the Present Day*, London: Pandora Press, 1987

Beerbohm, Max, *The Bodley Head Max Beerbohm* (ed. David Cecil), London, Sydney and Toronto: Bodley Head, 1970

Richard Belzer, *How to Be a Stand-Up Comic*, New York: Citadel Press, 1988

Berger, Phil, *The Last Laugh: The World of Stand-Up Comics*, New York: Cooper Square Press, 2000

Berle, Milton (with Haskel Frankel), *Milton Berle – An*

Autobiography, New York: Applause Theatre & Cinema Books, 1974

Bevan, Ian, *Top of the Bill: The Story of the London Palladium*, London: Frederick Muller, 1952

Brandreth, Gyles, *The Funniest Man on Earth: The Story of Dan Leno*, London: Hamish Hamilton, 1977

Brandwood, Neil, *Victoria Wood: The Biography*, London: Virgin Books, 2002

Bratton, J. S. (ed.), *Music Hall: Performance and Style*, Milton Keynes and Philadelphia: Oxford University Press 1986

Brecht, Bertolt, *Poems 1913–1956* (ed. John Willett and Ralph Manheim), London and New York: Methuen, 1987

Bruce, Frank, and Archie Foley (eds), *More Variety Days: Fairs, Fit-ups, Music Hall, Variety Theatre, Clubs, Cruises and Cabaret*, Edinburgh: Tod Press, 2000

Bruce, Kitty (ed.), *The Unpublished Lenny Bruce*, Philadelphia: Running Press, 1984

Cantril, Hadley, and Gordon W. Allport, *The Psychology of Radio*, New York and London: Harper and Brothers, 1935

Carter, Judy, *Stand-Up Comedy: The Book*, New York: Dell Publishing, 1989

Cook, William, *Ha Bloody Ha: Comedians Talking*, London: Fourth Estate, 1994

——, *The Comedy Store: The Club that Changed British Comedy*, London: Little, Brown, 2001

Davies, Russell (ed.), *The Kenneth Williams Diaries*, London: HarperCollins, 1993

Davison, Peter, *Popular Appeal in English Drama to 1850*, London and Basingstoke: Macmillan, 1982

Dawson, Les, *A Clown Too Many*, Glasgow: Collins, 1986

DiMeglio, John E., *Vaudeville USA*, Bowling Green, OH: Bowling Green University Popular Press, 1973

Dixon, Stephen, and Deirdre Falvey, *Gift of the Gag: The Explosion in Irish Comedy*, Belfast: Blackstaff Press, 1999

Double, Oliver, *Stand-Up! On being a Comedian*, London: Methuen, 1997

Douglas, Mary, *Implicit Meanings*, London: Routledge, 1999

Driver, Jim (ed.), *Funny Talk*, London: Do-Not Press, 1995

East, John M., *Max Miller: The Cheeky Chappie*, London: Robson Books, 1993

Enfield, Harry, *Harry Enfield and his Humorous Chums*, Harmondsworth: Penguin, 1997

Felstead, S. Theodore, *Stars Who Made the Halls: A Hundred Years of English Humour, Harmony and Hilarity*, London: Werner Laurie, 1946

Gammond, Peter (ed.), *Your Own, Your Very Own! A Music Hall Scrapbook*, London: Ian Allan, 1971

Gifford, Denis, *Victorian Comics*, London: George Allen & Unwin, 1976

——, *Encyclopaedia of Comic Characters*, Harlow: Longman, 1987

Glenn, Phillip, *Laughter in Inaction*, Cambridge: Cambridge University Press, 2003

Goffman, Erving, *The Presentation of Self in Everyday Life*, Harmondsworth: Penguin, 1971

Goldman, Albert (from the journalism of Lawrence Schiller), *Ladies and Gentlemen—Lenny Bruce!!*, Harmondsworth: Penguin, 1991

Gove, Philip Babcock, *Webster's Third New International Dictionary of the English Language Unabridged*, London: G. Bell & Sons, and Springfield MA: G. & C. Merriam, 1961

Green, Jonathon, *Cassell's Dictionary of Slang*, London: Cassell, 1998

Grenfell, Joyce, *Joyce Grenfell Requests the Pleasure*, London: Macmillan, 1976

Griffiths, Trevor, *Comedians*, London: Faber, 1976

Gross, John (ed.), *The Oxford Book of Essays*, Oxford and New York: Oxford University Press, 1992

Haddon, Archibald, *The Story of Music Hall*, London: Fleetway, 1935

Hample, Stuart, *Inside Woody Allen: Selections from the Comic Strip*, Sevenoaks, Kent: Coronet/Hodder & Stoughton, 1979

Harrop, John, *Acting*, London and New York: Routledge, 1992

Henry, Lenny, and Steve Parkhouse, *The Quest for the Big Woof*, Harmondsworth: Penguin, 1991

Hind, John, *The Comic Inquisition: Conversations with Great Comedians*, London: Virgin, 1991

Honri, Peter, *Working the Halls*, Farnborough, Hants: Saxon House, 1973

Howerd, Frankie, *On the Way I Lost it: An Autobiography*, London: Star/W. H. Allen, 1976

Hudd, Roy, *Roy Hudd's Book of Music-Hall, Variety and Showbiz Anecdotes*, London: Robson Books, 1994

Izzard, Eddie (with David Quantick and Steve Double), *Dress to Kill*, London: Virgin, 1998

King, Graham, and Ron Saxby, *The Wonderful World of Film Fun*, London: Clarkes New Press, 1985

Lahr, John, *Show and Tell*, Berkeley, Los Angeles and London: University of California Press, 2000

Lane, Lupino, *How to Become a Comedian*, London: Frederick Muller, 1945

Lewisohn, Mark, *Radio Times Guide to TV Comedy*, London: BBC Worldwide, 1998

Limon, John, *Stand-Up Comedy in Theory, or, Abjection in America*, Durham, NC and London: Duke University Press, 2000

Lorenz, Konrad, *On Aggression*, London: Methuen, 1967

Louvish, Simon, *Monkey Business: The Lives and Legends of the Marx Brothers*, London: Faber, 1999

Mackie, Albert D., *The Scotch Comedians: From Music Hall to Television*, Edinburgh: Ramsay Head Press, 1973

Mackintosh, Iain, *Architecture, Actor and Audience*, London and New York: Routledge, 1993

McCormick, Malcolm, *Billy Connolly: Bring on the Big Yin*, Glasgow and London: Collins, 1977

Marc, David, *Comic Visions: Television Comedy and American Culture*, Boston, London, Sydney and Wellington: Unwin Hyman, 1989

Midwinter, Eric, *Make 'Em Laugh: Famous Comedians and their Worlds*, London: George Allen & Unwin, 1979

Monkhouse, Bob, *Crying with Laughter*, London: Arrow, 1993

——, *Over the Limit: My Secret Diaries 1993–8*, London: Century, 1998

Morecambe, Gary, and Martin Sterling, *Morecambe and Wise: Behind the Sunshine*, London and Basingstoke: Pan, 1995

Nachman, Gerald, *Seriously Funny: The Rebel Comedians of the 1950s and 1960s*, New York: Pantheon, 2003

Napier, Valantyne, *Glossary of Terms Used in Variety, Vaudeville, Revue & Pantomime*, Westbury, Wilts: Badger Press, 1996

Nathan, David, *The Laughtermakers: A Quest for Comedy*, London: Peter Owen, 1971

Nicolson, Dave, *Bobby Thompson: A Private Audience*, Newcastle-upon-Tyne: TUPS Books, 1996

Nilsen, Alleen Pace, and Don L. F. Nilsen (eds), *Encyclopedia of 20th Century American Humor*, Phoenix, AZ: Oryx Press, 2000

O'Connor, Tom, *Take a Funny Turn: An Autobiography*, London: Robson Books, 1994

Oddey, Alison, *Performing Women: Stand-ups, Strumpets and Itinerants*, Houndmills and London: Macmillan, 1999

Parker, James, *Turned On: A Biography of Henry Rollins*, London: Phoenix House, 1998

Priestley, J. B., *Particular Pleasures*, London: Heinemann, 1975

Ramsden, Paul, *Learning to Teach in Higher Education*, London: Routledge, 1992

Ray, Ted, *Raising the Laughs*, London: Werner Laurie, 1952

Reinelt, Janelle, G., and Joseph R. Roach (eds), *Critical*

Theory and Performance, Ann Arbor: University of Michigan Press, 1992

Ripley, A. Crooks, *Vaudeville Pattern*, London: Brownlee, 1942

Sankey, Jay, *Zen and the Art of Stand-Up Comedy*, New York and London: Routledge, 1998

Sayle, Alexei, and Oscar Zarate, *Geoffrey the Tube Train and the Fat Comedian*, London: Methuen, 1987

Simpson, J. A., and E. S. C. Weiner (eds), *The Oxford English Dictionary* (2nd edn), Vol. XVI, Oxford: Clarendon Press, 1989

Skinner, Frank, *Frank Skinner*, London: Century, 2001

Slide, Anthony (ed.), *Selected Vaudeville Criticism*, Metuchen, NJ and London: Scarecrow Press, 1988

Stein, Charles W. (ed.), *American Vaudeville As Seen by Its Contemporaries*, New York: Knopf, 1984

Thompson, Ben, *Sunshine on Putty: The Golden Age of British Comedy from Vic Reeves to The Office*, London and New York: Fourth Estate, 2004

Took, Barry, *Star Turns: The Life and Times of Frankie Howerd and Benny Hill*, London: Weidenfeld and Nicolson, 1992

True, Cynthia, *American Scream: The Bill Hicks Story*, London: Sidgwick and Jackson, 2002

Tushingham, David (ed.), *Live 2: Not What I Am: The Experience of Performing*, London: Methuen, 1995

Wagg, Stephen (ed.), *Because I Tell a Joke or Two: Comedy, Politics and Social Difference*, London: Routledge, 1998

Watkins, Mel, *On the Real Side: A History of African American Comedy from Slavery to Chris Rock*, Chicago: Lawrence Hill, 1999

Willett, John (ed. and transl.), *Brecht on Theatre*, London: Methuen, 1978

Wilmut, Roger, *Kindly Leave the Stage: The Story of Variety, 1919–1960*, London: Methuen, 1985

Wilmut, Roger, and Peter Rosengard, *Didn't You Kill My Mother-in-Law? The Story of Alternative Comedy in Britain from the Comedy Store to Saturday Live*, London: Methuen, 1989

Zmuda, Bob (with Matthew Scott Hansen), *Andy Kaufman Revealed!*, London: Ebury Press, 1999

Articles

'Biggest Variety Boom for Years', *The Era*, vol. 101, no. 5207, 21 July 1938, p.1

'Copyright in Personality; VAF and Brussels Convention', *The Era*, vol. 101, no. 5207, 21 July 1938, p. 1

'Television and English', *Listener*, vol. LXXVI, no. 1950, 11 August 1966, p. 194

'Comedy Goes on the Curriculum', *Sunday Times*, 11 July 1999, p. 3

Barker, Clive, 'The "Image" in Show Business', *Theatre Quarterly*, vol. VIII, no. 29, Spring 1978, pp. 7–11

Billen, Andrew, 'I'd Die if my Parents Saw Potato Men', *The Times*, 16 March 2004, Features section p. 4

Burrell, Ian, 'Izzard Breaks Records with Rock and Roll Tour', *Independent*, 22 September 2003, p.6

Cavendish, Dominic, 'Muslim Makes Bin Laden a Laughing Matter; Dominic Cavendish Reports on a Stand-Up Comedienne in Demand on Both Sides of the Atlantic', *Daily Telegraph*, 18 October 2001, p. 11

Connor, John, 'Laughs in Store', *City Limits*, 4–11 May 1989, pp. 16–17

Cook, William, 'Funny Turn at the Arena; Newman and Baddiel Strive to Fill Wembley Arena with Laughs', *Guardian*, 13 December 1993, Features, p. 5

——, 'Rising to the Joke', *Guardian*, 22 February 2003, *The Guide* section, pp. 4–6

——, 'Ealing Live!', *Guardian*, 24 January 2004, *The Guide* section, p. 40

d'Antal, Stephen, 'His Fall From Grace Has Been Well Documented but Now the Shamed Entertainer is Trying to Make a New Life for Himself in New Zealand; Will

Barrymore Ever be Able to Run Away from his Past?',
Express, 24 April 2004, News p. 53

Drobot, Eve, 'No Laughing Matter, Yuk Yuk's Mark
Breslin: Better a Microphone than a Gun', *Descant*, vol.
18, Spring–Summer 1987, pp. 155–67

Duncan, Andrew, 'Lenny's New Face', *Radio Times*, 12–18
April 2003, pp. 26–8

——, 'Jack of All Tirades', *Radio Times*, 21–27 February
2004, pp. 22–4

Ellis, James, '60 Second Interview: Jeremy Hardy', *Metro*,
12 March 2002

Farndale, Nigel, 'Insincerely Yours: After Five Decades of
Irritating People in the Name of Light Entertainment,
Bob Monkhouse Has Finally Been Recognised as a
National Living Treasure. Nigel Farndale Tries to Work
out Why', *Sunday Telegraph Magazine*, 13 September
1998, p. 26

Gifford, Denis, 'Terry Wakefield: Film Funster', *Ally
Sloper*, vol. 1, no. 2, October 1976

Gill, A. A., 'The Devil's Work', *Sunday Times*, 9 August
1998, Features section

Hall, Julian, 'Edinburgh Festival 2003: Comedy: Shazia
Mirza and Patrick Monahan, Gilded Balloon, Teviot
00999', *Independent*, 21 August 2003, Comment section,
p. 14

Hamill, Denis, 'Ghost Story Comes with Punch Line',
Daily News (New York), 19 September 1999, Suburban
section, p. 4

Harrison, Andrew, 'This Much I Know: Bill Bailey,
Comedian and Actor, 39, London', *Observer Magazine*, 5
October 2003, p. 8

Hay, Malcolm, 'Preview: Cabaret – Tirade Secrets and the
Low-Down on the Stand-Ups', *Time Out*, 15-22
November 1989, p. 39

Hicks, Bill, 'Dear Bill', *Index on Censorship* ('The Last
Laugh' edition), vol. 29, no. 6, November/December
2000, issue 197, pp. 68–77

Kingston, Peter, 'King of Comedy', *Guardian*, 10 August 1999, *Guardian Education*, pp. 2–3

Krassner, Paul, 'The Busting of Lenny', *Index on Censorship* ('The Last Laugh' edition), vol. 29, no. 6, November/December 2000, issue 197, pp. 78–85

Lawson, Mark, 'The Unforgiven: An Evening with Michael Barrymore Was Bizarre and Unsettling', *Gurardian*, 20 September 2003, Leader pages, p. 24

Lee, Veronica, 'All Present and Politically Correct', *Observer*, 25 August 2002, Review section, p. 11

Logan, Brian, 'Be Truthful – and Funny Will Come. To Mark This Year's Inaugural Richard Pryor Award for Comedy, We Asked a Group of Comics to Put a Question to the Great Stand-Up. Brian Logan Introduces the Results', *Guardian*, 9 August 2004, Arts pages, p. 13

——, 'Edinburgh: How Was it for You?: As this Year's Festival Ends, Brian Logan Finds out Who Had a Blast and Who's on the Brink of Financial Ruin', *Guardian*, 30 August 2004, Features pages, p. 14

Merritt, Stephanie, 'Eddie? He's Forever Changing Gear: After a Few Serious Roles, the Comedian in Tights Returns in Fine Style', *Observer*, 30 November 2003, Review, p. 11

Middleton, Christopher, 'Silly Billy', *Radio Times*, 20–26 November 2004, pp. 34–5

Mikhail, Kate, 'Eddie Izzard, Comedian', *Observer Magazine*, 22 September 2002, p. 22

Mintz, Lawrence E., 'Standup Comedy as Social and Cultural Mediation', *American Quarterly*, vol. 37, no. 1, Spring 1985, pp. 71–80

Mulholland, Garry, 'When Eddie Met Henry', *Time Out*, 2–9 December 1998, pp. 22–5

Noble, Ross, 'Edinburgh Festival: Be Unprepared: Why Would a Comic Invent a New Act every Night? It's More Fun, says Ross Noble. Oh, and You Don't Have to Remember any Lines', *Guardian*, 8 August 2001, Features pages, p. 12

Norrick, Neal R., 'On the Conversational Performance of Narrative Jokes: Toward an Account of Timing', *Humor*, vol. 3, no. 14, 2001, pp. 255–73

O'Connell, Alex, 'Howard Read and Little Howard', *The Times*, 22 August 2003, Features, p. 21

O'Connor, John J., 'TV: Stendhal Drama and a Dance Series Begins', *New York Times*, 25 October 1982, Section C, p. 18

Philp, Myra, 'Audience Jeers Connolly's Sick Joke about Iraq Hostage; That's Just not Funny, Billy', *Express*, 6 October 2004, News section, p. 15

Russell, John, 'Catch a Rising Comic at Four Showcases', *New York Times*, 8 December 1978, Weekend section, pp. C1, C27

Salmon, Barry, 'Amazing First Week Silenced the Doubters', *Dewsbury Reporter*, 2 October 1998, pp. 10–11

——, 'Building the Dream', *Dewsbury Reporter*, 16 October 1998, p. 8

Sanghera, Sathnam, 'Funny Business; Some of Britain's Funniest People – Frank Skinner and Al Murray Among Them – Are Managed by the Toughest Team in the Show Business World. Sathnam Sanghera Meets the Men who even Frighten the BBC', *Mail on Sunday*, 10 February 2002, p. 36

Scott, Vernon, 'Scott's World; Newhart Adjusts', *United Press International*, 9 October 1984, Entertainment

—— (interview with Milton Berle), *United Press International*, 20 August 1991

Snoddy, Julia, 'Jongleurs Founders Sell Stake to Regent for £7m', *Guardian*, 8 August 2000, City pages, p. 19

Spanton, Tim, 'I've Got a Degree in Beckhamology', *Sun*, 14 August 2000

Sweeting, Adam, 'It's the Way He Tells 'em – Adam Sweeting on the Contradiction That is Billy Connolly', *Guardian*, 13 June 1991, Arts section

——, 'From Big Yin to Big Yank', *Guardian*, 2 December 1992, Features, p. 4

Thorncroft, Antony, 'Heard the One About: Antony Thorncroft Looks at a 20-year-old institution, the London Comedy Store', *Financial Times*, 21 May 1999, p. 18

Walker, Dave, 'But Seriously, Folks; Comedy Store Veterans Tell Their "True Hollywood Story" – and it's not Always for Laughs', *Times-Picayune*, 8 April 2001, Living: On the Air section, p. 1

Wansell, Geoffrey, 'What Killed Their Marriage?', *Daily Mail*, 26 October 2002, p. 38

Wareham, Mark, 'Sick with Laughter', *Mail on Sunday*, 3 October 2004, FB section, p. 80

Wigley, Allan, 'Pulling Fast One on Death Never Works', *Ottawa Sun*, 22 May 2004, Showbiz, p. 21

Wilson, Ollie, 'New Degrees of Comic Learning', *The Stage*, no. 6180, 23 September 1999, p. 27

Woods, Judith, '"Omega 3 Fatty Acids? Fantastic"; The Drink is not a Problem, the Weight Needs to Go and the Smoking is Cher's Fault. But Johnny Vegas Feels Good, He Tells Judith Woods', *Daily Telegraph*, 26 November 2003, p. 24

Zito, Tom, '"The Sleaze" is Pleased; John Belushi is Finding Fun in his New Movie-Star Fame', *Washington Post*, 8 September 1978, Style section, p. D1

Interviews

Shelley Berman, by telephone, 5 August 2004
Adam Bloom, by telephone, 29 June 2004
Jo Brand, Dulwich Picture Gallery, 1 April 2004
Rhona Cameron, by telephone, 19 March 2004
James Campbell, by telephone, 25 August 2004
Rhys Darby, by telephone, 30 June 2004
Omid Djalili, by telephone, 28 June 2004
Dave Gorman, by telephone, 29 June 2004
Jeremy Hardy, Streatham, 1 April 2004
Harry Hill, by telephone, 26 August 2004

Alex Horne, by telephone, 6 July 2004
Milton Jones, by telephone, 28 June 2004
Phill Jupitus, BBC Broadcasting House, London, 6 June 2004
Mark Lamarr, Chiswick, 14 July 2004
Shazia Mirza, by telephone, 28 June 2004
Ross Noble, Orchard Theatre, Dartford, 24 June 2004
Alexei Sayle, University of Kent, Canterbury, 21 November 2003
Mark Thomas, Clapham, 27 February 2004
Andre Vincent, central London, 14 July 2004

Unless otherwise attributed, all quotes from the above comedians are taken from these interviews

Live Shows

Bill Bailey, *Part Troll*, Wyndham's Theatre, 18 October 2003
Jello Biafra, Sheffield City Hall (Memorial Hall), 30 September 2001
Jo Brand, Stag Theatre, Sevenoaks, 10 May 2004
Roy 'Chubby' Brown, Margate Winter Gardens, 24 February 2004
James Campbell, Assembly Hall Theatre, Tunbridge Wells, 1 June 2004
Comedy Store, 26 February 2004
Billy Connolly, *Too Old to Die Young*, Carling Hammersmith Apollo, 29 September 2004
Jim Davidson, *Vote for Jim*, Winter Gardens, Margate, 25 October 2003
Jack Dee, Stag Theatre, Sevenoaks, 23 May 2004
Harry Hill, Battersea Arts Centre, 14 September 2004
Daniel Kitson, Brighton Dome Pavilion Theatre, 30 January 2004
Last Laugh Comedy Club, The Lescar, Hunters Bar, Sheffield, 4 May 1995

Dylan Moran, *Monster II*, Brighton Dome Concert Hall, 28 April 2004

Al Murray – The Pub Landlord, Gulbenkian Theatre, Canterbury, 31 January 2004

Ross Noble, *Noodlemeister*, Orchard Theatre, Dartford, 24 June 2004

Mark Thomas, Gulbenkian Theatre, Canterbury, 8 December 2004

Vinyl

Shelley Berman, *A Personal Appearance*, EMI Records, 1961, catalogue no. CLP 1512

Jello Biafra, *No More Cocoons*, Alternative Tentacles Records, 1987, catalogue no. VIRUS 59

Jasper Carrott, *A Pain in the Arm*, DJM Records, 1977, catalogue no. DJF 20518

Jasper Carrott, *The Unrecorded Jasper Carrott*, DJM Records, 1979, catalogue no. DJF 20560

Jasper Carrott, *The Stun (Carrott Tells All)*, DJM Records, 1983, catalogue no. DJF 20582

Frankie Howerd, *At the Establishment Club & at the BBC*, Decca, 1963, catalogue no. LK 4556

Jimmy Jones, *All the Breast: Best from Jimmy Jones*, JJ Records, 1979, catalogue no. JJ0002

Tom O'Connor, *Ace of Clubs*, North West Gramophone, 1975, catalogue no. NWG 75102

Mort Sahl, *1960 or Look Forward in Anger*, Verve Records, 1960, catalogue no. MG V-15004

Alexei Sayle, *Cak!*, Springtime Records, 1982, catalogue no. CAK 1

Jimmy Walker, *Dyn-O-Mite*, Buddah Records, 1975, catalogue no. BDS 5635

Various artists, *Fifty Years of Radio Comedy*, BBC Records, 1972, catalogue no. REC 138M

Various artists, *Great Radio Comedians*, BBC Records, 1973, catalogue no. REC 151M

Various artists, *Laugh with The Comedians*, Granada TV Records, 1971, catalogue no. GTV 1002

Audio cassettes

Woody Allen, *The Nightclub Years 1964–68*, EMI, 1990, catalogue no. ECC3

Jo Brand, *Jo Brand Live*, Laughing Stock, 1993, catalogue no. LAFFC 21

Ben Elton, *Live 1989*, Laughing Stock, 1993, catalogue no. LAFFC 16

Ted Ray, *Ray's a Laugh*, BBC Radio Collection, 1990, catalogue no. ZBBC 1117

Various artists, *The Golden Years of the Music Hall*, Saydisc, 1990, catalogue no. CSDL380

CDs

Shelley Berman, *Inside Shelley Berman*, Laugh.com, 2002, catalogue no. LGH1111

Shelley Berman, *Outside Shelley Berman*, Laugh.com, 2002, catalogue no. LGH1115

Lenny Bruce, *The Lenny Bruce Originals, Volume 2*, Fantasy, 1991, catalogue no. CDFA 526

Lenny Bruce, *The Historic 1962 Concert When Lenny Bruce Was Busted*, Viper's Nest, 1992, catalogue no. VN178

Lenny Bruce, *The Carnegie Hall Concert*, World Pacific/Capitol Records, 1995, catalogue no. CDP 7243 8 34020 2 1

Lenny Bruce, *To Is a Preposition; Come Is a Verb*, Knit Classics/Douglas Music, 2000, catalogue no. KCR-3019

George Carlin, *Class Clown*, Eardrum Records/Atlantic, 2000, catalogue no. 92923-2

Bill Cosby, *Why is there Air?*, Warner Bros. (no date given for CD release, album originally released 1965), catalogue no. 1606-2

Phyllis Diller, *The Best of Phyllis Diller*, Laugh.com, 2002, catalogue no. LGH1112

Dick Gregory, *Talks Turkey*, Vee Jay/Collectables/Rhino Entertainment, 2000, catalogue no. COL-CD-7163

Buddy Hackett, *The Original Chinese Waiter*, Laugh.com, 2002, catalogue no. LGH1107

Bill Hicks, *Arizona Bay*, Rykodisc, 1997, catalogue no. RCD 10352

Bill Hicks, *Rant in E-Minor*, Rykodisc, 1997, catalogue no. RCD 10353

Bill Hicks, *LoveLaughterAndTruth*, Rykodisc, 2002, catalogue no. RCD 10631

Bill Hicks, *Flying Saucer Tour Vol. 1 Pittsburgh 6/20/91*, Rykodisc, 2002, catalogue no. RCD 10632

Bill Hicks, *Live at the Oxford Playhouse 11.11.92*, Invasion Group, 2003, catalogue no. INVACD 1001

Dan Leno, *Recorded 1901–1903*, Windyridge, 2001, catalogue no. WINDYCDR1 (available from www.musichallcds.com/)

Steve Martin, *Let's Get Small*, Warner Bros. (no date given for CD release, album originally released 1977), catalogue no. 9 45694-2

Dylan Moran, *Monster – Live*, Sound Entertainment, 2004, catalogue no. TLCD 53

Bob Newhart, *'Something Like this . . .' The Bob Newhart Anthology*, Rhino/Warner Archives, 2001, catalogue no. R2 76742

Ross Noble, *The Official Bootlegs – Part 1*, Stunt Baby/Brian Records, 2001, catalogue no. RN001

Ross Noble, *The Official Bootlegs – Part 2*, Stunt Baby/Brian Records, 2003, catalogue no. RN002

Richard Pryor, *. . . And It's Deep, Too! The Complete Warner Bros. Recordings (1968–1992)*, Rhino/Warner Bros., 2000, catalogue no. RS 76655

Henry Rollins, *Sweatbox*, Quarterstick Records/Touch and Go Records, 1992, catalogue no. QS10CD

Henry Rollins, *A Rollins in the Wry*, Quarterstick Records, 2000, catalogue no. QS63CD

Mort Sahl, *At the hungry i*, Laugh.com, 2002, catalogue no. LGH 1122

Jerry Seinfeld, *I'm Telling You for the Last Time*, Universal Records, 1998, catalogue no. UD-53175

Mark Thomas, *Dambusters: Live 2001 Tour*, Laughing Stock, 2003, catalogue no. LAFFCD 0136

Robin Williams, *Reality . . . What a Concept*, Laugh.com, 2002, catalogue no. LGH 1104

Jonathan Winters, *Stuff'n Nonsense*, Laugh.com, 2001, catalogue no. LGH 1059

Steven Wright, *I Have a Pony*, WEA Records, no date, catalogue no. 7599253352 OMCD 1150

Henny Youngman, *Henny Youngman Himself*, Laugh.com, 2001, catalogue no. LGH 1008

Various artists, *The Comedy Store: 20th Birthday*, Uproar Entertainment, 1996, catalogue no. UP 3669

Various artists, *4 at the Store*, BBC Audiobooks, 2004, ISBN no. 0563523077

Various artists, *Gems of the Music Hall*, Flapper/Pavilion Records, 1993, catalogue no. PAST CD 7005

Various artists, *Music Hall Alive: Edwardian Stars Recorded 1938 & 1948*, Music Hall Masters, 2003, catalogue no. MHM022/3 (available from www.mysite. wanadoo-members.co.uk/musichallmasters)

Various artists, *Stand-Up Great Britain*, Laughing Stock, 2000, catalogue no. LAFF CD 105

Videos

Lenny Bruce, *Lenny Bruce Without Tears*, Vision Entertainment/Time Warner, 1992, catalogue no. 50328-3

Billy Connolly, *Two Bites of Billy*, VVL, 1995, catalogue no. 6362523

Jack Dee, *Live in London*, VVL/Polygram, 1997, catalogue no. 0475823

Eddie Izzard, *Definite Article*, VVL, 1996, catalogue no. 0431903

Eddie Izzard, *Glorious*, VVL, 1997, catalogue no. 0476043

Eddie Izzard, *Dress to Kill*, VVL, 1998, catalogue no.0579863

Phill Jupitus, *Live – Quadrophobia*, VVL, 2000, catalogue no. 0740533

Andy Kaufman, *Andy Kaufman Plays Carnegie Hall*, Paramount, 2000, catalogue no.839693

Phil Kay, *That Philkay Video*, Colour TV, 2000, catalogue no. JW112

Mark Lamarr, *Uncensored and Live*, VVL, 1997, catalogue no. 0474343

Eddie Murphy, *Delirious!*, CIC Video/Eddie Murphy Television, 1983, catalogue no. VHR 2162

Robert Newman, *Resistance is Fertile*, Laughing Stock, 2001, catalogue no. LAFFV 0123

Richard Pryor, *Here and Now*, Parkfield Entertainment/ Columbia Pictures, 1989, catalogue no. CVT 21140

Bobby Thompson, *The Little Waster*, Tyne Tees Television/ Mawson & Wareham Music, 1986, catalogue no. MWMV1003

Vaudeville, Winstar TV & Video, 1999, catalogue no. WHE71199

DVDs

Steve Coogan, *Steve Coogan Live: The Man Who Thinks He's it*, Universal, 2000, catalogue no. 902 020 2

Bill Hicks, *Totally Bill Hicks*, VCI/4 DVD, 2001, catalogue no. VCD0162

Harry Hill, *'First Class Scamp' Live at the London Palladium*, VVL, 2000, catalogue no. 9020192

Eddie Izzard, *Circle*, Universal, 2000, catalogue no. VFC 39359

Eddie Izzard, *Sexie*, Universal Pictures Video, 2003, catalogue no. 8208905

Richard Pryor, *Live in Concert*, Revolver Entertainment, 2004, catalogue no. REVD1806

Chris Rock, *Bring the Pain*, Dreamworks, 2002, catalogue no. 0044504009

Johnny Vegas, *Who's Ready for Ice Cream?*, Universal, 2003, catalogue no. 8209129

Television

Arena ('Oooh, er Missus! The Frankie Howerd Story'), BBC2, 1 June 1990

Bernard's Bombay Dream, Channel 4, 26 June 2003

Bill Bailey Live, Channel 4, 2 January 1998

Bob Hope at 100, BBC1, 12 August 2003

Dave Allen, BBC1, Saturdays, 6 January–10 February 1990

Face to Face, BBC2, 12 January 1998

Friday Night Live, Channel 4, 26 February 1988

Funny Business, BBC2, 29 November 1992

Hurrah for Cancer, BBC3, 28 October 2004

Jack Dee Live, Channel 4, 13 October 1995

Jack Dee Live at the Apollo, BBC1, 27 September 2004

Kings of Black Comedy, Channel 4, 9 March 2002

Lee Evans – Wired and Wonderful, Live at Wembley, BBC1, 19 September 2003

Lenny Bruce: Swear to Tell the Truth, BBC4, 3 June 2003

Lenny – Live and Unleashed, BBC1, 27 December 1990

Live Floor Show, BBC2, 8 February 2003; 15 March 2003

The Mark Thomas Comedy Product, Channel 4, 29 March 1996

Pebble Mill, BBC1, 20 April 1994

Ross Noble – Unrealtime, BBC2, 21 February 2004

Saturday Live, ITV, 1 June 1996

The South Bank Show, ITV, 24 January 1991; 4 September 1992; 5 December 1993; 15 September 1996; 26 September 1999

Stand-Up America, BBC2, 7 July 1987; 22 February 2003; 1 March 2003; 15 March 2003

The Stand-Up Show, BBC1, 18 March 1995; 8 April 1995; 18 November 1995

Stand-Up with Alan Davies, BBC1, 19 June 2000; 26 June
2000; 3 July 2000
TX: 'Je Suis a Stand-Up' – Eddie Izzard Abroad . . ., BBC2,
7 December 1996
We Know Where You Live. Live!, Channel 4, 16 June 2001

Radio

In the Psychiatrist's Chair, BBC Radio 4, 19 August 1987
Pillories of the State, BBC Radio 4, 28 January 2001

Internet

Jeffrey Drake, 'Point Man against Censorship':
www.rambozo.com/index.php?p=articles&c=3&a=jello-
interview (accessed 7/9/04)
William J. Briggs, 'How Much is a Celebrity Name Worth?':
www.sphvalue.com/vm1099-3.html (25/2/03)
'History of the Show': www.johnnycarson.com/carson/
did_you_know/history/index.jsp (27/9/04)
www.pub122.ezboard.com/fwordoriginsorgfrm8.showMes
sage?topicID=464.topic (27/9/04)
www.newyork.citysearch.com/profile/7390572 (30/9/04)
www.improv.com/index.cfm?fuseaction=aboutUs.home%
20title= (30/9/04)
www.spitfiretour.org/zack.html (7/9/04)
www.andykaufmanreturns.blogspot.com/ (1/10/04)
www.livejournal.com/community/eddieizzard/ (11/10/04)
www.auntiemomo.com/cakeordeath/open.html (16/11/04)
www.humourversity.com/frame.html (22/11/04)
www.comedyworkshops.com/ (22/11/04)
www.comicstriplive.com/class.asp (22/11/04)
www.thecomedyschool.com/ (22/11/04)
www.newagenda.org.uk/ (22/11/04)

Other

Holborn Empire poster from week beginning 17 December 1934, reproduced on a facsimile postcard produced by the Badger Press, Westbury, Wiltshire (available from www.vaudeville-postcards.com)

Pathé News interview with Reg Dixon (entitled 'Reg Dixon Hometown') dating from 1950–59, available via www.britishpathe.com

Tour programme for Eddie Izzard's *Sexie*, 2003